(Continued)

Authorizing Readers

RESISTANCE AND RESPECT IN THE TEACHING OF LITERATURE

Peter J. Rabinowitz and Michael W. Smith

FOREWORD BY WAYNE C. BOOTH

Teachers College, Columbia University
New York and London

National Council of
Teachers of English
Urbana, Illinois

Published simultaneously by Teachers College Press, 1234 Amsterdam Avenue, New York, NY 10027 and the National Council of Teachers of English

Library of Congress Cataloging-in-Publication Data

Rabinowitz, Peter J., 1944–
    Authorizing readers : resistance and respect in the teaching of literature / Peter J. Rabinowitz and Michael W. Smith ; foreword by Wayne C. Booth.
        p.   cm. — (Language and literacy series)
    Includes bibliographical references and index.
    ISBN 0-8077-3690-2 (cloth : alk. paper). — ISBN 0-8077-3689-9 (paper : alk. paper)
        1. Literature—Study and teaching (Secondary)   2. Reader response criticism.
    I. Smith, Michael W. (Michael William), 1954–   .   II. Title.   III. Series: Language and literacy series (New York, N.Y.)
    PN59.R25   1997
    807'.1'273—dc21   97-31022

ISBN 0-8077-3689-9 (paper)
ISBN 0-8077-3690-2 (cloth)
NCTE Stock No. 40890

Printed on acid-free paper
Manufactured in the United States of America

05 04 03 02 01 00 99 98   8 7 6 5 4 3 2 1

To our parents

CONTENTS

FOREWORD

FAIRLY EARLY in this century John Dewey annoyed many philosophers and educators by arguing that theory and practice could never be effectively separated. Though scores of prominent thinkers have since embraced his effort at fusion, the comfortable habit of pretending that the two are separable continues to thrive. The results have been especially destructive in the study and teaching of literature.

For too many, the practice of teaching has been viewed as subordinate to scholarship, criticism, pursuit of theoretical questions, or the currently fashionable cultural critique. Teaching is, of course, necessary, somewhere down the line, but the real rewards are properly reserved for the "scholars" who teach advanced students a few hours a week. There's nothing new in this: In my four years of graduate work, in the forties, none of my teachers even mentioned that I should be preparing for a first job that would inevitably be—teaching.

The rich dialogue that Rabinowitz and Smith offer, uniting theory and practice, is not between "an impractical theorist" and "an untheoretical practitioner." It is true that if one simply looked at their previous publications, one might make the mistake of reducing Rabinowitz to a "narratologist" and Smith to a practical, nontheoretical "educationist" or "pursuer of teaching technique." Rabinowitz's book *Before Reading* is one of the most perceptive and useful discussions of how readers read and how they might read better if they thought harder about how texts work. Smith's publications have been mostly about how teachers can better engage students in genuine "transactions" with texts—and with their teacher and fellow students. But as their dialogue progresses, one sees not only that each of them has always been engaged in both theory and practice, but also that in writing the book together, they have been learning all the way. Smith's ideas about teaching have been modified by Rabinowitz's pursuit of his distinction between the "authorial audience" and the "narrative audience"; his attempts to teach the "right reading" based on the teacher's laborious re-reading have shifted to the teaching of "interpretative strategies" that yield not students who have learned the one right reading but more fully engaged students who have learned how and why to ask useful questions about any text. Similarly, Rabinowitz's confidence in many of his theoretical distinctions has diminished as he has encountered Smith's detailed accounts of actual reading responses, and he has been led to further thought about his past impositions of "indubitable" assumptions. By the end, he is a lot less confident about any one method than he felt before they began their project.

Both authors, after decades of work on both sides of the fake split, have thus brought the consequences of those decades of practice into a splendidly provocative debate: rival teaching practices, based on rival theories of teaching, confronting rival theories of what "literature" is, of why we bother to teach it in the first place, and of what kinds of reading are most worth pursuing. The authors steadily relate challenging theoretical issues to pedagogical issues of the most threatening kind: how to turn nonreaders into responsible, critical readers; how to deal with the overwhelming range of abilities and interests and cultural backgrounds of present-day students; how to move students from where they are to where the teacher is, without turning "where the teacher is" into a dogmatic and destructively elitist platform, actually banning the students from the show. Slicing through the false dichotomies that corrupt too much current debate, the authors deal in fresh ways with questions of multiculturalism; with battles about "the canon"; with quarrels between those "reader-response" critics who have celebrated "resistant" reading and defenders of "the author" and authorial intentions who have insisted on "respect" for authorial intentions, and with current anxieties about how dwelling on theoretical questions can destroy students' pleasurable engagement with literary texts.

At the center is always the essential problem that too many "higher level" teachers of literature have ignored: how to bridge the gap between what teachers know, or think they know, and what the students at a given stage are capable of taking in. If we accept the authors' commitment to a genuinely democratic education—education that enables everyone to rise as far as possible in the art of first really "taking in" and then effectively criticizing what texts offer them—then we have to find ways of ensuring that this or that elite does not work in destructive ways to impose "standards" that are not only self-serving but destructive of independent growth.

Facing the problem honestly produces interesting tensions throughout the book between two thoroughly plausible views of what constitutes "right reading" and the best way to create the "right" kind of readers. On the one hand, is it not obvious that students should be taught how to show full *respect* for textual "intentions" of all kinds, "literary" or not? Can teachers claim to have taught well if their students have not learned how to discover what authors are really *trying* to say? If students learn simply to impose their presuppositions on a text, what's the point of their reading it?—they come out no different from what they were when they went in. On the other hand, is it not obvious that students should be taught the critical skills of *resisting* both what authors intend and what teachers see as the right reading (or at least as the range of acceptable ones)? Should not teachers be aware that when they impose their "informed" readings on students, insisting on their own, better-informed view of what authors are up to, they may not just kill students' interests and violate students' spirit—they may even overlook legitimate readings that only the students can offer?

Though each of the authors here has a somewhat different view of these two potentially contradictory goals, the book is a major effort to show how the best versions of each goal can be reconciled: every good teacher of "reading" or "literature" or "English" should pursue both the legitimate forms of respect for authorial intentions (not what the flesh-and-blood author might have hoped for, but what the text actually requires of the attentive reader) *and* the best forms of resistance (not just resistance to what one happens not to like or understand, but resistance to genuine intellectual, ethical, and political deficiencies implicit in the text's intentions). Students' growth, just like teachers', occurs when both goals are pursued with close attention and unflagging vigor.

What we have in this book, then, is a rich encounter with the paradox faced by serious teachers: I am a teacher, I am paid *as* a teacher, because I have something to teach; I have a duty, as the authors here put it, to help students to get from where they are to where I am. Yet "where I am" may be the greatest obstacle to my succeeding: My world is not their world, my presuppositions may not be their presuppositions, and my knowledge of the text, based on laborious re-reading, may be precisely what will kill their engagement with it.

In short, this book provides the best discussion I have read of two related questions: "Why teach literature in the first place?" and "How can you do it not just effectively, in the sense of winning converts to your view of things, but in the sense of producing full ethical and intellectual development in students?" Learning from each other as they go, disagreeing and then working toward agreement, Rabinowitz and Smith teach me just how many of my assumptions and practices have been questionable and how much I still have to learn about a challenging, immensely difficult profession that in my (dogmatic) view is unsurpassed in its importance.

Wayne C. Booth
University of Chicago

PREFACE

ONE OF THE RECURRING symbols of the winter holiday season—less familiar than Christmas trees, menorahs, or the New Year's ball at Times Square, but just as regular—is the flurry of reports in the mass media about the Modern Language Association convention. It's a predictable ritual, in which the titles of four or five of the most apparently outlandish papers are set forth as proof that literary academics—theorists in particular—engage in nothing more than disputing arcane points that have little bearing on the "real world."

It is not only auto mechanics, lawyers, and members of Congress who have accepted this image. Secondary school teachers of literature, too, seem prepared to believe that literary theory is somehow unconnected to their lives. As Applebee (1993) noted: "In our case studies of programs with reputations for excellence, we also asked teachers directly about their familiarity with recent developments in literary theory. Some 72 percent of these teachers reported little or no familiarity with contemporary literary theory. As one teacher put it, 'These are far removed from those of us who work the front lines!'" (pp. 121–122).

It's easy to understand why literary theory has developed this reputation. Much of it *is* difficult, much of it *is* jargon-ridden and poorly written (sometimes aggressively so), and, frankly, much of it *is* divorced from the concerns that made Peter Rabinowitz and me (and, we presume, many of our readers) turn to literature in the first place. When you add to this the increasing number of broadsides against "theory" from neoconservatives—attacks often based on caricatures of what theorists are doing—it's hardly surprising that theory is suspect, even among people whose lives are centered around literature. But, as we argue here, this easy dismissal of literary theory impoverishes our reading and our classroom practice. "Theory" (and, as Peter explains in Chapter 1, there is some debate about its meaning) should not be the province of elite intellectuals at research universities: It has value for improving the pedagogical practice of anyone who teaches literature at any level.

Peter and I know this from experience, for as our readings of each other's work over the years have confirmed, theory and practice can have a positive symbiotic relationship. We came to this intellectual exchange with very different backgrounds and interests. Peter is a literary theorist—more particularly, a narrative theorist—who has taught at the college level since the late 1960s, most of that time at Hamilton, a private liberal arts college in central New York. I am an English educator at Rutgers University who taught high school for more than 10 years. As I have read Peter's theoretical work on how readers read, I have often been struck by how he has articulated a theoretical point of which I previously had had only a tacit understanding. I have been able to use this articulated understanding to help me reflect on my teaching. In addition, Peter has also advanced ideas that were new to me, ideas that have both challenged the way that I have taught and opened new directions for my thinking. Although Peter's primary research is in theory, he is a classroom teacher, too (indeed, many of his students are only a year out of high school). So he's been interested in my investigations of how students read literature and of how teachers can help students have more meaningful transactions with texts and has used them to gain a deeper understanding of issues he has confronted in his own teaching. Our friendly, though sometimes contentious, conversations also suggest that my examinations of and theorizing about what happens when readers come together to talk about texts, both in and out of school, have challenged, supported, and extended his ideas.

This book is an attempt to convey something of the spirit of that continuing intellectual conversation. In so doing, we hope our example will challenge the separation of theory and practice by bringing them into an explicit dialogue. Specifically, this volume alternates a series of theoretical examinations of the nature of literary reading written by Peter with a series of discussions of the educational and ethical implications of those explorations written by me. What results is not in any way intended as a survey of current literary theories: This is not the place to go if you want to find a quick definition of *deconstruction* or if you want to construct a bibliography of the best recent essays in postcolonial theory. It is, rather, an exploration of a particular theoretical perspective—one we are both committed to—and a consideration of how that perspective plays out in practice, particularly in pedagogical practice.

Our perspective is grounded in the importance of envisioning the author as a necessary participant in literary transactions. We recognize that much recent research and theory in both reading and response to literature has placed the spotlight on students as meaning makers and has done much to dispel the image of students as passive recipients of knowledge; and we suspect that most of our readers will share a belief in the importance of students' being active and engaged readers and interested and active participants in classroom discussions. At first glance, our emphasis on the importance of the author may seem to put us at odds with most reader-centered theorists and student-centered teachers. The central argument of this book, however, is that authorial reading is not only compatible with but also essential to truly progressive practice and truly engaged readers.

Our book is about authorizing readers in two senses. Like most contemporary teachers and theorists, we use the phrase *authorizing readers* to mean giving readers power, freeing them from passively accepting their teachers' interpretations. But at the same time the phrase carries for us a second meaning, one that limits readers' freedom, at least for a time. In that second sense of *authorizing*, we mean helping readers develop the conventional knowledge they need to engage intelligently with authors. We believe that that such engagement depends on paying authors and their characters some initial respect. These two meanings are not, however, at odds with each other: Indeed, our argument hinges on the belief that the first is dependent on the second. For only after readers learn how to respect authors can they resist them. Such resistance is an assertion of readers' authority in the strongest sense.

More specifically, the first two chapters of the book set out the basic theoretical conceptions and pedagogical arguments. First, Peter explains his notion of the multiple audiences of any fictional text and describes what he calls "reading as authorial audience." His explanation of what readers have to do to read authorially and what they gain by doing so challenges the argument of those who associate authorial reading with naiveté and simplicity. In Chapter 2, I argue that associating authorial reading with teacher-dominated discussion comes from limited conceptions of the nature of authorial reading and demonstrate how discussions in which participants work to develop authorial readings can be democratic in ways that other discussions of literature cannot. In Chapter 3 Peter extends his theoretical argument by pointing out the ways in which critiques of authorial reading that emphasize the individuality of the reader fail to recognize both the extent to which reading literature is a conventional act and the extent to which authors are constrained by those conventions. In Chapter 4 I extend my pedagogical argument by demonstrating that teachers can help students learn conventions through engaging and humane instruction. This argument questions the tendency to celebrate teaching that is designed to elicit students' responses while being suspicious of teaching that is designed to educate students' responses. In Chapter 5 Peter argues that this suspicion is rooted at least partially in confusing the acts of reading and re-reading and discusses how this confusion distorts the politics of the classroom. In Chapter 6, I explain how Peter's arguments have led me to an uncomfortable reconsideration of the political implications of my own teaching. Our final two chapters offer another kind of political argument as we focus on the implications of our ideas for the reading of what is commonly termed multicultural literature. In these chapters we reverse our order of presentation. In Chapter 7 I build upon the ethical dimension of my pedagogical argument and explain why authorial reading is necessary to do sensitive readings of multicultural literature. In Chapter 8 Peter challenges what he sees as my overly romantic view that any reader can do a sensitive reading of any text by arguing that readers have the obligation to recognize when they are deliberately excluded from a text's intended audience.

Because *Authorizing Readers* is a conversation and not a jointly authored monologue, readers will notice differences from chapter to chapter. For example, Peter writes with/against a variety of literary theorists who have influential voices in the very intense theoretical conversations of the last two decades or so; the books and films he writes about, while an eclectic mix of the canonical and the offbeat, tend to be the sorts of books and films that are taught in colleges; and his concerns are primarily focused on the interaction of the reader and the author, through the medium of the text. For him, the relationship between reading and the classroom is more or less accidental (his word), and he is therefore concerned with classroom practice largely to the extent that it helps students to get at texts in profitable ways. In contrast, I focus on those theorists who seem to me to have had the greatest impact on how secondary school teachers think about their teaching; I draw my examples, for the most part, from a much different group of texts, and I am far more concerned than Peter is with the classroom (or the book discussion group) as an important community in its own right. Moreover, although our theoretical and political orientations are very similar, they are not identical, and through the course of the book we'll explore our disagreements. Readers will undoubtedly note stylistic differences as well. Like Twain in *Huckleberry Finn*, we "make this explanation for the reason that without it many readers would suppose that [we] were trying to talk alike and not succeeding."

Although this book is presented as a conversation between the two of us, in fact it is only a small part of a much larger conversation that we have had with students, colleagues, friends, and family. Wayne C. Booth, Wayne Otto, Michael Rabinowitz, Nancy Sorkin Rabinowitz, and Jeff Wilhelm—as well as Sarah Biondello, Carol Collins, Lyn Grossman, and Karen Osborne at Teachers College Press—read, and quarreled with, earlier drafts of the entire manuscript. Many others have made their imprint on this book by reading portions of it, responding to papers we have presented, or providing research assistance. Although it would be impossible to name all of them, the list would certainly have to include the following: Judy Abel, Ann Ardis, Jamie Barlowe, Sheridan Blau, Katheryn Doran, Eli Goldblatt, Lydia Hamessley, Tieka Harris, Elizabeth Jensen, Hilde Lowenstein, Amie Macdonald, Anne Marcoline, Jim Marshall, Maureen Miller, Alan Nadel, Karen Osborne, James Phelan, Jay Reise, David H. Richter, Christine Rosalia, Kara Stanek, Dorothy Strickland, Priscilla Walton, Joan Wolek, and two anonymous reviewers from Teachers College Press. Thanks to all.

Michael W. Smith

WHERE WE ARE WHEN WE READ

Peter J. Rabinowitz

RECENTLY, TOWARD THE END of an intense first-year seminar on the political, cultural, and ecological consequences of living with atomic weapons, I found myself working through Walter Miller's apocalyptic *Canticle for Leibowitz* with my students. The novel chronicles the rise and fall of a new civilization following a massive nuclear war; and although I had positive (though vague) memories of having read it in high school in the early 1960s, I found, upon re-reading, that it made me profoundly uncomfortable. In particular, I was disturbed by what I felt to be Miller's reliance on Catholic doctrine (including images of rebirth) as a way of cushioning his readers from the horrors of nuclear destruction.

I was especially troubled by the last section of the book, which mounts a strong attack on euthanasia and suicide, even for those suffering severe radiation burns. Nonetheless (or, more accurately, as a result), we were having a spirited discussion about the conflicting demands of science and religion in the field of medical ethics. Suddenly, "Eli" (one of my best students, although one who had apparently not paid too much attention to the novel or to the discussion that day) blurted out that he really liked the book because, as a Jew, he appreciated the way the Jewish author had "spoofed Catholicism."

I wish I could boast that I seized that opportunity to make a lasting impact on my class. But in fact, as so often happens under pressure, I made a wrong turn. I told Eli that he was simply wrong, that Walter Miller was a serious Catholic, that the early versions of its material had even appeared in *Catholic Digest*—and then returned to the discussion of ethics he had disrupted.

I suspect that Eli had two responses. First, he probably felt my manner was dismissive, even authoritarian—and in this belief, he was regrettably right: I didn't attempt to prove my claim that the book was not a spoof but simply made an assertion, relying on my authority as a teacher to carry the point. Second, I suspect that he would have liked me to praise his interpretation, to tell him that he had offered a valuable perspective on the text—and here he was definitely wrong.

Helping ourselves as teachers negotiate between those two responses—finding a theoretical frame that can help us simultaneously to
teach our students to respect authors and the texts they produce without
falling back on authoritarian pedagogy—is the central aim of this book.
Michael Smith and I use the word *respect* advisedly. Respecting authors
does not mean deifying them, agreeing with them, or even liking them.
Tolstoy's Pozdnyshev, the narrator of *The Kreutzer Sonata,* finds the first
movement of the Beethoven violin sonata from which the novel takes its
name "a terrible thing." Yet he still recognizes that "to clap a little, and
then to eat ices and talk of the latest scandal" is an inappropriate response
to a performance (Tolstoy, 1889/1960, pp. 219–220). Respect, in our usage,
is compatible with the most contentious talking back, and even with firm
resistance to the text. To put it somewhat differently: Our general purpose
in this book is to provide a theoretical framework and some practical
applications that will allow a classroom practice that takes students and
their interpretive practices seriously without falling into an interpretive
relativism in which literary texts mean what we want them to mean—at
its most extreme, the kind of solipsistic position represented by Stanley
Fish's (1980) famous claim that *Lycidas* and *The Waste Land* are different
poems only "because I have decided that they will be" (p. 170). Geoffrey
Hartman (1993) has rightly observed that much theory of the "purer kind
. . . shifts attention away from 'reading aright,' or the discovery of a meaningful intention (ethical, historical, aesthetic), toward language as a medium that can never be as transparently communicative as the word 'intention' suggests" (p. 41). Michael and I are convinced that such a shift is
not in the best interests of our students. As Barbara Christian (1985) aptly
put it: "The least we owe the writer, I think, is an acknowledgement of
her labor. After all, writing is intention, is at bottom, work" (p. xi).

HARD THEORY, EASY INFERENCES

Two clarifications are necessary before I can continue. First, a definition.
In our use of the words *theory* and *theoretical,* Michael and I are resisting
an increasingly common tendency to narrow these general terms so that
they refer to a very particular (and forbidding) kind of theory, what's
loosely been labeled "High Theory." Diana Fuss (1994) describes the trend
well: "Theory in its present formulation no longer stands in for, meto-
nymically, all of what has conventionally come under the sign of 'knowledge.' . . . Theory is concerned less with the dispassionate transmission
of knowledge than with the ideological and institutional conditions of its
performance" (p. 103). We, in contrast, are using the term *theory* in a way

closer to that proposed by Jonathan Arac (1994): "I understand *theory* as the deliberate thinking about the principles of activities that are already somewhat familiar" (p. 169). In so doing, we are making not only an intellectual point, but a political point as well. It is not simply that the narrow use of the term distorts our sense of the range of ways in which theory can be deployed; more important, it does so in a hierarchical and exclusionary way by privileging certain kinds of research and interpretive practice at certain kinds of academic institutions. David B. Downing, Patricia Harkin, and James J. Sosnoski (1994) put it well: "It *appears* that very little of what counts as 'theory' can take place in other than the most privileged and elite institutions" (p. 14). One consequence is that even those high-theoretical practices that claim to serve "as a critique of . . . structures of oppression" in fact enforce an academic hierarchy through their excessive difficulty and their consequent "aggrandizement by exclusion" (p. 14).

Second, when I call on Hartman, Arac, and Downing, Harkin, and Sosnoski for support in this way, I do so with some trepidation. Theoretical alliances are tricky matters that, especially in the current, contentious climate, are susceptible to the "Two or Three Things I Know About Her" Syndrome. This phenomenon was made especially vivid during a class I taught a few years back, when one of my students, well known for her post-hippie attire and her ardent vegetarianism, told the class she was against abortion. It was an electrical moment, since everyone in the room had assumed that, once they had access to a few signs of her cultural preferences, they could readily fill in the rest.

Such a gesture of easy extrapolation is understandable and even perhaps forgivable among first-year college students, but it's repeated with alarming regularity in professional critical debates as well. It's appropriate in this regard that the critical terrain is so often described in military terms: Annette Kolodny (1980) described dancing through the minefield, I referred in the previous paragraph to "theoretical alliances," the popular press refers routinely to the culture wars. For such metaphors both nourish and are nourished by assumptions of easy extrapolation. Once someone leans on Paul de Man for support, we believe we can place her on the critical mapping of friends and enemies.

To be sure, it is common to read complaints that someone on "the other side" is being oversimplistic in the way he or she lumps all of *his or her* presumed enemies together. But both among critics who view themselves as traditionalists and critics who view themselves as oppositional (whatever those terms might mean), we can find depressing examples of the same homogenizing practices. George Will (1991/1994), for instance, reduces the Modern Language Association to a group of "academic

Marxists" who share the belief in the doctrines that "writers . . . are captives of the conditioning of their class, sex, race," that "culture is oppressive," and that Emily Dickinson's poetry "exult[s] clitoral masturbation" (pp. 286–287). At a rather different point in the critical spectrum, Donald Morton (1990) loosely refers to "the line of William Bennett, Allan Bloom, and E. D. Hirsch" as if they all shared a single perspective (p. 59).

In this context, it is increasingly necessary to state not only where you stand but also where you do not. Thus it's probably necessary to point out that while I share Hartman's (1993) concern about possible consequences of too great a stress on High Theory, it doesn't follow that I assent to his claim that "it is illogical, in terms of our mission, to displace the literary from the center of attention, and to allow ethics or politics to swallow just about everything" (p. 43). "The literary" is a loaded term, especially in the wake of the Russian formalist interests in "literariness." And once the "literary" is placed at the "center," it is too easy to return to a kind of formalism that, to my mind, is not conducive to a democratic classroom. (Just what can replace that formalism will be clearer as we move on.) The same principle works in reverse as well: When Michael and I disagree with certain elements in a critic's arguments, it does not necessarily imply full-scale opposition. Thus, although we find ourselves disputing Robert Probst at several points in the book, that's not because we find little or nothing to agree with in his work. Indeed, it's because we've learned so much from him, and find ourselves so closely allied to him on so many issues, that we believe these points of difference to be especially revealing.

ANNA'S PERFUME: THE ACTUAL AND AUTHORIAL AUDIENCES

Fundamental to my argument are two interlocking sets of principles, one (the subject of this chapter) about where "the reader" stands when reading and the other (which is elaborated in Chapter 3) about the kinds of activities in which readers engage. To begin: Where are we when we read? From what position do we take in a text? This is not a simple question, in part because "the reader" never reads from a single, unified position. Especially when reading fiction, readers find themselves playing several simultaneous roles. First is the role that Eli was playing most forcefully—what I have elsewhere (Rabinowitz, 1987/1997) called the "actual audience." Each reader comes to a book with a complex and often internally inconsistent set of beliefs, expectations, experiences, desires, and needs. According to current mythology, this was the dimension of the reader that was most forcefully banned from the classroom during the days of "New Criticism," when students were trained to transcend what I. A. Richards (1929) called their *"mnemonic irrelevances"*—the "misleading effects of the reader's being reminded of some personal scene or adventure, erratic associations, the interference of emotional reverberations from a past which may have nothing to do with the poem" (p. 13). And it was consequently the dimension that was most vigorously championed by the subjective reader-critics who helped lead the assault on New Criticism and whose arguments had such a powerful impact on classroom practice in the 1970s and 1980s. As David Bleich put it in *Readings and Feelings* (1975), "the role of personality in response is the most fundamental fact of criticism" (p. 4). Or, to quote Norman Holland (1975), "Each reader builds up an experience from a literary work that is . . . a variation upon his identity theme" (p. 286).

Every individual reader is different from every other reader. As a result, no writer can ever be sure of what his or her readers will be like. At the same time, however, no author can make any rhetorical decisions (conscious or unconscious) without relying on prior assumptions about precisely what values, experiences, habits, and familiarity with artistic conventions his or her readers will bring to the text. In *Canticle for Leibowitz*, for instance, Miller made his choices based on the assumption that his readers would know something about Catholic doctrine, that they would catch his Biblical allusions, that they would be sufficiently familiar with Western European history to appreciate the ways in which that history is recapitulated in the post-Holocaust world of his novel, and that they would understand enough about electrical engineering to recognize the ironic gap between the old circuit designs that Brother Francis finds and his blundering attempt to interpret what they mean. He also expected that his readers would have the emotional and ethical capacity to respond, with horrified sympathy, to the description of Mrs. Grales, the two-headed woman who seeks a baptism for her second head—and that they would have internalized the kind of reading strategies that would allow them to recognize the parallels among the three parts of the novel.

How could Miller have made such assumptions without knowing who, in particular, would read his books? How could he have planned for the students in my class, none of whom had even been born when he wrote his novel? As authors usually do, he used his best judgment and designed his novel for a hypothetical audience that I call the *authorial audience*. It is the underlying argument of this book that in order to read intelligently, we need to come to share the characteristics of the authorial audience, at least provisionally, while we're reading. To the extent that we do not, our reading experience will be more or less seriously flawed.

Let me give a small example that has vexed me for years. Toward the beginning of the 1899 short story "Lady with a Dog," when the protagonist Gurov begins his affair with Anna in Yalta, Chekhov specifically notes the presence of Japanese scents in her hotel room. As a moderately experienced reader of Chekhov, I am confident that he expected me to take this detail as a reflection on Anna. But what, in particular, does it reflect? Is it a sign of her social position? her naiveté? her repressed romanticism? her approachability? her unapproachability? I can't answer, because I don't know enough about the cultural conventions within which Chekhov was working. Among other things, I don't know whether, for a turn-of-the-century Russian, Japanese perfume was cheap or was a sign of good taste, much less whether its semiotic significance changed when you vacationed in Yalta. The resonance of the detail therefore passes me by.

Of course, there will always be a gap between the actual and the authorial audience. There will always be references we do not understand, expectations we do not meet, attitudes we do not share, experiences we have missed. Any reading will therefore, of necessity, be imperfect. In part because we are interested in different kinds of interpretive communities, Michael and I often differ on where to draw the line between the imperfect and the unacceptable. In particular, since he is more concerned than I am with classroom community as an end in itself, he is more apt to be lenient toward imperfections that produce good conversations than I am. Nonetheless, we do both believe that, other things being equal, the smaller the gap, the better the reading. Let me stress that this does not mean that we are proposing a hierarchial, historically oriented classroom in which the teacher's primary task is to fill passive students with information about the work's context, silencing them on the grounds that until they *fully* understand a text, they have nothing of substance to offer to any discussion of interpretation. We are not interested in imposing what Dianne F. Sadoff (1994) has rightly criticized as "prescriptive or normative commentary about literature" (p. 15). But it is our contention, for reasons that Michael will develop in detail in Chapter 2, that the gap between authorial and actual audience *is* a barrier both to good reading and to a truly democratic pedagogical environment, and that while the gap between actual audience and authorial audience can never be completely bridged, we owe it to the texts that we read, and the classrooms in which we discuss them, to try to reduce it as much as possible. Partiality is inevitable, and recognizing that inevitability frees us from the obligation to defer our responses and our judgments until we can claim to know a text completely. But that inevitability does not free us from the need to make a good-faith effort to respect the text's fundamental requests—nor from the obligation to change our responses and judgments in the face of greater knowledge.

The concept of the authorial audience is easily confused with similar terms, such as *intention* and *implied reader.* It is therefore useful to clarify its scope. First, something that Michael keeps reminding me that I have sometimes failed to emphasize in my earlier writings: Although the authorial audience has cognitive components, the authorial audience is not reducible to a cognitive category. As Eli's inability to recognize the moral frame of *Canticle for Leibowitz* makes clear, it has ethical dimensions, in the broadest sense of "ethical" (such as the sense outlined by Booth [1988]) as well. Dostoyevsky's *Crime and Punishment* not only assumes a reader with the interpretive strategies necessary to untangle the philosophical threads of Raskolnikov's "great man" theory. It also assumes a reader who is capable of responding to his character in certain ways—a reader who can both judge his moral flaws correctly and, at the same time, appreciate his virtues sufficiently to appreciate his moral reformation at the end. The authorial audience has what might loosely be called aesthetic components, too. Authors usually write for readers who are capable of taking *pleasure* in certain aspects of their texts. Gerard Manley Hopkins's poems will have little impact on a reader who cannot appreciate the purely sonic qualities of language.

It is here that our position most clearly veers away from the often similar position outlined by E. D. Hirsch, Jr., in *Validity in Interpretation* (1967). Hirsch makes the valuable distinction between meaning (defined as "what the author meant by his use of a particular sign sequence") and significance (defined as "a relationship between that meaning and a person, or a conception, or a situation, or indeed anything imaginable") (p. 8). His argument that understanding the meaning should precede discussions of significance parallels our claims that judgments about—including resistance to—a text should follow the act of joining the authorial audience. But it often seems that for Hirsch meaning is largely a cognitive category—whereas the authorial audience goes well beyond that. Thus I would argue that a reader cannot seriously oppose the racial politics of *Gone with the Wind* without first joining the authorial audience. But this requires more than understanding, cognitively, what Margaret Mitchell "meant" when she wrote her text. Serious opposition also requires experiencing (at least provisionally), and coming to terms with, the ways in which the novel manipulates the emotions of the authorial audience—for instance, the way it creates sympathy for the Klan—and the ways in which these feelings as authorial audience and the reader's knowledge and experience as actual audience come into conflict. To resist the politics of this text in any significant way, one needs to respect Mitchell's art sufficiently to understand its pull.

Our position is thus consistent with (although it does not necessarily entail) a variety of different ideological positions. It is consonant, for instance, with Henry Giroux's notion (1994), following Grossberg, of a pedagogy centering, among other things, on "understand[ing] how issues regarding audience, address, and reception configure within cultural circuits of power to produce particular subject positions and secure specific forms of authority" (p. 49). It is equally consistent with Wayne Booth's more traditional humanist arguments in *The Rhetoric of Fiction* (1983b) and *The Company We Keep* (1988).

Second, the authorial audience is not an inner psychological category. Indeed, this is one of the things that distinguishes the concept from authorial intention. To be sure, there is considerable overlap between the two. But "authorial audience" refers to publicly available social practice rather than to private mental processes. It is reasonable, for instance, for viewers to assume that, as the authorial audience of Nikita Mikhalkov's 1994 film *Burnt by the Sun*, they are expected to associate the black car, even on its first appearance, with sinister forces. It's possible to do so, however, without making any hypotheses about the author/director's interior psychological state. We do not need to know, for instance, anything about his own childhood experiences with black cars—any more than we need to psychoanalyze Edgar Allan Poe in order to recognize that the threat of being buried alive carries a negative valence in his stories.

One consequence of thinking about the authorial audience rather than authorial intention is that it reveals the extent to which authors, as well as readers, are under certain kinds of constraints. For if the authorial audience exists on the level of social practice, an author—if he or she is to be readable—cannot simply write in any way of his or her own choosing: The social nature of the authorial audience puts significant checks on the author's creative freedom. I will return to this issue in the final section of Chapter 3.

In separating the notion of authorial audience from psychology, I am not arguing that private processes are an illegitimate focus of study. Henry Louis Gates, Jr.'s eloquent essay about James Baldwin, "The Welcome Table" (1993), argues that "Desperate to be 'one of us,' to be loved by us, Baldwin allowed himself to mouth a script that was not his own" (p. 58). That observation offers valuable insight into Baldwin's pained later years and the way that pain influenced his writing. But Gates's insights are quite different from the understanding of those "scripts" that comes from reading them as authorial audience. Furthermore, they are secondary—not in the sense of "less important" but in the sense of "dependent upon." That is, Gates's discussion points to contradictions in Baldwin's writings, a contradiction between what was and was not "his own"; and seeing that contradiction requires a prior understanding of what his texts were "mouthing" to the audience he was writing for. Without that understanding in place, the contradiction doesn't exist.

Third, the authorial audience is not a purely textual category—and this is one of the differences between the authorial audience and the "implied reader." The implied reader is the reader one can logically infer from textual features—but the authorial audience may well be more highly specified than any textual features allow us to determine. Thus, to return to Anna's perfume: Chekhov's text implies, quite clearly, a reader who knows that Japanese scents have significance; but the text implies nothing about what that significance is. Indeed, it is because of the gap between the implied reader and the authorial audience that something in addition to formal understanding—historical background, generic experiences, ethical sensitivity—is usually required before we can understand a text.

"DON'T TELL CHUCK": WRITING FOR AND WRITING AROUND

The authorial audience is not the only audience for whom an author designs his or her text. Authors sometimes have to soothe their editors before they can even make initial contact with their readers. Authors also sometimes play one audience off against another. In 1996, for instance, physicist Alan D. Sokal published an article, "Transgressing the Boundaries: Towards a Transformative Hermeneutics of Quantum Gravity," in the prestigious postmodern journal *Social Text*. After its appearance, he announced that it had not been a serious essay at all, but rather a parody of the excesses of postmodern thought, intended as an "experiment" to determine "prevailing intellectual standards." "Would a leading North American journal of cultural studies," he wondered, "publish an article liberally salted with nonsense if (a) it sounded good and (b) it flattered the editors' ideological preconceptions?" There were at least two intended audiences here. On the one hand, he was testing the editors of the journal, offering them "an opportunity to demonstrate their intellectual rigor"; at the same time, he "intentionally wrote the article so that any competent physicist or mathematician (or undergraduate physics or math major) would realize that it is a spoof" (Sokal, 1996b, pp. 62–64).

The voluminous responses to the hoax are a worthy subject of inquiry in themselves. But for the purposes of my argument here, two points are revealing. First, this small scandal reminds us that not every audience an author presupposes is the "authorial audience." The editors of the journal were intended dupes; it's only the "competent" readers who were Sokal's authorial audience. Second, and perhaps more important, even though they never stated it in these terms, nearly everyone in this debate, including (perhaps especially) those committed to postmodern notions of textuality, seemed happy to analyze the complex rhetoric of the affair by leaning on arguments that were grounded in the authorial audience or in the authorial intention behind the prank. Thus the editors of the journal had the following "initial responses" when they found they had been taken:

> One suspected that Sokal's parody was nothing of the sort, and that his admission represented a change of heart, or a folding of his intellectual resolve. Another was less convinced that Sokal knew very much about what he was attempting to expose. A third was pleasantly astonished to learn that the journal is taken seriously enough to be considered a target of a hoax, especially a hoax by a physicist. (Robbins & Ross, 1996, p. 54)

Even more striking, from this perspective, is Stanley Fish's op-ed piece in the *New York Times*. Fish has made his career to a large extent by minimizing the importance of authorial reading. Indeed, much of his work has erased the difference between author and reader by arguing that interpretive strategies are strategies "not for reading (in the conventional sense) but for writing texts, for constituting their properties and assigning their intentions" (1980, p. 171). In other words, in much of Fish's mature theorizing, it is the reader, not the author, who creates both meaning and intention in a text. But Fish criticized Sokal in part because "he carefully packaged his deception so as not to be detected except by someone who began with a deep and corrosive attitude of suspicion" (1996, p. A23). Fish was thus not only hinging his argument on the notion that the author makes the meaning but was going a step further, criticizing what we call the authorial audience on ethical grounds. Stanley Fish promoting *trust* as the key term in the reader/text exchange? The contradiction was gleefully seized upon by many readers of Fish's work.

Hoaxes are a limited rhetorical genre—but multiple presumed audiences emerge in other situations as well. When dealing with volatile issues in repressive times, for instance, authors often have to pay attention to censors of one sort or another. Thus, from the 1930s until the 1960s, Hollywood writers wishing to touch on politically or sexually sensitive issues had to write in a way that would placate not only the Hays Office (the self-censoring board created in 1922 by the Hollywood studios to circumvent outside interference) or its successors but also producers and often actors as well. Gore Vidal describes having to keep the underlying dynamic of *Ben-Hur* from Charlton Heston, who would not have appreciated it:

> I proposed the notion that the two had been adolescent lovers and now Messala has returned from Rome wanting to revive the love affair but Ben-Hur does not. He has read Leviticus and knows an abomination when he sees

one. I told [director William] Wyler, "This is what's going on *underneath* the scene—they *seem* to be talking about politics, but Messala is really trying to rekindle a love affair," and Wyler was startled. We discussed the matter, and then he sighed, "Well. Anything is better than what we've got in the way of motivation, but don't tell Chuck." (Quoted in Russo, 1987, pp. 76–77; see also Vidal, 1995, pp. 304–306)

Understanding texts written under pressure, like understanding hoaxes, requires taking all of the competing audiences into account. There's no way to tell why things are coded as they are without knowing the constraints under which writers are working. Still, the authorial audience has a different status from that of other audiences in an author's mind, and while it's not always easy, in practice, to disentangle them, it is possible to distinguish, in theory, the audience a writer writes *for* and the audience he or she is writing *around*. I will return to this issue in Chapter 8.

It is also important to recognize that works with multiple authors sometimes aim at multiple authorial audiences. This situation comes up, for instance, in this very volume. Michael's imagined readers are primarily concerned with classroom dynamics and are interested in theoretical issues largely for their impact on pedagogy. My authorial audience is more interested in the theoretical issues per se, and is more patient with analyses that do not seem to have immediate pedagogical payoffs. The texts most familiar to our presumed readers are different, too, so we are apt to look in different places for examples. And although we have both tried to broaden our accessibility, we recognize the inherent difficulties a project like this one imposes on its actual audience, which is asked to switch gears with regularity.

More important, we find multiple authorial audiences in film adaptations or musical settings of literary works—especially where one author has misunderstood (or repressed) the intended meaning of the other. Tchaikovsky's profound misunderstanding of Pushkin's *Eugene Onegin* makes his opera a rhetorical maze; as Lydia Hamessley (1994) points out, in Henry Lawes's settings of Katherine Philips's poetry, the music attempts to control the poetry. Even in such complex cases, though, the notion of authorial audience, while it needs to be pluralized, is still essential to analysis.

ONRUSHING ENGINES: GETTING OUT OF THE WAY OF TEXTS

In arguing for the primacy of authorial reading, I am not recapitulating claims for universality. It is not the case that all actual readers can join the authorial audience, nor is it even the case that all actual readers *should* join the authorial audience of all texts. An individual actual reader, for instance, may be intentionally excluded by a text. That is, the authorial audience may not include me, not accidentally because I lack knowledge about Japanese perfume, but purposefully because the author has wished to cast me as someone outside his or her readership. Sometimes this is an intellectual exclusion: I feel this way, for instance, when I try to get into *Finnegans Wake*. More important these days, however (and I realize the distinctions are hazy), are political or ethical exclusions. In particular, members of privileged groups reading or writing about texts by marginalized writers—White critics confronting Black texts, straight critics confronting gay texts—often find themselves in uncomfortable positions.

We can see symptoms of dis-ease about the ethics of trying to join an authorial audience that may in fact be trying to exclude him in Richard Shusterman's (1995) *Critical Inquiry* dialogue with Tim Brennan. Shusterman, a "white, Oxford-trained, philosophy professor (and not simply a Jew but an Israeli)" found himself questioning his authority to interpret rap. He therefore felt he needed the "symbolic permission of a leading African-American critic, Houston Baker" before he could write on the subject—and even that failed to solve the crisis of legitimation (pp. 150–151). Similarly, Brennan (1995) felt the need to preface *his* remarks with the affirmation that he did not want to be seen as trying to be part of the "social process of African-American self-definition and recognition" (p. 159).

I do not know whether Brennan and Shusterman in fact should have been writing the essays that they wrote, or whether they were, in fact, taking on texts from which they had been properly excluded. But I do know that dealing seriously with such difficulties, which we address in more detail in Chapters 7 and 8, is no trivial matter for teachers, especially as reading lists become more multicultural. And stressing the notion of authorial reading, far from eliding these difficulties, is in fact especially valuable in part because it helps us conceptualize them. Neither Brennan nor Shusterman could possibly come to grips with their dilemma without coming to grips with their relationships to the authorial audiences of the texts in question. And even if it is sometimes morally inappropriate for some actual reader to join the authorial audience, that ethical choice has its cost. For if you cannot, or do not, join the authorial audience, you are in some major respect outside the text.

Let me emphasize again that joining the authorial audience is not the same thing as *accepting* the position of the authorial audience. In *The Resisting Reader* (1978), for instance, Judith Fetterley calls for readers to resist certain texts, and, as the echo in our subtitle suggests, we believe her advice is sound. So is Susan S. Lanser's call for a practice that helps students "stand outside rather than within textually or professorial inscribed reader positions, to question and critique the curriculum" (1994, p. 65). Critical readers—in the best sense of "critical"—need to question the ideology proposed by the texts they read. But you cannot step *beyond* the authorial audience without first recognizing it; and it is therefore not inconsistent that, although Fetterley does not use my terminology, her analyses start out with attempts to reconstruct authorial readings. And it is thus appropriate that when James Phelan disputes her critique, he does so not by disputing her complaints about sexist portrayals but rather by questioning her description of the novel's progression as seen by the authorial audience (1989, pp. 165–188). As Phelan insists, critical reading involves questioning the values of the texts you engage; but you can't begin to do so unless you first determine the authorial audience.

Let me start with a simple example. You're sitting at lunch with a colleague who says, "Hey! I just heard a good one. Why won't a barracuda eat an IRS agent?" You reply, "I don't know. Why?" Your friend chuckles: "Professional courtesy!" Now imagine the same scenario, but substituting the word *librarian* for IRS *agent*. Now imagine a third version, substituting the word *Jew*.

Certainly, it would be possible to perform a purely formal analysis of these jokes, much in the way Vladimir Propp (1928/1970) analyzed Russian fairy tales; but such an analysis, which might well underscore their formal similarities (indeed, their formal identity), would not get to the issue either of their values or, for that matter, of their effectiveness. Bringing in the authorial audience, however, allows us to go considerably further.

First, it would remind us that jokes all depend on generic expertise. All versions assume that the audience will be familiar with the genre of the joke; if the actual audience is expecting a scientific answer to the question, the exchange will puzzle rather than amuse. I return to the notion of genre in Chapter 3.

Second, approaching the jokes in terms of the authorial audience provides one of the clearest avenues to understanding the failure of the middle version. Although it remains formally correct, this variant assumes an authorial audience that believes that librarians are an especially vicious class of people—in other words, it assumes an authorial audience that doesn't exist in the culture at large. This version might serve a function for the teller, as a way of expressing a personal animus; it might serve, for the actual audience, as a revelation of the teller's eccentricities; it might conceivably work as a joke in some very specific actual community under some very specific circumstances. But for all intents and purposes, the joke has no public existence *as a joke* because its authorial audience is so eccentric.

Third, and most interesting: The strongest way to deal seriously with the immorality of the third version is to recognize, to begin with, the values that it presupposes in its audience. That is, only after we understand the audience experience presumed by the joke, only after we confront what sort of person would in fact have that experience, and only after we recognize such people really do have a significant presence in our culture can we come to terms with the key difference between the second and third versions: The problem with the third is not simply that it expresses a personal animosity but that it taps into a larger culture of anti-Semitism. And we can learn something significant about that anti-Semitism and about how to resist it by putting ourselves, momentarily, in the position of the authorial audience. And who knows? Perhaps this experience might illuminate the dynamics of the first version—the "safe" one—and encourage those of us who laughed at it thoughtlessly to reconsider our reaction and think about the political ramifications of such a quick, anti-tax response.

The same is true of more substantial texts. You can't begin to explore the macho ideology of Hemingway's story "Fifty Grand" or the Cold War male hysteria of Mickey Spillane's *I, the Jury* without first taking account of the beliefs and attitudes that the authors expected in their readers. Joining the authorial audience, in other words, is a provisional testing, not a permanent adopting, of a perspective. It does not require any ultimate assenting to the author's point of view—and as I have stressed, it certainly does not stand in the way of vigorous disagreement with an author or a text. On the contrary, it's what makes talking back possible in the first place.

For example, it's possible, even admirable, for an actual reader of Jane Austen's *Sense and Sensibility* to question whether Marianne's marriage to Colonel Brandon really *is* a reward—or whether Marianne is, rather, selling out to repressive social conventions. But to resist Jane Austen's perspective on domesticity requires first respecting her art sufficiently to sort out the ironies of her complex description of Marianne's decision, "with no sentiment superior to strong esteem and lively friendship, voluntarily to give her hand to another!—and *that* other, a man . . . who still sought the constitutional safeguard of a flannel waistcoat" (1811/1933, p. 378). And sorting out that irony requires understanding the precise meaning of "sentiment" for the authorial audience—as well as recognizing the social implications of a flannel waistcoat. Likewise, it was perfectly appropriate for Eli to resist the Catholic underpinnings of *Canticle for Leibowitz*. But disagreement requires initial common ground.

Without prior understanding, there is nothing to disagree *with*, and debate and dispute are replaced with talking at cross purposes. The reader will simply be engaged in a straw-person argument.

I would not need to be so emphatic if William R. Schroeder (1986) had been correct when he insisted, with some dismay, that "the authorial intention theory seems to be gaining currency again" (p. 14). I see no evidence of such a shift. Even critics who claim to be aiming at rhetorical analysis often ignore one side of the rhetorical equation by dismissing the author. In the opening chapter of *Sodometries,* for instance, Jonathan Goldberg (1992) analyzes a political T-shirt supporting the Gulf War, building in part both upon claims about what the shirt assumes is in the mind of its audience and upon claims about what is involved in reading the shirt "properly" (p. 5). But at no point in his analysis does he consider the shirt as an object made *by someone* with some more or less specific audience in mind; he works instead with a textualized audience that is quite divorced from any authorial presence and quite divorced from any political reality. It is for a similar reason—the way failure to consider the authorial audience depoliticizes interpretation—that I disagree with Isaiah Smithson (1994) when, following Culler, he formulates what he sees as the central critical dichotomy of the day by distinguishing between critics who are engaged in "interrogating cultural phenomena" and those who are engaged in "elucidating literary masterpieces" (p. 1). His heart is with the former—but I would argue, as I would argue with Goldberg, that you cannot interrogate cultural phenomena without first elucidating the objects involved, whether they be masterpieces or not.

In the past, I've stressed that there are many kinds of readings that do not require joining the authorial audience even as a first step. But under the pressure of constant conversations with Michael, I've grown increasingly skeptical of how many there really are. Certainly, there are aspects of *literary study,* study of the institution of literature broadly construed, that do not involve reading as authorial audience because they do not involve any interpretive activities at all—in fact, because they do not require reading at all. One can chart out what texts are included in anthologies without getting into problems of interpretation. It is even possible, as Janice Radway (1984) has demonstrated, to survey the reactions of actual readers without probing the question of what the texts meant for the readers they were designed for.

But these are circumscribed fields of inquiry. And most other critical investigations that attempt to circumvent reading as authorial audience find themselves reduced to either incoherence or triviality. Take, for instance, the operations of censors. Censors often act on the assumption that certain superficial "facts" about a text, regardless of the interpretive scheme from which they were expected to be read, are sufficient grounds for silencing. We can see this most clearly in attempts to regulate appropriate language. I remember being chastised by a colleague on the staff of *Fanfare*, a record magazine for which I regularly write, because in an interview with Count Alexander Labinsky, I had quoted his use of the word *fuck*. It had been a difficult interview to write up, and the choices I made about language were made, either rightly or wrongly, in terms of my perceptions both of my audience and of the way I believed my interviewee wished to present himself to that audience. For my colleague, however, it was an open-and-shut case. Certain words are, as they are for the Federal Communications Commission (FCC) (at least at certain times of day), simply taboo. It's because of the same kind of thinking that Hemingway could, in *A Farewell to Arms*, refer to being kicked in the scrotum, but not in the balls (Hemingway & Perkins, 1996, p. 75).

Motion Picture Association of America (MPAA) regulations about sex, violence, and language are on the surface more subtle, because they supposedly take context into account. As Jack Valenti (1996), head of the ratings board, puts it, "In making their evaluation, the ratings board does not look at snippets of film in isolation but considers the film in its entirety." But there is a curious literalism in the principle that "The rating board can make its decisions only by what is seen on the screen, not by what is imagined or thought." And it is perhaps no surprise that, as a consequence, the language policy ultimately falls back on the variation of the taboo-words principle enunciated by my colleague: "A film's single use of one of the harsher sexually-derived words, though only as an expletive, shall initially require the Rating Board to issue that film at least a PG-13 rating. More than one such expletive must lead the Rating Board to issue a film an R rating, as must even one of these words used in a sexual context."

Not much subtler are many of the arguments about the use of the word *nigger* in *Huckleberry Finn* or *Show Boat*. I am not here taking a position on whether or not Twain's novel should be taught in high school or college literature classes or whether the Kern/Hammerstein musical should be produced unaltered. My point is rather that you cannot even begin to discuss these questions without first investigating the authorial audience and how that word is supposed to be taken in the text. It is, for instance, only by taking the authorial audience into account that we can distinguish the use of the word *nigger* in Twain and Hammerstein from its use in Joseph Conrad, Charles Chesnutt, Thomas Dixon, Jr., Dick Gregory, or Spike Lee.

It might seem a paradox, in fact, to write an essay condemning Twain's use of the word *nigger*—since the essay itself would commit the same sin. Many critics would, I believe, get around this problem by evoking the traditional philosophical distinction between use and mention. The word *nigger* is *used*, for instance, when someone writes "Kill all the niggers" on a bathroom wall; the word is *mentioned* in the sentence *"Nigger* is an offensive word." Apparently, there is widespread agreement that mention has a different ethical status than use, especially when the mention itself is further cushioned by the use of such arch euphemisms as "the N-word." (I recall hearing a young boy breathlessly complaining to his soccer coach that a member of the other team had "used the asshole-word.") I have no problem with the principle that mention and use demand different ethical evaluations. But I would argue that in many cases, the difference between author and narrator generates the same distinction. When Jason begins his section of *The Sound and the Fury* with "Once a bitch, always a bitch" (Faulkner, 1929/1990, p. 180), Jason is using the term *bitch*, but Faulkner is only mentioning it. Is the same thing happening in Twain? Perhaps, and perhaps not; but we can't tell simply by looking at the words on the page. We need to think more deeply about the author/reader exchange, which ultimately requires coming to terms with the authorial audience.

Once again, let me stress that considering the authorial audience does not answer the question of whether or not *Huckleberry Finn* should be taught. It only provides the grounds on which it is possible to have a serious discussion of the question. It is a first step, not a last step.

In sum, it is difficult to talk seriously about language in a text without considering the authorial audience. It is even more difficult to imagine such a detour in any study that involves confronting the ideology of what is represented in an imaginative text—for representation is necessarily representation from a particular point of view, and attitudes toward what is represented can only be analyzed seriously when that point of view is taken into account. In particular, although he used different terminology, Wayne Booth (1974) confirms that failure to join the authorial audience almost inevitably results in a failure to gauge irony. Misreading irony takes many shapes: whether failing to recognize irony when it is there, or imputing it (as in Eli's case) when it is not, or, more subtly, by misconstruing its angle and scope. In her novel *Show Boat*, Edna Ferber describes melodrama as plays in which "innocence wore golden curls. Wickedness wore black. Love triumphed, right conquered, virtue was rewarded, evil punished" (1926/1958, p. 65) and in which "onrushing engines were cheated of their victims" (p. 102). Understanding these passages requires not only recognizing her mockery but also coming to terms with a certain nostalgic sympathy as well.

More generally, the disregard for the importance of authorial readings has led to a widespread inability to distinguish representation and endorsement. Thus, for instance, Susan McClary (1991) argues that Bizet's *Carmen* "articulates . . . a whole range of late nineteenth-century symptoms of cultural paranoia" (p. 63) and that through its "deadly narrative strategies" (p. 79), it causes "the listener not only to accept Carmen's death as 'inevitable,' but actually to *desire* it" (p. 62). McClary, one of the sharpest musicologists around, is undoubtedly correct about what the opera represents. But the key interpretive issue is not *whether* the late nineteenth century's paranoia appears in the opera but rather *how* its symptoms are represented. The meaning of the "Gypsy-as-outsider" trope, after all, was strongly contested in nineteenth-century culture. There's the contrast, for instance, between the "Gypsy-as-threat" in Jane Austen's *Emma* and the "Gypsy-as-anti-philistine-ideal" in Pushkin's poem *The Gypsies*—an idealization that may be uncomfortably racist for many contemporary readers, too, but one that is nonetheless significantly different in the values expected of its authorial audience. And no discussion of where a text positions its reader can avoid coming to terms with what baggage it expects its reader to be carrying.

But even critical activity that goes well beyond what is generally construed as "interpretation"—even much purely formal analysis—requires coming to terms with the authorial audience. Indeed, it may well be that formal studies hinge on the authorial audience as much as interpretive studies do. Is *Measure for Measure* a comedy or a tragedy? Could one begin to answer that question without confronting Shakespeare's expectations about his audience's fears and anxieties about syphilis? Or its attitudes toward marriage as an institution? Can one, for that matter, perform a formalist metrical analysis on a poem without knowing the rules of pronunciation shared by the author's expected audience? This does not necessarily mean that one needs to support what Catherine Addison (1994) calls the "pernicious" doctrine that "poems should be pronounced as their authors would have pronounced them" (p. 672)—only that the expected pronunciation provides the grid against which any individual reader's interpretations takes on its significance.

Study of the authorial audience, as I have suggested, is especially important in cultural studies. For instance, if one wished to follow Isaiah Smithson's (1994) definition—"culture studies is committed to understanding how texts acquire meaning, examining the relations among texts and the nation's several cultures, expressing dissent based on these investigations, and fostering social change" (p. 9)—it would be necessary, as a first step, to deal with authorial reading, which is a prerequisite to understanding the process by which texts acquire meaning. I would certainly agree with Zavarzadeh and Morton (1991) that literariness does not exist in inherent "internal properties" of texts but rather in the procedures by which we take them in; but while this means that literature is not "a discourse *inherently* different from other discourses" (p. 9, emphasis added), it does not follow that literature's noninherent differences from other discourses are minimal or can be ignored. That is, while many in cultural studies might disagree, literary texts *do* take their meanings in ways quite different from the ways other cultural artifacts take their meanings. Global interpretive skills that do not take the difference between literary and nonliterary texts into account are unlikely to serve their interrogators well. One major aspect of this difference will be clarified in the last section of this chapter.

CAIRO'S PERFUME: THE TEACHER'S ROLE

As I have suggested above, my own interests in this issue have been primarily theoretical. But working with Michael has made me increasingly sensitive to the pedagogical dimensions of my work. Specifically, the difference between joining the authorial audience and assessing the authorial audience from our perspective as actual audience is of pedagogical, as well as theoretical, importance, for the questions one can ask about each step are quite different, and there is a major difference in the types of classroom interaction they involve. Recently, while I was teaching *The Maltese Falcon*, my class stumbled over one passage because several students didn't understand that Joel Cairo (the character played by Peter Lorre in the film) was being coded as gay. In the discussion, two different sets of questions became intermingled. The first was a series of what might be called reading-skill questions: How did I "know" that the authorial audience read him as gay? How could I convince my class that I was not "overinterpreting"? What were the signals in the text that would have been obvious to the readers for whom Hammett was writing? The second was a set of interpretive questions: How do we feel about the treatment of the character? What can the particular agreed-upon signals for homosexuality—for instance, perfume—tell us about attitudes in the 1920s?

This distinction may seem at first similar to Robert Scholes's (1985b) distinction between interpretation—"what the teacher knows and you don't," or, less coyly, calling "upon all texts to stand and yield their hidden meanings" (p. 40)—and criticism. In fact, however, my first step also includes much of what Scholes includes in criticism—"discovering the codes that are invoked by a text and exposing the means by which a text seeks to control our responses to it" (p. 42). In any case, I believe (although Michael does not fully agree with me here) that distinguishing these two sets of questions is important, not only because it clarifies what's at stake but also because each of them leads to a different kind of class activity, *participation* and *discussion.* It is of course possible for a class to approach the first question—the one about the nature of the authorial audience—in an interactive way, where the students and the teacher both talk. But that is still not really a situation in which democratic discussion is possible, because it is not a question about which students can develop their own lines of thought. It's similar, in that regard, to having music students count out the rhythm of a piece of music in order to determine the meter—they're engaged, but not really discussing, and to a large extent, this is an area where the teacher has authority because he or she usually has greater knowledge. As a "liberal-minded" teacher, I often aim at giving a Socratic veneer to such moments—but it's possible that I'm simply being dishonest. As Paula Treichler (1994) remarks, "No utopian pedagogical forms exist: sometimes the assertion of authority, hierarchy, and propriety brings us as close to utopia as a particular classroom ever will" (p. 93). As I've said, Michael and I disagree about the pedagogical consequences here. At least at the high school level, he is less apt simply to *tell* students what is at stake. In contrast, although I try (not always successfully) to avoid the kind of authoritarian gestures with which I answered Eli, I do not feel that there is much to be gained by discussing whether (as opposed to explaining in detail how I know that) Cairo is being portrayed as a homosexual or not.

The second, interpretative, set of questions, in contrast, is one where students and teachers *can* engage, if not as equals, then certainly as partners in a democratic inquiry. But that second set of questions is only possible once the answer to the first set of questions is in place. I think making this distinction offers, among other things, a way out of the familiar teaching dilemma that Gerald Graff (1994) has labeled "the bully/wimp syndrome." Graff sometimes feels he is dominating his classes and sometimes feels as if he is letting them down by simply letting them chatter on. "When I assert myself aggressively, I feel as if I am imposing my authority on students, turning them into passive receivers of intellectual bank deposits. But when I hold back I feel I am defaulting on my responsibilities, and I wonder what I am doing teaching at all" (p. 181). Graff's by-now-famous solution is to teach the conflicts by bringing in counterauthorities—but that still leaves students in a secondary position, watching the experts battle it out. Centering the classroom on reading as authorial audience is more liberating because it recognizes and celebrates those areas where students do, in fact, have significant material to offer to the class.

To put it differently: I agree with Lawrence Grossberg's (1994) critique of "hierarchical" pedagogical practices where "the teacher assumes that he or she understands the real meanings of particular texts and practices, the real relations of power embodied within them, and the real interests of the different social groups brought together in the classroom or in the broader society" (p. 16). But I would not want (nor would Grossberg) to let that critique intimidate me and deter me from telling students what I *do* know about the texts in question.

AT LILLAS PASTIA'S TAVERN: THE NARRATIVE AUDIENCE

In terms of requiring their readers to join their authorial audiences, *Canticle for Leibowitz* and *Sense and Sensibility* are not unlike any other public communication. Physicists and journalists, too, write with an authorial audience in mind, and they run into parallel problems when their actual readers fail to join it. With striking understatement, James Wilkinson (1996) has argued that "few of the [historical] sources that have survived, however credible, supply the background historians need to interpret them. Many eyewitness accounts assume, consciously or not, that the audience has pertinent supplemental information" (p. 83). That is not only true of ancient texts. In order to make sense of the editorials written after the first use of atomic weapons, it's necessary to know the scientific beliefs that the writers assumed their readers would hold.

But fiction, because of its imitative nature, brings yet a third audience into play. For fictional narratives are imitations, in the specific sense that they appear to be something that they are not. This does not mean that fiction is necessarily mimetic in the narrow traditional sense—fiction is assuredly not always (perhaps not ever) a mirror of "reality." But fiction is always playing a special kind of double game, which entails a complex relationship with the world outside it. Prosper Mérimée's novella *Carmen*, for instance, appears to be a memoir of a traveling archaeologist who in turn relates the life story of an imprisoned murderer. One way of conceptualizing this duality is to recognize that, since a novel is usually an imitation of some nonfictional form (often biography or memoir), so the narrator (whether dramatized or not) is an imitation of an author. And just as an actual author always writes for a hypothetical authorial audience, so a narrator always writes for an imitation audience that I call the *narrative audience*. To read fiction, we must not only join the authorial audience (which recognizes what it reads as an invented artifact and hence treats the characters as constructs—stressing what James Phelan [1989] calls their synthetic dimension) but also *pretend* to be members of the narrative audience (which takes what it reads as history and treats the characters as real—stressing what Phelan calls their mimetic dimension). This narrative audience is an audience that, in the case of *Canticle for Leibowitz*, believes that a massive nuclear war actually did take place—one that, in the case of *Sense and Sensibility*, believes, less extravagantly, that a woman named Marianne Dashwood really existed and that she is a person worth caring about.

The experience of fictional works is thus always at least double. We can treat the work neither purely as what it is nor purely as what it appears to be but must in fact hold these competing (and mutually incompatible) perspectives simultaneously in our consciousness. We are hardly responding appropriately if we pull out an atlas to find the exact location of the monastery that serves as the principal setting of *Canticle*; but neither should we refuse to sympathize with Abbot Zerchi's agonies over medical ethics merely because he is an invented character. The intended response treats *Canticle for Leibowitz* as both "real" and "unreal" at once. Similarly, we are not reading *Carmen* intelligently if we treat the story as "real" and try to make a reservation at the tavern of Lillas Pastia where Carmen sets up a rendezvous with Don José on his release from prison. But at the same time, I wouldn't want my students to close off sympathy for the pain Carmen suffers under Don José's attempts at sexual control simply because she's not a "real" person.

Thus, for instance, the authorial audience of *The Rape of Shavi*, Buchi Emecheta's parodic gloss on *Lost Horizon*, has a great deal of information, both literary-technical and historical-cultural, at its disposal. It understands how to distinguish different points of view in a novel, for instance, and it knows, at least in general, the historical-cultural relationship between Europe and Africa. The narrative audience has that information, too; but in addition, the narrative audience believes in the existence of a country called "Shavi" with a large, readily accessible supply of stones as hard as diamonds—beliefs that the authorial audience does *not* share.

Distinguishing the authorial from the narrative audience is not simply a matter of assuming that what is represented in the text is imaginary. It might be foolish to try to book a reservation at Lillas Pastia's; but many people *do* take the Dashiell Hammett tour in San Francisco, a tour that traces over locales featured in *The Maltese Falcon*. Rather, distinguishing these two audiences involves a far more intricate process of sorting out— a process that can easily go wrong in practice.

As I've suggested, these two audiences can have a variety of relations to one another. Different authors, and the same authors in different texts or even different parts of the same text, aim for different balances between the two, to radically different effects. The dense historical texture of Margaret Walker's Civil War novel *Jubilee*, for instance, solidifies our alliance with the characters and their fate. In contrast, the closing of Nabokov's *Bend Sinister* hits us as it does at least in part because our compassion for Krug, whose son has been tortured and killed by a totalitarian regime, is abruptly undermined by the intervention of the author, who exposes the fabricated nature of the narrative audience by informing his readers that the character is only an artistic creation, that his immortality was "a play upon words," and that "death was but a question of style" (1947/1960, pp. 210–211). The authorial/narrative distinction helps us understand, as well, the nuanced effect of Hitchcock's *Psycho*, which depends on our relationship both to the characters and to the actors who play them. As Thomas Allen Nelson (1982) puts it, "In *Psycho* Hitchcock . . . teases us, especially the males in the audience, into a voyeuristic longing to gaze with Norman Bates (Anthony Perkins) on the erotically inviting body of Janet Leigh, which Hollywood in *its* prurience had enticingly hidden from view for many years" (p. 24). Likewise, the authorial/narrative distinction helps us understand how we are intended to read symbolism. Some symbols—for instance, Virginia Woolf's lighthouse—are aimed at the authorial level; but other symbols, like the secret message proving immortality at the end of Nabokov's short story "The Vane Sisters," are intended to work on the narrative level alone.

Both the authorial and the narrative audience are abstractions, but they are abstractions in radically different senses. The authorial audience is a hypothetical construction of what the author expects his or her readers to be like; the narrative audience, on the other hand, is an imaginative creation by the author—something he or she hopes to convince the readers to pretend to become. To add to the complexity, the authorial and narrative audiences are not parallel but are in a sense hierarchical; that is, *one aspect of joining the authorial audience is pretending to join the narrative audience.* When Michael and I speak, throughout this book, of reading authorially, then, we are *not* speaking of a reading that ignores our participation as narrative audience. We are, rather, talking about a kind of reading that involves participation on both levels, balanced according to the demands of that particular text.

In describing fiction in the way that I do, I am not taking a position on the essence of "literature." My view is compatible with a wide range of competing conceptions—with many views of literature as creating worlds of the imagination, and with John Beverley's (1993) position that literature has a strong "connection with the formation of the modern state and the conditions of maintaining and redefining capitalist hegemony, particularly in situations of colonial or neocolonial domination" (p. xiii). It's likewise consistent with the notion that the distinction between literature and nonliterature is historically variable and that the lines between the two differ according to time and place. But Michael and I do believe that for all its complexity and variability, the distinction between fiction and nonfiction is a crucial one and one that can be best understood in terms of the operations of the reader.

In stressing that fiction is inherently different from nonfiction, I am consciously working against the grain of an increasing tendency to use *fiction* in a loose sense, meaning something like "crafted" or "ideologically inflected," to refer to all human creations. This is the sense in which Annette Kolodny, for instance, used the term when she claimed that "literary history . . . is a fiction" (1980, p. 8). I agree fully with her point: History is constructed as much from the concerns of the present as from the "facts" of the past. But because of her formulation, she makes that point at considerable cost: She mystifies the distinction between the ways historians and journalists invent and the ways novelists invent. (For an excellent recent discussion, see Lehman (1998]). Similarly, Alvin Kernan (1993), even as he is trying to defend literature from postmodern critiques, falls into the same trap: "Nor are we likely soon to forget what theory has painfully taught us, that all forms of discourse are fictional in at least some sense" (p. 25).

Kernan (1993) quickly tries to restore the distinction, and he does so in terms of truth: "Literary texts . . . differ from other types of texts in being self-consciously aware that they are not trying to be faithful to some prior literal truth" (p. 25). I am taking a different tack: Fiction is different from nonfiction, not because it has a different relation to literal truth (a position that begs for a postmodern attack) but because it calls on different conventions of reading. Specifically, fiction calls on the reader to play the part both of authorial and of narrative audience. In describing it in this way, I am trying to maintain the fiction/nonfiction distinction without falling into the binary hierarchy attacked by many postmodern critics, especially those involved in cultural studies. Jane Gallop (1993), for instance, sees the turn from literary studies to cultural studies as a recognition that literature should be "looked at as one among various signifying practices rather than as a privileged site of 'culture'" (p. 66). I would argue, however, that denying fiction's rhetorical differences is a counterproductive means of challenging its privilege. Whether or not literature is the privileged site of culture, it operates—at least in its fictional manifestations—in a way quite different from, say, architecture and city planning.

The tendency to treat fiction as just one signifying practice obscures the distinction between narrative and authorial levels, and consequently obscures what's at stake in many literary disputes. This is not only true of the disputes of professional critics; although the specific terminology may be technical, the distinction itself is crucial from the earliest reading experiences as well. Recently, I was listening to a group of 13-year-old girls at a birthday party arguing, with considerable passion, about whether Walt Disney's Goofy was or was not a dog. The anti-dog faction called on the undeniable evidence that Goofy walked on two legs and talked, in contrast to Pluto, who did not; and since Pluto was a dog, Goofy could not be. Instead, they maintained, he was a cow. This claim brought about the counterclaim that he had no horns.

Two key theoretical points are in order here. First, there is no way the discussion could have continued as anything but the shouting match that it was without some effort to determine the nature of the narrative audience—that is, to determine what authorial-level information was in fact applicable on the narrative level. That is, none of the girls disputed that the actual and authorial audiences believe that a dog cannot stand on two legs and talk; the real question, although it was never precisely clarified, was whether or not this belief carried over to the narrative level.

Second, distinguishing the authorial and narrative levels does not answer the interesting and important questions about a text (in the Disney case, the question of why, on the narrative level, dogs are divided into two classes). Rather, it is what makes intelligent formulation of those questions possible in the first place. And while this particular case appears trivial, at least to those not engaged in the dispute, it's paralleled by numerous other literary disputes with more substantial weight. A class can't discuss the psychosexual dynamics of James's *The Turn of the Screw* without first determining whether the authorial audience's nonbelief in ghosts carries over to the narrative audience; but even once a group has decided on the answer to that question, the important questions have not yet been answered—they've only been made available to be asked.

Among other things, this model helps us distinguish three different kinds of misreading (and I realize the term is problematic), or mispositionings, with regard to texts. First, we have what might be called the Quixotic or "Different Drummer" reading—a reader might not be in the authorial audience at all, either through a short-circuit in his or her attempt to join (my own situation, say, in trying to read medieval texts that rely heavily on fine points of Christian doctrine) or, more interesting, through a principled refusal to accept the author's authority, such as Roland Barthes's preference for "writerly" texts in which "the reader [is] no longer a consumer, but a producer of the text" (1970/1974, p. 4); as he puts it, "The birth of the reader must be at the cost of the death of the Author" (1968/1977, p. 148). Quixotic readings have become increasingly au courant, in a variety of forms besides Barthes's playful production of plurality. They're found, for instance, in the wake of the extreme versions of subjective criticism that are often assumed to represent "reader-response criticism." David Bleich (1975), for instance, insists that "reading is a wholly subjective process and . . . the nature of what is perceived is determined by the rules of the personality of the perceiver"(p. 3). Quixotic readings are also found in the wake of the various kinds of skepticism loosely associated with deconstruction and the criticism of Stanley Fish (1980), who argues that "interpretation is not the art of construing but the art of constructing. Interpreters do not decode poems; they make them" (p. 327). Whatever its theoretical merits, such principled disdain for the authorial audience makes it difficult, even impossible, for readers, especially young and inexperienced readers, to be educated, molded, or discomfited by the texts that they read—for as soon as they assume the role of both writer and reader, they meet no one but themselves. It's not simply that such a position makes it difficult to come to agreement—it also makes it difficult to come to meaningful disagreement with a text. A reader can always stage a debate with his or her own invention of an author—but such debates remain monologues, limited to the reader's own prior conceptions. One cannot meaningfully take issue with Walter Miller's arguments about euthanasia, for instance, unless one understands where he is to begin with—and that requires recognizing, as Eli could not, that his text is not ironic on this score.

Second, it's possible—in what we might call an Emma-Bovary reading—to overemphasize the narrative audience, forgetting that we are reading a work of art. Few readers are quite as naive as, say, the backwoodsman in Edna Ferber's *Show Boat* for whom theater, having "come late into the life of [his] literal mind," was indistinguishable from reality, and who threatens to shoot the villain in the melodrama on the stage (1926/1958, p. 101). And fewer readers still have the experience of Woody Allen's Kugelmass ("The Kugelmass Episode"), who actually enters Flaubert's novel and has an affair with Emma Bovary. Still, modern Western literature is full of cautionary tales about readers who are seduced by the mimetic level of texts—not only Flaubert's Emma but also Pushkin's Tatyana and Twain's Tom Sawyer fall prey to the lure of the narrative audience. We all have had students who have been so caught up in the characters and plot that they have failed to recognize the artistic drive behind it; and we've all read newspaper editorials and popular opinion pieces about violence on television that fail in the same way.

Third—and prodding from Michael has revealed my own insensitivities on this score—one can engage in more or less extreme forms of Blimberism. Blimber was the teacher in Dickens's *Dombey and Son* who believed that "all the fancies of the poets, and lessons of the sages, were a mere collection of words and grammar, and had no other meaning in the world" (1846–48/1907, pp. 134–35). Few critics today go to such lengths, but many do underestimate the importance of the narrative audience, treating the text as a semiotic construct without serious mimetic interaction with human lives. As I have argued in more detail elsewhere (Rabinowitz, 1996), we can see this in many contemporary interpretations of Conrad's *Heart of Darkness*. While an earlier generation of critics tended to universalize the novella as a statement about human nature, in university settings readers are now increasingly likely to explore more postmodern claims. Because of a growing dissatisfaction with Enlightenment humanism, many academic readers steer away from universal "moral themes," making novels, even apparently mimetic novels, seem concerned largely with issues of language or interpretation or rhetoric—for instance, what Charles Reeves (1985) calls "narratability" (p. 291). Peter Brooks (1984), to give one famous example, describes Marlow's "ethical pronouncements" as a cover-up that, instead of illuminating our understanding, hides "a starker and possibly contradictory truth" (p. 248). Such an approach could well lead to engagement on the narrative level, to ethical claims, and to a deeper understanding of the politics of imperialism. But Brooks turns out to be more concerned with the rhetorical workings of the cover-up than with the political situation that is covered up. In his hands the novel therefore turns into a self-reflexive deliberation that "is ultimately most of all about transmission" (p. 261): "One finally needs to read *Heart of Darkness* as act of narration even more than as narrative or as story" (p. 261).

Brooks is not exceptional. In many other readings, too, Conrad's novella nearly dissolves into self-referentiality. Thus, Donald M. Kartiganer (1988) recognizes the novel's connection with the colonial enterprise. But he ends up diluting its political significance by insisting on the "centrality of interpretation" in the novel's thematic interests (p. 167). His reading, in other words, skirts the narrative level, ultimately turning Marlow's tale into a tract about itself, "a formulation of criteria" for its own reading (p. 167).

At its worst, as Michael has consistently urged me to recognize, such Blimberism leads to arrogance and a dehumanizing view of other people; in this case, for instance, it turns the suffering of the Africans so vividly described in the novel into a mere instrument for something else. And this interpretive move has political, as well as literary, consequences. After all, whether you think Conrad is a racist or an anti-imperialist or both, it is precisely his description of the outrages of imperialist looting of Africa that might prompt serious consideration of colonialism and racism. Thus, for instance, Marlow describes the prisoners of a chain gang: "I could see every rib, the joints of their limbs were like knots in a rope" (1899/1996, p. 30). Or think of the dying workers he sees in the grove, "black shadows of disease and starvation. . . . Brought from all the recesses of the coast in all the legality of time contracts, lost in uncongenial surroundings, fed on unfamiliar food, they sickened, became inefficient, and were then allowed to crawl away" (p. 32).

What ethical acts are we, as readers, performing when we escape from the pain of the text, distancing ourselves from the narrative audience by treating these concrete images of pain as but stepping stones to a discussion of something more abstract and implicitly more important, like "narratability"? Neal Oxenhandler (1984) aptly describes what is at stake: "The impulse to mimetic reading is not merely a reprehensible tic; it is the acknowledgement of our link with the poet as denizens of the same world, as pilgrims through the same history" (p. 44)—and, one might add, our link with characters as well.

The lines separating these types of misreading are not precise. Michael sometimes sees my formalist concerns leading me into Blimberism—I find issues of narratability, in fact, quite compelling. I sometimes see his humanitarian concerns pushing him to a Bovaryism that treats the characters as more important than the author. Although we map the possibilities in somewhat different ways, however, we both agree that intelligent reading involves a delicate and complex balancing act. If we are to engage in serious communication with a fictional text, we need to be able to juggle our roles as the authorial audience the author has expected with our roles as the narrative audience he or she has created. But intelligent reading involves a step beyond absorbing great literature as if it were the repository for the wisdom of the ages: To read a work responsibly involves taking on this double role without, at the same time, abandoning our actual selves. Eli's reading was not wrong because his own anti-Catholicism was engaged—it was wrong because it wasn't engaged *with* anything.

AUTHORIAL READING AND THE ETHICS OF TEACHING

Michael W. Smith

So what? If Eli was engaged and if *A Canticle for Leibowitz* was what motivated his engagement, why isn't that enough for us as teachers? Both Peter and I would offer an answer that's grounded in politics, though those answers would be somewhat different. As a theorist Peter is primarily concerned with how readers recognize the ideologies that inform a text and the impact that a text can have on a reader's ideology. Eli's reading, therefore, was problematic to Peter, on the one hand, because Eli didn't respect Miller, which made it impossible for Eli to learn from him. Trying on Miller's anti-euthanasia stance might have persuaded Eli of its value. At the very least it would have taught Eli something about how such a stance might be grounded. On the other hand, Eli's reading was problematic to Peter because it made it impossible for Eli to assert his resistance to Miller. If he had taken Miller's anti-euthanasia stance seriously and still rejected it, Eli would have had to articulate and defend his own beliefs, something his flip response didn't require him to do. Making such a defense would not only have been likely to clarify and strengthen Eli's own ethical position, it would also have resulted in his asserting a kind of declaration of readerly independence that is an important step in everyone's development as a reader.

I share Peter's concerns. But as a teacher and teacher educator, I'm also concerned with the politics of the classroom, a concern I have in common with other reader-centered teachers and theorists. I recognize, however, that arguing for the value of authorial reading will evoke for some a return to the bad old days in which teachers performed on texts in front of passive students. In this chapter, I begin by explaining why I think that worry is unfounded. More specifically, I argue that authorial reading allows resistance both to teachers and to authors and so undermines traditional classroom hierarchies. In the second part of the chapter, I extend Peter's discussion of the importance of authorial reading by arguing that authorial reading provides a foundation for truly democratic classroom discourse because it enables students to work together on the common project of interpreting a text.

AUTHORIAL READING AND PROGRESSIVE PRACTICE

Recent critiques of the New Criticism as the theoretical foundation for the teaching of literature center on the way that it authorizes teachers at the expense of students. Robert Probst (1992a), whose writing against the New Criticism has been extremely influential in schools of education, explains that the chief assumption of the New Criticism is that the literary work sets the norms by which it should be read; that is, a literary text dictates its own reading. Later he argues that this assumption has unfortunate consequences for students:

> First of all, it assures them that they will fail. They may fail more or less badly, but they are doomed to fail. . . . Our individuality, our unique perception and valuation of the world, prevents us from fully grasping those norms—whatever they may be—implicit within the literary work. The conception of the "real poem" as a structure of norms leaves us, like poor Tantalus, clutching at grapes that forever elude us.
>
> And although, by definition, all of us are deficient, some are more deficient than others. The notion of the genuine poem establishes a hierarchy of readers, with the most renowned critic at the top, other published scholars a rung or two below. . . other professors and teachers several steps further down the ladder, and finally, at the bottom, most deficient of all, the student. (p. 55)

If students are indeed on the bottom of the ladder, unfortunate pedagogical consequences will certainly ensue. The hierarchy Probst describes helps explain why James D. Marshall (Marshall, Smagorinsky, & Smith, 1995) found that students play a much less significant role in classroom discussions of literature than do teachers. (Marshall found that even in upper-track classrooms, teachers tended to slot students' responses into an interpretive frame that the teachers were developing and elaborating.) The hierarchy Probst describes helps explain why students are content to parrot their teachers' interpretations in essays rather than to offer their own.

In response to what they see as the inevitable and problematic hierarchy that results from a pedagogy grounded in the New Criticism, Probst and others call for a more reader-based pedagogy. Although I don't want to be reductive, I think that the difference between these pedagogies can be illustrated by posing the central question of each. New Critics would have readers ask "What does this mean?" Reader-response critics in the Probst tradition would substitute "What does this mean to me?"

Interestingly, although these questions are very different, the central question of reader-response theory seems to me to be informed by a hallmark of the New Criticism, the very theory it purports to critique. Like the New Critics, response theorists seem to worry about the authorial fallacy, for they pay little or no attention to the intelligence that created the literary text. In Chapter 1, Peter explains why he thinks it's impossible for readers to answer the New Critical question and why it's insufficient for them to answer the reader-response question. He offers a third question as an alternative: "What would this mean for the audience the author was writing for and how do I feel about that?"

The reluctance to consider the author seems to stem from a belief that reading authorially is the same sort of elusive goal as searching for the "true poem" and as such carries with it the same pedagogical consequences. After all, asking what a text means and asking what a text means to its intended readers may seem on the surface to be similar questions. This belief is problematic for two important reasons. First, it conflates imputing authorial intent with what Peter calls playing the authorial audience. Second, it ignores the role of the narrative audience in reading authorially. Each of these problems has important implications for teaching. Let me take them in turn.

As Peter explains, the notion of authorial audience is not intended to avoid the issue of authorial intention but rather to recast the question so that our interest becomes a category of social convention rather than psychology. An example may make the consequences of this point clear. An invitation to a wedding indicating that the reception will be "black tie" invokes a whole set of social conventions. Even paraphrasing the invitation requires conventional knowledge. The invitation means that a man should wear a tuxedo and a woman an evening gown. (A black tie alone would certainly be inappropriate.) But it also means that the reception is likely to be in the evening, that we probably shouldn't bring our children, and that we might want to spend a little bit more than usual on a gift. What it doesn't mean is that the person who invited us really wants us to come. We make many inferences that we can feel relatively sure of, but none of them has to do with the psychology of the sender.

Once we've respected the conventions invoked by the invitation, we can comment on them. We could, for example, criticize the sender for pretension (a pretension that may require guests to spend more money than they can comfortably afford) or admire the sender for adding solemnity to a ceremony that is too often treated cavalierly in our culture. But we cannot make either of these essentially political critiques without reading the invitation in a conventional way. We believe that what is true for wedding invitations is also true for literature: Our students can only make a political commentary on a literary text if they understand the codes and conventions that text invokes.

Both the potential for criticism and the potential for admiration that I noted above help establish why authorial reading confounds the hierarchy that Probst so rightly decries. The potential for political critique confounds the hierarchy because political critiques are not grounded in literary knowledge, a kind of knowledge that will certainly be unequally distributed. My experience as a coordinator for a People and Stories/ Gente y Cuentos program at an adult education center in Camden, New Jersey, bears this out. People and Stories/Gente y Cuentos, a program directed by Sarah Hirschman and Pat Andre and funded by the New Jersey Council for the Humanities, sponsors the discussion of multicultural literature at a variety of nontraditional sites: women's shelters, prisons, and other social service organizations. My group was made up of students studying to take their Graduate Equivalency Diploma (GED) exam and their teachers. Over 90% of the students with whom I worked were African American.

One of the stories we discussed in my group was "Everyday Use" by Alice Walker (1973). The story is narrated by the African American mother of two daughters and set in rural Georgia in what appears to be the late 1960s. The story begins as the narrator and her younger daughter wait for the arrival of the older daughter for a visit. The two daughters stand in stark contrast. Dee, the older, has a style and sensibilities that pushed her away from home, first through attending a school in the city and later by leaving home and forging an African identity. In contrast, her sister Maggie is shy and frightened. Her mother describes her walk this way: "Have you ever seen a lame animal, perhaps a dog run over by some careless person rich enough to own a car, sidle up to someone who is ignorant enough to be kind to him?" (p. 49). During the visit, Dee, who has renamed herself Wangero Leewanika Kemanjo, asks for quilts her grandmother made, quilts her mother had promised to Maggie. She argues for the quilts, which she plans to display on her walls, by saying, "Maggie can't appreciate these quilts! She'd probably be backward enough to put them to everyday use" (p. 57). Her mother retorts that it doesn't matter that Maggie might wear the quilts out for "She can always make some more. . . . Maggie knows how to quilt" (p. 58). Maggie, however, is willing to give up the quilts. She says, "She can have them, Mama. . . . I can 'member Grandma Dee without the quilts" (p. 58). But the narrator remains firm in her decision to give the quilts to Maggie.

Dee/Wangero leaves after criticizing her mother and sister for not understanding their heritage and for being content to live as they always have. The story closes with the narrator and Maggie sitting next to each other on a bench, "just enjoying, until it was time to go in the house and go to bed" (p. 59).

Doing an authorial reading of the story requires readers to recognize the codes and conventions the author used in creating it. One clear example of what this means for "Everyday Use" is noticing that Dee/Wangero invokes the title of the story in her complaint about Maggie. Realizing that titles have a privileged position helps us understand that Walker wants readers to give these lines a special attention and to recognize that she is making an ironic commentary on the criticism that Dee/Wangero offers of her sister.

However, it doesn't mean that that's the last thing readers ought to do. Our discussion began slowly. There was some talk about how ungrateful the older sister was and how you should never treat your mama that way. But then someone said something like the following: "I know that that girl wasn't good to her family, but sometimes there are things more important. You have to think about the race. And the only way we are going to change things is if people do things like go away to school. And hang up quilts for us to be proud of." This was a powerful political critique of the story, one on which the group focused for most of an hour.

In our discussion of "Everyday Use" the knowledge that mattered was not literary knowledge, a kind of knowledge of which I had a disproportionate amount. What counted in that discussion was the experience that the participants had had in having their consciousness raised by people who weren't willing to go along with the ways things had always been or the strength that they had been able to draw from their families or the ways they had worked to make change in their communities. What counted was what Eli Goldblatt (1995) has called in his study of young urban writers the home institutions upon which the participants could draw. Because that was what counted, my literary knowledge didn't place me above the other participants in a hierarchy of readers.

I would be naive to believe that all students will feel comfortable in drawing upon their home institutions to offer political critiques of texts, especially when those home institutions have seldom been legitimatized in schools. However, authorial reading can undermine the hierarchy Probst discusses for another reason as well. Authorial reading brings another authority into the classroom, and students can use that authority to resist the teacher.

Let's go back to Peter's discussion of *A Canticle for Leibowitz* for an example. In Chapter 1, Peter made his political critique of Miller's Catholic sensibilities clear. Now let's imagine that one of Peter's students was a Catholic who shared Miller's views on euthanasia. Resisting Peter by drawing upon the student's own Catholicism may have been exceedingly difficult. After all, people of faith are not often embraced by the academy. (I'd argue the authorial audience posited by Eli in his comment on the text could be characterized by a shared belief in the value of spoofing religion.) But authors have status in the academy, so if the student had done an authorial reading, the student could use Miller as a way to resist Peter. The student could have pointed to how in Miller's view the two-headed woman had the potential for salvation and weighed that salvation against the horror of her present circumstance.

That's not to say that authorial reading places authors beyond critique. In fact, when we recognize the importance of playing the narrative audience as one dimension of authorial reading, we see that authorial reading can confound that hierarchy as well.

Peter's discussion of the narrative audience makes it clear than we are not reading authorially unless we give characters, at least provisionally, the same kind of respect we ought to give the real people who populate our lives. Paying that respect is the foundation for the ethical implications of literature.

What gives stories their ethical force is that they are usually centered on characters' efforts to face moral choices. As Wayne Booth (1988) explains, "In tracing those efforts, we readers stretch our own capacities for thinking about how life should be lived" (p. 187). Robert Coles (1989) provides a moving testimony to Booth's position in *The Call of Stories* by quoting one of his students:

> When I have some big moral issue, some question to tackle, I think I try to remember what my folks have said, or I imagine them in my situation—or even more these days I think of [characters in books I've read]. Those folks, they're people for me ... they really speak to me—there's a lot of me in them, or vice versa. I don't know how to put it, but they're voices, and they help me make choices. I hope when I decide "the big ones" they'll be in there pitching. (p. 203)

Playing the narrative audience is what gives characters a voice.

As Bakhtin (1984) points out, when characters have voices, they may not only speak to readers, they may speak against authors. He uses the term *polyphonic* to describe texts in which characters are *"not only objects of authorial discourse but also subjects of their own directly signifying discourse"* (Bakhtin, 1984, p. 7, emphasis in original). That is, in polyphonic novels characters take on a life of their own as *"fully valid voices"* (p. 6, emphasis in original). Understanding that playing the narrative audience is an essential element of an authorial reading makes it clear that authorial readings are not monologic, for playing the narrative audience requires readers to consider characters as active subjects. This understanding establishes again the intimate relationship between respect and resistance. If readers respect characters, they can recognize when characters resist authors. They may even create polyphony where none was intended.

Vipond and Hunt (1984) make a similar point in a different way. They argue that what they call point-driven reading (they use the term *dialogic reading* in their more recent work) depends in part on what they call transactional strategies, strategies built on the recognition that the text was constructed by "an intentional being who is responsible for it" (p. 272). This recognition allows readers "to notice discrepancies—that is, *ironies*—between the implied values and beliefs of the author as against the values and beliefs of the characters" (p. 272, emphasis in original). For example, the discussion of "Everyday Use" was built on noticing the discrepancy between Walker and Dee/Wangero and discussing how we should feel about it.

Although our discussion was political, it was not marked by the kind of political talk that has made "Don't talk about religion or politics" a chestnut for people hosting a dinner party. I'll be talking more about this in the second section of this chapter, but I think it's important to note that our discussion was rooted in the story and that this helped it be more than an occasion for making speeches about the political positions people had before they read the story. Perhaps most importantly, the story made us take seriously the cost in human terms of the positions we were taking. We saw how Dee/Wangero's choices alienated her from her family. We saw Maggie's shyness and the "real smile" she flashes at the close of the story. But we also felt the limited future she faces.

Playing the narrative audience can result in readers' resisting authors for other reasons as well. In Peter's discussion of *Heart of Darkness,* he critiques readers who fail to play the narrative audience because their failure to do so "turns the suffering of the Africans so vividly described in the novel into a mere instrument for something else." But readers are not the only ones susceptible to that failure. Authors may display a similar "arrogant and dehumanizing" attitude to their own creations. If readers play the narrative audience, they are in a position to critique authors for that arrogance, as another look at *Huckleberry Finn* suggests.

When Peter explains why the notion of an authorial audience is crucial to the discussion of whether *Huckleberry Finn* is racist, he centers his argument on Twain's use/mention of the word *nigger.* It seems to me that a much more powerful critique of the novel is the way Tom treats Jim as Tom orchestrates Jim's escape. If readers have played the narrative audience and have come to care about Jim, Tom's actions are cruel rather than funny. If readers believe that Twain expects them to ignore or not care about the way Tom victimizes Jim so that he can use Jim as a tool for his satire of the romantic literature that influenced Tom, they have grounds to call the book racist.

When students play the narrative audience and grant characters their voices, they may hear talk that calls authors' privilege into question. When they play the narrative audience, texts are not simply objects of art and authors the geniuses who created them. Authors are people who have a special kind of power over others, their characters, and with that power comes the obligation to use it humanely. If they play the narrative audience, students will not only experience Twain's masterful use of dialect but will also hold him responsible for how he uses Jim. If they play the narrative audience, students will not only see the beauty of Shakespeare's language but will also hold him responsible for how he uses Shylock.

Of course, if students had to be forced to do authorial readings and to play the narrative audience, these benefits would be undermined. However, my study of 16 eighth-graders talking with their student teacher in one-on-one conversations about two stories as they read them together suggests that students value authorial reading. While they were reading, the students in my study accepted the idea that the characters about whom they were reading were worthy of their attention and concern, as their responses to Morley Callaghan's "All the Years of Her Life" (1971) suggest.

The story opens with a young man being caught shoplifting by the druggist who employs him. When the druggist calls the young man's mother, the young man worries about the kind of scene she'll cause when she arrives at the store. But the young man is surprised. His mother demonstrates a "kind of patient dignity" and the druggist fires the boy without calling the police (p. 86). When they leave the store, the boy attempts to speak to his mother, but she cuts him off, saying "Don't speak to me. You've disgraced me again and again" (p. 88). The story concludes with the young man's realizing the hardships he had caused his mother as he watched her sitting at the kitchen table straining to drink her tea.

One student began her final remarks on the story this way:

> I think he probably won't get in trouble anymore. I am not sure if that really wasn't just an act she put on, but I think if he does, he probably won't as often. . . . He is starting to think about, I don't

know, that what he does doesn't only affect him anymore. It affects his mom too.

Another student took a slightly different tack:

> I, I, I like at the ending cause it is just like cause, um, um, like my mom, she either sits down and watches TV. Like his momma at the end gets something to eat and that's something, that's something to do, right? Like watch TV. That's something to do and fix, um, a cup of tea. That's something to do and, um, like, feel sorry for what I did. And he is kind of like sorry for what he did.

Although the first student bases her remark primarily on the text and the second bases his on personal experience, both seem to me to be marked by how they regard Alfred, the young man, as much more than ink on paper. Because they speak of him in this way, it is possible that Alfred will speak to them when they think about their relationship with their parents.

Recognizing the importance of the narrative audience will also help make it unlikely that what Peter called students' "participation" will overwhelm their "discussion." Peter argues in the previous chapter that there are times when students simply won't recognize the semiotic significance of a detail, as in his students' failing to recognize that Joel Cairo was being coded as gay, and that on those occasions students can only participate in their teachers' exposition of the significance of the detail. To be sure, students will misread. In "All the Years of Her Life," for example, the narrator comments that "Mrs. Higgins [the boy's mother] must have been going to bed when [the druggist] telephoned, for her hair was tucked loosely under her hat, and her hand at her throat held her light coat tight across her chest so her dress would not show" (p. 86). Two students in my study read these details as signaling that the mother was going to try to get her son out of trouble by trying to seduce the druggist. Teaching the story to these students, therefore, would certainly involve creating an experience or a sequence of questions that would help them understand that the author meant no such thing by these details. However, what's far more important to the story is how she must have felt as she rushed to get ready, what it took for her to make her appeal, whether she should have bailed her son out yet again, and so on. All of these questions are eminently discussible.

Authorial reading, then, confounds hierarchies that have long existed in classrooms. Authorial reading challenges the privileged position of teachers both by promoting political discussions in which the unequal distribution of literary knowledge in the classroom has little impact and by allowing (but not forcing) students to use the authority of the author to resist the authority of the teacher. Authorial reading also challenges the privileged position of the author. The New Critical question "What does this mean?" doesn't allow students to resist authors because their energies are devoted to discovering meaning. The reader-response question "What does this mean to me?" doesn't allow resistance because, as Peter points out in the previous chapter, it does not provide anything to resist. In contrast, the authorial-reading question "What would this mean for the audience the author was writing for and how do I feel about that?" encourages resistance both because it provides something to resist and because it gives students something to resist with: their home institutions and their concern for the characters.

Further, if we see progressive instruction in literature as helping students "to identify with the other, to empathize with others' thoughts and feelings and to develop the capacity for ethical respect" (Giroux, 1992, p. 7), then we have to recognize that authorial reading is consistent with the aims of progressive education in a way that at least some response-centered instruction may not be.

Consider, for example, the pedagogical ideas of David Bleich (1975, 1978, 1988), a subjectivist critic Peter discusses in Chapter 1, whose work is laudable for his attention to the pedagogical consequences of his theoretical arguments. Bleich bases his approach, what I have elsewhere called autobiographical writing against reading (Smith, 1992a), on the assumption that "all people, young and old, think about themselves most of the time and think about the world in terms of themselves" (Bleich, 1975, p. 4). Although Bleich's thinking has evolved to placing increasing emphasis on intersubjective meanings, his primary goal remains to help students develop their self-awareness. His method is based in large measure on having students write response statements in which they explore the personal associations they experienced while they read. These response statements then become the primary texts that the class will study. What follows is an excerpt of a response statement from one of his students on Melville's "Bartleby the Scrivener," which he cites in *The Double Perspective:*

> The character of Bartleby reminds me of my friend J. She used to sit in the secretarial lounge and constantly study. Her entire life was concerned with Russian linguistics. She rarely went out drinking . . . . I have tried to understand her odd personality for six years. (Bleich, 1988, p. 134)

In this response statement, the student quickly leaves the story behind. I would argue that doing so is problematic for two reasons. In the first place, she gives little ethical respect to the other most distinct in his otherness: Bartleby. And in the second place, by ignoring the author, she is violating a fundamental principle of ethical behavior. Although it's certainly not fashionable to quote E. D. Hirsch, I think he offers a powerful explanation of why that is so. Hirsch (1976) argues that when we simply use an author's words for our own purposes without respecting his or her intentions, we

> transgress what Charles Stevenson in another context called "the ethics of language," just as we transgress ethical norms when we use another person merely for our own ends. Kant held it to be a foundation of moral action that men should be conceived as ends in themselves, and not as instruments of other men. This imperative is transferable to the words of men because speech is an extension and expression of men in the social domain, and also because when we fail to conjoin a man's intention to his words we lose the soul of speech, which is to convey meaning and to understand what is intended to be conveyed. (p. 90)

I am arguing, then, that encouraging authorial reading is not a return to the Dark Ages. Rather, because it challenges traditional hierarchies and promotes an ethical respect for others, both authors and their characters, authorial reading can be at the center of progressive practice.

I know that my emphasis on the narrative audience makes Peter a little nervous. He fears that I'll fall into Emma Bovary's trap. However, I think that Peter misunderstands Emma's problem. It's not that she believed too much in the characters about whom she read. Rather it's that her beliefs about those characters went unchallenged. Another reason that authorial reading can be the basis of progressive instruction is that it allows a class to work together on a common project. What Emma needed was something that a pedagogy grounded on authorial reading could provide: the opportunity for truly democratic discussions of literature.

AUTHORIAL READING AND DEMOCRATIC DISCUSSIONS

Competing Notions of Democracy in the Teaching of Literature

Whenever the discussion of how we should teach literature addresses ethical issues, people get uncomfortable. Whose ethics should inform our teaching? The censorship controversies that abound throughout the country establish that the question is far from settled. However, even in an age of relativism, one principle seems to be shared by virtually everyone concerned with American education: the importance of democratic class-rooms. What's not shared is the particular vision of democracy to which people refer. In fact, at least three competing visions of democracy are often cited in discussions of teaching literature. I want to turn now to an examination of each of these visions and an to explanation of why each one seems to me to be problematic. I will go on to offer an alternative vision of democratic teaching grounded in the work of John Dewey and explain why I believe that authorial reading is so important to achieving that vision.

One thing that was quickly lost in the furor surrounding E. D. Hirsch's *Cultural Literacy* (1987) was his belief in the democratic character of his recommendations. Hirsch argued that people who are not culturally liter-ate can neither do the reading they need to do to make informed political decisions nor frame their oral or written arguments in ways that would give those arguments a hearing in the public arena. Of course, Hirsch's position has been attacked for its narrow and parochial view of what's worth knowing. But what's more important to my argument here is that Hirsch's notion of democratic education suffers from two flaws. In the first place, it equates democracy with democratic governing. And since it does so, it emphasizes the future at the expense of the present. Dewey's (1916/1944) view of democracy seems to me to be much more compel-ling. He states it succinctly: "A democracy is more than a form of govern-ment; it is primarily a mode of associated living, of conjoint communi-cated experience" (p. 87). If one imagines democracy as a way of living rather than as a mode of governing, democratic education must do more than prepare students to participate in governing. Rather it must engage them in meaningful associated living. That means that teachers can no longer justify their curricular and instructional decisions on the premise that they will be good for students in the future, what I've come to call the cod-liver-oil approach to teaching. Dewey has convinced me of the importance of focusing instead on the quality of the immediate experi-ence that students are having. As he explains, "It is not of course a ques-tion of whether education should prepare for the future. If education is growth, it must progressively realize present possibilities, and thus make individuals better fitted to cope with later requirements" (p. 56). It seems to me that Hirsch's failure to recognize the importance of present possi-bilities is at the heart of his advocating a curriculum that runs the risk of alienating many students.

Louise Rosenblatt offers a substantially different view of why literary education is important for democracy, but it's one that also seems to me to be flawed. Rosenblatt (1995) recently articulated a position that has marked her work since *Literature as Exploration*. In her response to Alan Purves's critique of the impact of her transactional theory on educational thought, she explains, "Why have I felt it important to clarify these theoretical matters? Because in a democracy we need citizens with the imaginative capacity to put themselves into the place of others and see the human implications of ideas" (p. 353). Rosenblatt's arguments have certainly found a more appreciative audience among teachers than have Hirsch's. But although her ideas may be more humane, I don't think that they are more democratic, for Rosenblatt also neglects the importance of conjoint experience. As John Willinsky (1991) points out, even Rosenblatt's attention to empathy is rooted "in an understanding of the self" (p. 122), an argument Willinsky advances by citing the following passage from *Literature as Exploration:*

> During the aesthetic experience, we can transcend the limitations of time and place. We can participate in the tensions, the conflicts in values, the choices, of the characters we have conjured up by means of the texts. Reflection on these, and awareness of our own responses to them can lead to self-understanding, self-criticism, perhaps a clarification or a reinforcement of values. (Quoted in Willinsky, p. 123)

I am not saying that these are trivial goals. I am saying that it is not at all clear to me how they are democratic goals.

Another appeal to democracy seems to me to come as a consequence of teachers' and theorists' recognizing the profound influence of a reader's personal experience on that reader's transaction with a text. Such a recognition will be central to my contention that discussions that have authorial reading as a major purpose will have a democratic character. But not all reader-based theories lead in that direction, as a return to the literary theories of David Bleich reveals. As I noted previously, Bleich's belief in the centrality of the personality of the reader leads him to propose that students write response statements in which they explore the unique personal associations evoked by a text and that these response statements be the focus of subsequent discussion. This approach has anti-democratic implications, at least in Dewey's terms. Although Bleich calls for students to work together to help each other gain personal insights, something essential is missing. Dewey (1897/1964) explains that "the best and deepest moral training is precisely that which one gets through having to enter into proper relations with others in a unity of work and thought" (p. 431). Bleich's theories are built on the belief that no such unity can exist.

One reason that reader-based theories may seem to be democratic is that they break down the hierarchy that Probst notes by suggesting that no reading is better than another. In Stanley Fish's (1983) response to Wayne Booth's *A Rhetoric of Irony*, he goes so far as to argue that a literal reading of an ironic text cannot be seen as mistaken for it is a consequence of the interpretive community to which the reader belongs. Booth (1983a) explains a significant problem with Fish's view:

> The curious assumption running through [Fish's] examples seems to be that criticism should operate on the principle of one man–one vote. No matter who the man or woman might be who performs a reading, no matter how little experience with a given genre a judgment may spring from, no matter what forms of inattention, prejudice, ignorance, inexperience, or emotional crippling have been at work. If someone calls "Hold!" Fish will report a new proof for the nonexistence of stability. As soon as anyone disputes "the presence of an incongruity, by adding one more to our list of alternative readings, by revising our sense of an author's beliefs—the entire edifice trembles, and the debate over whether an utterance is ironic, or over which of several ironic meanings is the right one, will begin again." ("Short People" 178) Here is democratic criticism with a vengeance. (p. 206)

And here is a "democratic" criticism that denies a fundamental precept of democracy. When Booth introduces the concept of ironic reconstruction, he uses the notion of *topoi* or "common places." The successful interpreter of irony, in essence, rejects the place that an author appears to be offering, for a "higher and firmer location" (Booth, 1974, p. 36). In a democratic society we ought not pretend that everyone's circumstances are equal; we ought not, to extend Booth's metaphor, pretend that all dwellings are equal. Fish would have us approve, or at the very least ignore, substandard dwellings. Dewey, on the other hand, would have us work together to improve them.

Toward a Common Project: John Dewey and the Politics of Authorial Reading

What I'm calling for, then, is for teachers of literature to work to make their classrooms democratic communities and to recognize how working together on authorial readings can assist in achieving this goal. In making this call I recognize that the term *community* is problematic. As Joseph Harris (1989) explains, because *community* does not have what Raymond Williams calls a "positive opposing" term, it can quickly become empty and sentimental. To avoid that sentimentality, Harris calls on literacy researchers "to center our study . . . on the everyday struggles and mishaps of the talk in our classrooms" and to "reserve our uses of community to describe the workings of such specific and local groups" (p. 20). In Harris's view, students in classrooms rarely have the kind of shared values that the term *community* implies. Instead, he notes that, as in a city, members of classrooms are likely to be linked only by the fact that they share a physical space.

One of the reasons that Dewey's vision of democracy is so compelling to me is that it doesn't begin with the idealized vision of shared values that Harris critiques. What Dewey (1916/1944) does begin with is the belief that people are social beings: "Individuals are certainly interested, at times, in having their own way, and their own way may go contrary to the ways of others. But they are also interested, and chiefly interested upon the whole, in entering into the activities of others and taking part in conjoint and cooperative doings" (p. 24). This doesn't mean that communities are homogeneous. In fact, as Stephen Fishman (1993) notes, Dewey believed that healthy communities "possess members whose unique functions. . . complement one another" (p. 319). Fishman goes on to discuss how such communities can be formed: "Occasions must be provided for people to share their differences. When people understand enough about differences in their lives, according to Dewey, they will find their common interests" (p. 320). My research on patterns of discourse in discussions of literature suggests that discussions that work to develop authorial readings can be the kind of occasion that Fishman and Dewey urge teachers to provide.

In my study of the discourse of two adult book clubs (a description I use to designate the age of participants, not the reading material they discussed), I found that one of the primary benefits the adults recognized was the way their discussions helped them learn about each other. As one man noted about his club:

> I guess if people were to say well what is it about? What do you guys do there? I guess I could say I get to know my friends a lot better through these books and how they relate or react to them. That's primarily, I guess, one of the big enjoyments, and then the, the other one would be again, the, the idea that I get to see their, the perspectives they might take on life's events, within the book, and then relate them to their *own* life's events or experiences.

A member of the women's club I studied made a similar point about her club: "I think what's beautiful about this group is that it doesn't become a therapy session and yet . . . people are fairly open in showing how they relate to the book and what their experience has been similar to it without it becoming a bleeding-heart session."

Suggesting that it's important for readers to bring their lives to the literature they read is hardly a radical call. But consider for a minute what keeps the discussions from becoming a "bleeding-heart session." It seems to me that it's the book. Both speakers explain that participants relate their lives to the book. They do not speak of using the book as a springboard for a personal discussion. For example, in the excerpt below one adult uses his life experience to do an authorial reading of *A Theft* by Saul Bellow:

> Bellow was saying that . . ., the whole, Clara is—thinks she found her inner self but she's misled. And that's that's that's the deal, is that we all think we find our inner selves at various times but, we, but we usually find out that we haven't really come right on target. And nobody really, I mean I know that I don't know the little [his name] that's deep down inside me because it changes all the time, and I, sometimes I think I'm right on target, and then other times I realize that I really don't know what's going on.

The clubs that I studied sought "meaningful moral or psychological insights," which, according to Elizabeth Long (1987), is a goal that is characteristic of adult reading groups. Seeking these insights, insights that are at the heart of both the authorial and narrative audience, can be a common project, what Dewey would call a conjoint activity.

Sarah Allen's (1995) study of the way her seventh- and eighth-graders talk about books supports the notion of how much students value similar insights. Allen critiques the work that James Marshall, Peter Smagorinsky, and I did in our analysis of large-group discussions, small-group discussions, and discussions that take place out of school (the two studies I mentioned above were my contributions to our collaboration). She argues that because we regarded the discussions we studied as a unitary discourse, we failed to recognize the shifts in patterns of talk that occurred. Allen contends that the discussions in her class feature at least three different kinds of discourse: the discourse of the discipline, the discourse of engagement, and the discourse of understanding. Each discourse has its own rules for participation. For example, when students mark their response as belonging to the discourse of the discipline, they get to perform their disciplinary knowledge for the teacher without interruption. In the discourse of engagement, they share the experience they had while they read. This discourse only allows affirmations in response. The discourse of understanding, however, allows for challenge and collaborative turns.

In the following excerpt from a class discussion of Maya Angelou's *I*

Know Why The Caged Bird Sings, students begin in the discourse of engagement and then move to the discourse of understanding:

> STUDENT 1: I hate Delores.
> (Laughter)
> STUDENT 2: I hate her, too.
> STUDENT 1: She's so mean.
> STUDENT 3: She was so mean. She was *so* something my *daughter* like . . .
> (Voices overlap)
> STUDENT 2: I don't understand that.
> STUDENT 4: I thought he was furious and then they just drove away.
> (Voices overlap)
> TEACHER: It was a joke.
> STUDENT 2: He wanted to leave her with some man.
> (Voices overlap)
> TEACHER: It was a joke.
> STUDENT 5: It was? It was so weird. I thought. . .
> STUDENT 1: A joke.
> STUDENT 2: No one ever laughed.
> STUDENT 6: That's the kind of thing that makes sense when you were just playing around with each other and stuff like that, but when you read it in a book it's so serious most of the time you don't get it.

What seems to happen in this brief excerpt is that students begin by sharing their visceral reactions to a character, chiming in with each other to indicate support. Allen sees this as the discourse of engagement. But the character of the conversation seems to shift when student 2 says "I don't understand that." The class immediately stops sharing their visceral reactions, seemingly indicating that the search for understanding takes precedence. The collaborative nature of the discourse of understanding is suggested by the fact that two students question the teacher's "It was a joke" explanation. (In the discourse of the discipline, the teacher is never challenged.)

Discussions aimed at developing authorial readings, then, can provide the opportunity for working on a common project because readers value them. What happens as a consequence is that differences within the group become resources to participants because those differences help them achieve a goal that they value.

The adults I studied came to value the different ways of thinking and reading the other club members employed. As one of the men noted, the discussions help "you to figure out how other people think." One of his colleagues elaborated that point when he noted:

> Well, I think there are things that, that different people tend to focus on that they bring to the table that makes it interesting. For instance, Harold always seems to be able to, to bring in a religious interpretation into things. That I may not see. And both he and Richards tend to do a little bit of research into, into symbols and symbolism, and Richards tends to pick up on people's names and the way that they're used very often, and I don't pick up on in the same kind of detail that they do, and really enjoy being able to get that feedback. We all have a different way of approaching literature I think. And I think that really makes it interesting for me.

But there's more at stake than ways of reading. Both the adults and the eighth-graders that I studied used their lives to help them make sense of their reading far more often than students are characteristically called upon to do in traditional classroom discussions of literature. The book club member quoted above explains why that might be important:

> And you get pieces of the strong points of other people's back-grounds that can help bring more into those ideas, can help those ideas grow, you know, a knowledge base that somebody else has that, that maybe I *don't* have I'm able to tap into.

His comment suggests the complementarity of which Dewey speaks. His comment also suggests that he came to appreciate this complementarity because he and the other club members were working together on a common project.

I heard this play out on a recent discussion of Julia Alvarez's *How the García Girls Lost Their Accents* on the local National Public Radio outlet. At one point in the discussion, the panel and callers were discussing the racial politics of the book by examining how the García family treated their Haitian maid. One of the panelists was explaining his experiences as a light-skinned Dominican in order to shed light on the family's relationship to this woman. After he finished, a caller, also a Dominican, began a long statement about the racial politics of the island. After he had gone on for a while, the host interrupted him with a "Have you read the book?"—effectively shutting him off, though he answered in the affirmative. What is striking to me is that a very long conversational turn was appreciated when it shed light on the racial politics of the book, but a turn of no greater length was experienced as speechifying, as an intrusion upon the discussion, because it addressed the racial politics of the island.

In the first case, the ethnicity of the speaker was appreciated because it shed light on the matter at hand. In the second case, the ethnicity of the speaker gave rise to a suspicion that he was pursuing a point of limited personal interest.

Peter and I know that our project of rehabilitating authors as essential participants in literary conversations will seem to some to be reactionary. However, because authorial readings are necessary if students are to offer political critiques of texts, to pay an ethical respect to others different from themselves (more on that in Chapters 7 and 8), and to engage with each other in common projects, we think that our theory of the importance of authorial reading can ground truly progressive practice. This social and political emphasis is at odds with the characterization of progressive practice as that which celebrates the individuality of the reader. As Peter explains in Chapter 3, such a celebration minimizes the extent to which the reading and writing of literature are conventional acts. As I argue in Chapter 4, it also fails to recognize that students can learn interpretive conventions through humane and student-centered instruction.

CHAPTER THREE

WHAT READERS DO WHEN THEY READ / WHAT AUTHORS DO WHEN THEY WRITE

Peter J. Rabinowitz

TOWARD THE END of the previous chapter, Michael pointed out that the adults in his reading group "came to value the different ways of thinking and reading the other club members employed." One of them points out, as an example, that he appreciates Harold because he knows how "to bring in a religious interpretation into things" and Richards because he "tends to pick up on people's names and the way that they're used very often." This stress on *ways* of reading reminds us that the notions of actual, authorial, and narrative audience—which can be conceptualized as positions a reader inhabits while reading a text—only get us part way to understanding the act of reading; reading is also an activity, a way of doing things with a text once you have a position with regard to it. And not just any things. Neither the religious interpretations nor the names seem odd; but we would probably be surprised if the informant had said he appreciated Harold because he knows how to tie everything to his model train hobby or Richards because he's able to pick out all the uses of the letter *q* in a text. What makes certain ways of reading seem more persuasive than others?

"IT IS NOT REQUIRED OF A GENTLEMAN": RULE-GOVERNED READING

In this chapter, I argue that reading demands participation in a conventional, rule-governed activity. There are two axioms buried in this claim. First, reading is an *activity*. There would be no need to point this out, except that the word *reading* has taken on a double life. It refers to both an action ("I'm reading Conrad's *The Secret Sharer*") and to the *result* of that action ("In James Phelan's reading [1996] of *The Secret Sharer*, the Captain's feelings for Leggatt stem from 'mutual sexual attraction'" [123]). And to the extent that we are teaching reading, we are ideally teaching the activity, not the product—process rather than result. That is, when we teach *The Secret Sharer* our primary aim should be to help students learn how to *experience* Conrad's novel actively, not to provide them with information about *what* it means.

But when I talk about process rather than result, I am not suggesting that there is nothing concrete and substantive to be taught. The second axiom reminds us that the activity of reading is rule-governed and that, since the rules are conventional, they need somehow to be learned. Furthermore, unless we're talking about reading as recitation, reading inevitably starts out as a cognitive activity. As we have pointed out in the first two chapters, reading is not exclusively a cognitive activity, nor even primarily a cognitive activity; but it is *initially* a cognitive activity.

Recognizing this distinction between first and final steps reveals another difference between the kind of pedagogy Michael and I are suggesting here and the one urged by Robert Probst. In Chapter 2, Michael raises some ethical objections to Probst's proposals, centering on Probst's implied conflation of authorial intention and what we would call reading as authorial audience, as well as on his tendency to ignore the narrative audience. I believe, however, that there are cognitive objections as well. In developing his alternative to a pedagogy based on the New Critical "notion of the genuine poem" (1992a, p. 55), Probst—developing some of Louise Rosenblatt's ideas—proposes a pedagogy based on the notion that "producing interpretations is not the only possibility" for classroom activity (1992a, p. 60). He opts instead for a classroom based on the notion that "our readings *are* the poems" (1992a, p. 57), a classroom in which "correctness becomes . . . a virtually useless concept" (1992a, p. 59).

Probst does, of course, agree that there are certain matters on which a student can be demonstrably wrong. A student may misread a word, for instance. But Probst believes that "the literary transaction is first of all, a way of knowing something about the self" (1992a, p. 63), secondarily a way of knowing about others in the class, and only in a very subsidiary way a matter of knowing about texts—and even when seeking that kind of knowledge, it is only "occasionally appropriate" to try to determine "the intention and assumptions of the author" (1992a, 70). He offers (1992b), as one example, a description of different student reactions to Stephen Dunn's "The Sacred," a poem about a student who, when asked by a teacher if he had a sacred place, talked about his car.

I find Probst's "first of all" confusing, because it conflates importance with chronological priority, hence obscuring the difference between first steps and most important steps. Probst is right that discussion of the Dunn poem will be better if the students are able to talk about their own memories of cars and sacred places; he's right that "if we are restricted to what is there, in the text, ... we may be deprived of the material we need to respond fully to the text" (1992b, p. 69); and he's right that if you start with the belief that reading is "nothing more than the drawing of defensible inferences about authors' intentions" (1992a, p. 63), you are unlikely to end up with interesting readings or an interesting classroom. Critics (including students) certainly need to go further. But Probst's attack on correctness hinges on the fallacy that *starting* with "correct" readings (whether they be authorial readings or New Critical readings) means that such readings are necessarily deemed the most important thing and that readers will then go no further. I would argue, in contrast, that unless self-exploration is founded upon an authorial reading *as a cognitive first step* (rather than the only step), it's not, in the end, a literary self-exploration at all. Thus I don't see that the question "what does Dunn think?" (1992b, p. 69) necessarily *restricts* a student's exploration of either the poem or the issues that it raises. Most of what Probst describes going on in his ideal classroom would have been able to take place without the poem at all, merely by having a sensitive teacher ask students how they feel about the special space within their cars. By bringing Dunn's voice into the conversation, students have someone else to talk with and, if they wish, to resist; and if well handled by a teacher, the authorial voice can serve to sharpen their self explorations.

In order to clarify why this is so, it is perhaps necessary to be more specific about the activity involved in reading: Interpretation begins as a *transformation,* the turning of one text into another. This is true on the simplest level: To be able to read the phrase "Hamilton routs Pioneers"—which just happened to be the random headline visible after my teenage son finished with the paper on the day I drafted this paragraph—involves the capacity to transform it into an equivalent sentence such as "Hamilton's basketball team beat the Utica College basketball team last night." And that's even truer when we're talking about literary texts than when we're talking about newspaper headlines: Reading "Everyday Use" involves being able, for instance, to transform the discussion about quilts into a discussion of broader political questions. Of course, as Michael's description of his discussion of Walker's story makes clear, we do not want to suggest that such transformation is the *only* thing you can or should do with that text. But I would argue that anyone who is incapable of making such an initial transformation is, in a real sense, incapable of reading the text and thus incapable of engaging in the political arguments that ensue.

In other words, despite the New Critical denunciation of "the heresy of paraphrase," reading cannot take place *without* paraphrase. Paraphrase, though, is not a random or private action. Especially to the extent that we are talking about reading as something that can take place in a community such as a classroom or reading group, we're talking about something that can be both shared and taught. Even the most personal acts of reading, the individual "perspectives . . . on life's events" that Michael's informant sought in his book club, must be grounded on communal *rule-governed* procedures of transformation if they are to be shared with others.

For about a decade, I relied on a favorite metaphor for this transformation: Reading is like putting together an unassembled swingset. On one level, the text, like the swingset, is a collection of concrete objects—and there can be considerable agreement among the members of a group as to what the individual pieces are. And when it's completed, it offers opportunities for intellectual and emotional pleasure and exercise—both for individuals and for groups—as well as possible dangers, although the precise nature of those opportunities and risks will depend on the specific swingset at hand.

Of course, it is always possible to do something eccentric with the unassembled pieces. You can use a post as a bat for a game of stickball or as a prop for a broken window, just as you can use a scene in a novel in some idiosyncratic enterprise—you can read passages from Stephen King novels, for instance, as a way of summoning up personal childhood memories of summer camp in Maine; you can also follow the path of Alex, in Anthony Burgess's *Clockwork Orange,* who—in his own inimitable slang—describes the pleasures of the Gospels, reading "all about the scourging and the crowning with thorns and then the cross veshch [thing]" in order to imagine "helping in and even taking charge of the tolchocking [beating] and the nailing in" (1988, p. 92). But in a significant sense, this isn't playing with the swingset. You're not really using the swingset until you've assembled it. And while the swingset may come with some directions (here's where the rule-governed procedures of transformation come in), you can't perform the task unless you know beforehand what directions *are,* unless you have certain tools at your disposal, and—most important—unless you have some general prior sense about what sort of object you are aiming at constructing.

Michael has convinced me, however, that the swingset metaphor is too narrow because it plays down the importance of genre. As he suggests, some works of literature are unassembled swingsets, but others are unassembled gas grills, while still others are unassembled bookcases. This expansion of the metaphor highlights several characteristics of literary texts. First, texts can have a wide variety of intended uses: Some are more playful than others, some are more dangerous, some are more utilitarian. Second, while experience with one kind of text is certainly helpful as you approach another (once you have put together several gas grills, you're better prepared to handle not only a charcoal grill but a new bicycle as well), different kinds of texts really can call upon fundamentally different kinds of skills. Many kinds of objects require the knowledge that screws are tightened by turning them clockwise. But furniture kits require sanding and gluing; putting together electronic equipment requires facility with solder. Likewise, sonnets require a kind of metrical analysis that is close to useless when tackling a novel by Ian Fleming. Finally, to the extent that any successful act of reading always requires knowing beforehand the sort of object you are trying to build, different genres set up different frameworks within which to work. If you've never seen a dollhouse, your experience with bicycles won't give you much preliminary sense of shape; if you've never read a nineteenth-century sentimental novel, your experiences with Samuel Beckett will not give you much initial guidance, either.

Even with proper preparation, of course, there is no guarantee that you'll put the grill or the bicycle together correctly, or even that it *can* be put together correctly. The object itself, for instance, may be missing some of the requisite parts. True, a good manufacturer, like a good editor, should have some quality control system in place; but the pressures of production (and, in a literary text, the pressures of politics) may sometimes result in missing pieces. According to Gavin Lambert, who wrote the screenplay for the film *Inside Daisy Clover,* director Robert Mulligan "got more and more nervous about the lines being too explicit, and several of them were cut, making it all not very intelligible" (quoted in Russo, 1987, p. 152). Or you may misinterpret the instructions and put it together the wrong way. But *trying* to put the pieces together correctly—reading as authorial audience—seems a necessary first step toward any serious use of the grill. As I've said before, I am not arguing that putting a gas grill together is a sufficient activity (although it can be fun in the way doing a jigsaw puzzle is fun); but it's a necessary activity in the sense that it is what gets you to the point where the interesting things start to happen. As Michael points out about his discussion of "Everyday Use," what *counted* in the discussion was the controversy started by the person who said that sometimes certain things are more important than being good to your family. But that discussion only became possible because an authorial reading had preceded it.

As should be clear, in claiming that authorial reading is a necessary first step, I am not urging interpretive uniformity in our classes. But we do need to distinguish interest in the personal from encouragement of the idiosyncratic. Literature, of course—and I'd agree with Probst here—cannot be reduced to a Blimberian collection of facts. But knowledge of interpretive procedure is more or less concrete, and it is valuable, even necessary, in the sense that it has to precede the use of the text to affect knowledge of self and other; and although Michael and I disagree on this point (see Chapter 4), I would argue that it has to precede the pleasures that literature can bring—at least, if you are interested in sharing those pleasures with others in your reading community. As I've said, claiming that studying interpretive procedures is prior to the study of ethics or pleasure does not mean either that it is more important or that it provides the main motivation for studying. Rather, learning interpretive procedures is the *enabling* act that allows other literary work to take place. And as Michael's research, including the research he describes in Chapter 4, has suggested, it's quite possible to teach the rules of those procedures to students, either directly or tacitly.

To be sure, conventions operate with different degrees of rigidity. In this regard interpretive conventions are less like the rules for chess than like precepts of etiquette, as Michael suggests with his apt analysis of wedding invitations in Chapter 2. Interpretive conventions are not always formulated explicitly or sharply, although there is always profit to be made from guidebooks that let you in on what you "need" to know. They are not always severely enforced, although public acts of humiliation (whether in a classroom or at the country club) can easily influence behavior. They are historically contingent, although there's always some continuity in the practices of a given culture. And different sorts of occasions allow both different practices and different degrees of stringency. In her 1911 guide to etiquette, for instance, Mrs. E. B Duffey remarked that "it is not required of a gentleman in a railway car to relinquish his seat in favor of a lady" but that the situation is "different" in streetcars (pp. 91–92). More important, like rules of behavior—note how Mrs. Duffey's advice turns on issues of gender—rules of reading carry with them certain effects that can be broadly described as "political," in the sense that they reflect and influence the systems of power relationships (implicit and explicit) among various social, economic, and cultural groups.

Because my research has been directed more toward the act of interpretation than toward classroom dynamics, I had not noticed another way in which the rules of reading can be described as "political." But Michael's discussion of democracy in Chapter 2 has also made me acutely aware that these rules have another political dimension as well: for one of the things that students in a literature classroom do come to share is a repertoire of techniques of reading. It is in part this shared repertoire that makes possible what Fishman (1993) calls "occasions . . . for people to share their differences" (p. 320). To put it in other terms: Agreements about how to make sense of texts are a valuable resource, for they permit readers to have meaningful discussions even when they have very different responses to and evaluations of the texts that they read. And this, as Michael demonstrates, allows them to learn about one another. Michael suggests that what saves these book discussions from falling into what one participant called "a bleeding-heart session" is "the book." I'd modify his claim and suggest that it's the initial agreement about and respect for the rules of the game of interpretation—for it's only when there is some kind of initial agreement (what Stanley Fish [1980] calls an interpretive community) that anything like "the book" exists for the group in the first place.

PUTTING THINGS IN ORDER

There are so many rules governing social behavior that most people who have written about them have found it advisable to sort them according to what are assumed to be useful and appropriate categories. Mrs. Duffey, for instance, found it useful to break down "Etiquette for Courtship" into rules governing conduct of gentlemen toward ladies, conduct of ladies toward gentlemen, "premature declaration" (p. 126), and the duties of rejected suitors. There are a similarly vast number of interpretive rules for reading, and, in *Before Reading* (Rabinowitz, 1987/1997), I suggested four rough categories to keep them under control: rules of notice, signification, configuration, and coherence. Let me take each in turn.

First, rules of notice. There has been a long and pernicious tradition of critical insistence that it is possible, even necessary, to account for everything that happens in a novel. William R. Schroeder (1986), for instance, claims that "an interpretation is *complete* when all the elements of the text are incorporated in a nonarbitrary fashion" (p. 22). And when, for instance, Florence Ridley (1963) braces up her interpretation of Conrad's *Heart of Darkness* with the claim that, unlike the readings of other critics, hers "take[s] into consideration all of its parts" (p. 44), she is falling back on the same critical gesture. But as Schroeder admits, it is a principle that cannot be sustained in practice. For as should be clear to anyone who has ever tried to cut through the dense prose of Conrad's short novel, there is always more in any substantial text than any reader can deal with.

In fact, in order to read, we have to decide when to skip, when to skim, and when to be especially alert. The best we can hope to do, as readers, is not to miss what's consequential. Schroeder (1986), in modifying his position, makes precisely this claim: "A reading can legitimately be faulted if *important* elements are not explained" (p. 22, emphasis added). But in order to put this into practice, we need some system for determining what constitutes importance. And to do this well, we rely on rules that allow us to decide what counts as a narrative high point. Some of these rules apply quite broadly: One rule governing most modern Western narratives, for instance, stresses the ending—so it's not surprising that so many essays have centered on the final image in Fitzgerald's *The Great Gatsby*. Likewise, the readers in Michael's People and Stories/ Gente Y Cuentos program knew they were supposed to pay special attention when, in Walker's "Everyday Use," Dee/Wangero uses the phrase "everyday use" in her complaint about Maggie. As he suggests, that is because of a general rule that in most serious works of fiction, titles are stressed, and we know to pay special attention when they are repeated in the text. This rule, for instance, gives special emphasis to the conclusion of the next-to-last chapter of Harper Lee's *To Kill a Mockingbird*, where Scout confirms her acceptance of Mr. Tate's version of Bob Ewell's death by saying, "'Well, it'd be sort of like shootin' a mockingbird, wouldn't it?'" (1960/1962, p. 279). Other rules, in contrast, apply only to small groups of texts. Details about train schedules are more likely to be important in an Agatha Christie novel than in literature at large; dates are especially important in epistolary novels. Some rules are even author-specific: Viewers of Hitchcock films, for instance, know to look for the director's appearance on the screen; and as Robert Scholes (1985b) points out about Hemingway, "Whenever Ernest says, 'very,' watch out!" (p. 45).

Thus, I wouldn't feel chagrined if, during a discussion of Henry James's *Turn of the Screw*, a student question revealed that I didn't have the slightest idea what kind of sound the wheels make as the governess turns into the avenue on her first arrival at Bly. Given the authorial audience of that text, it's not an especially memorable detail. But I was certainly taken aback when one of my students wrote a paper on the significance of an event in Willa Cather's *Song of the Lark* that I had not noticed: the moment when Thea throws a copy of Tolstoy's *Kreutzer Sonata* down with disgust. I was embarrassed that I had skimmed over that detail, not because of some general injunction to incorporate "everything" into an interpretation, but because of a more specific understanding that in this kind of text—a highly-wrought and artistically self-conscious novel about the development of an opera singer—the main character's responses to other works of art, especially other works of art about the moral impact of music, are worthy of notice.

Second, once they have used rules of notice to highlight certain details, readers use what I call rules of signification to wrest particular meanings from them. We would use rules of signification to determine just what that mockingbird means in Harper Lee's novel—in fact, to determine that the mockingbird reference, in contrast to one of Hitchcock's ritual appearances, is figurative in the first place. Likewise, rules of signification tell us when it is appropriate to assume that snow has symbolic overtones (as in Hemingway's "The Snows of Kilimanjaro" or Joyce's "The Dead") and when snow is just a meteorological fact (as in the final section of Chekhov's "Lady with a Dog," when Gurov is explaining to his daughter why it doesn't thunder in winter). Rules of signification also allow us to determine who is talking in passages using interior monologue or "style indirect libre."

Rules of signification are especially difficult to handle, because they are highly susceptible to changes in history and geography, and dictionaries rarely track down the subtle shifts in vernacular meanings of words. It is through application of rules of signification that, as I suggested in the first chapter, the reader of *The Maltese Falcon* is expected to interpret Joel Cairo's glossy hair, his elegant tie-clip, his fawn spats, his "short, mincing, bobbing steps," and his "fragrance of chypre" as confirmation of the fact that Effie Perine's description of him as "queer" does, in fact, refer to his sexual orientation (Hammett, 1930/1989, p. 42). Likewise, it is through rules of signification that Michael's readers of Walker's "Everyday Use" can draw conclusions about Dee's character from the fact that she has changed her name. But these literary facts evoke this meaning only in texts written in a limited sociocultural milieu. Likewise, rules of signification are also highly susceptible to differences from text to text: given the Catholic emphasis of *A Canticle for Leibowitz*, it's reasonable to assume a religious halo in the fact that the two-headed woman is named "Mrs. Grales." It's not quite so obvious whether Raymond Chandler's intended audience would have the same associations with "Mrs. Grayle" in *Farewell, My Lovely*. Application of the wrong rules of signification can seriously distort the overall meaning of a text—as is demonstrated by the students in Michael's class, who, trying to come to terms with "All the Years of Her Life," misread the details of Mrs. Higgins's appearance ("her hair was tucked loosely under her hat, and her hand at her throat held her light coat tight across her chest so her dress would not show") as an indication that she was trying to seduce the druggist.

Third, by applying rules of configuration, readers can—during the act of reading—assemble the details and their significances generated by the first two sets of rules into some more or less familiar patterns, thus allowing them to make predictions about what is to come. Rules of configuration are what make literary expectations possible. Once we have the combination of James Bond, a megalomaniac villain in a secure fortress, and a threat to some major hub of civilization, we know that Bond will enter the villain's domain, will be captured, and will escape at the last moment. There are more specific rules as well: For instance, the rule that I call the Rule of Magnetic Opposition. This rule, which fuels our interpretation of many texts centering on intense binary psychological conflict, encourages readers to expect that the distance between the protagonist and the villain will progressively shrink. Specifically, we are invited to expect that when the villain offers an invitation to explore psychic depths, the protagonist will be tempted and ultimately corrupted. The Rule of Magnetic Opposition sets up expectations in such canonical texts as *Heart of Darkness* and, more problematically, Dostoyevsky's *The Idiot*. And it is a crucial element that generates expectations in such contemporary psychological thrillers as the films *Black Widow, Love Crimes,* and *Silence of the Lambs* (where the villains seduce not only the heroines, but the viewers as well) and in James Ellroy's singularly perverse novel *The Big Nowhere*. It is important to remember, though, that while rules of configuration provide a normative frame against which to measure the events of a particular text, they give meaning in two distinct ways: They create effects both when the text fulfills expectations and when it refuses to do so. I'll return to the effects of nonfulfillment later in this chapter.

Finally, there are rules of coherence, which allow us, once we have finished reading, to fit the text together as a whole. As Annette Kolodny (1980) puts it, "In our heart of hearts, of course, most critics are really structuralists (whether or not they accept the label) because what we are seeking are patterns (or structures) that can order and explain the otherwise inchoate" (p. 17). Kolodny, less concerned with authorial reading than I am, goes on to claim, "Thus, we invent, or believe we discover, relational patternings in the texts we read which promise transcendence from difficulty and perplexity to clarity and coherence" (p. 17). I'd put it differently: Authors and the readers they write for share communal norms that allow them to share relational patternings in texts. Particularly important are rules that allow us to distil some larger theme from the work—that allow us, for instance, to decide that *Hamlet* is a play "about" repressed Oedipal desires.

For many critics, including the New Critics, rules of coherence are by far the most important rules of interpretation. Schroeder (1986), for instance, defines "an interpretation of a narrative text" as "a series of hypotheses that coherently explain the organization and elements of the text and that thereby elucidate the text's thematic implications" (p. 10). If you are not guided by the criteria of coherence and completeness, he argues, you're "not doing interpretation" (p. 16). This faith in coherence has been vigorously disputed by deconstructionists, although in many ways their arguments, too, place coherence at the center of literary structure—even though it is the text's lack of coherence that is underscored. I have rather different reasons for believing that the emphasis on coherence is limiting, reasons I discuss in detail in Chapter 5.

I would argue that any act of reading, no matter how arbitrary, involves the application of *some* rules of notice, signification, configuration, and coherence. What distinguishes authorial reading, as we conceptualize it, from other kinds of reading is not the fact that it involves application of interpretive rules but rather the particular interpretive rules that are invoked. That is, authorial reading requires applying those rules that the authorial audience would apply—and it is the choice of these rules, rather than other rules, that distinguishes authorial reading from several other kinds of reading.

Most obviously, the choice of rules distinguishes authorial from what I earlier called Quixotic reading or idiosyncratic reading—reading in which a reader applies rules that are not shareable, in the sense that there is no persuasive reason for anyone else to apply them to the text in question. Michael discusses such a Quixotic reading in Chapter 2, when he talked about Bleich's student who was reminded of her Russian linguist friend when she read "Bartleby the Scrivener." Although I agree with Michael's criticism of the student, I'd frame the problem in a slightly different way. Michael saw the student as leaving the story behind; I'd see it as a case of leaving behind the agreed-upon procedures for reading the story.

In any case, the choice of one possible set of rules over another not only distinguishes authorial reading from idiosyncratic reading; it also distinguishes it from what might be called Institutional Reading—the application of interpretive procedures that are widely shared (perhaps, in certain interpretive communities, even enforced) but that do not happen to be those of the authorial audience. Freudian or Lacanian readings, for instance, are often Institutional Readings: They may reveal insights into the way the world operates, but unless they occur alongside authorial readings, they make their points by binding and gagging the author. Similarly, many of the interpretations of *Heart of Darkness* that I discuss in Chapter 1—for instance, Peter Brooks's (1984) claim that the novel "is ultimately most of all about transmission" (p. 261)—are Institutional Readings that serve to mute the political angle suggested by Conrad's (1986) own expression of the "idea" of the book: "the criminality of inefficiency and pure selfishness when tackling the civilizing work in Africa" (pp. 139–140).

Let me make it clear that Institutional Readings are often valuable, especially for texts that we wish to resist. Applying a feminist perspective, say, to Dashiell Hammett's *The Maltese Falcon* shows up certain underlying patterns of masculine power in the way the story is told (see Rabinowitz, 1994b). But our understanding of those patterns—our sense of their strength and our ability to resist them (if we wish)—is stronger if we know whether Hammett is praising them, criticizing them, or simply unaware of them. And that requires, as we have suggested elsewhere in this book, that the Institutional Reading be placed against the authorial reading.

Furthermore, and perhaps more important, Institutional Readings often have a stifling effect on the reader's ability to find something new in a text, for at their worst, they turn into Procrustean Readings that so radically preinterpret the text that the reader knows what he or she will find even before picking up the text. Take, for instance, J. Hillis Miller's allegorical reading strategies: According to Miller (1989), everything in Henry James's *What Maisie Knew* "stands for something else, but ultimately this 'something else' is the act of reading itself" (p. 96). Furthermore, the novel teaches us about "the impossibility of reading" (p. 97) and hence teaches us that we are "eternally alone" and that "the thematic assertions of even the most apparently morally concerned literature" are irrelevant (p. 98). But Miller does not present this simply as a particular interpretation of a particular text. Although he admits that "whether or not the same conclusions would follow from the reading of other works could only be determined by reading them," he calls this "a potentially [!!] interminable process" and offers a totalizing claim nonetheless: "I claim . . . that analogous results would universally follow" (p. 98). I suspect that he is right; that is, his interpretive strategies are so powerful that we can know the moral meanings they will uncover, even in texts we have never even heard of, much less read.

Authorial readings are, I believe, most important when you are reading on your own. In a classroom, a book club, or any other situation where discussion is possible, the eccentric reader or the Institutional Reader has some possibility of hearing other voices that can serve as a corrective. When reading alone, however, the only voice with which you can engage is the author's. If that voice is silenced by your initial choice of reading techniques, you are apt to end up talking to yourself.

DIFFERENT OCCASIONS, DIFFERENT KINDS OF TEXTS

Let me stress again that while application of some rules in each of the four categories is necessary to make sense of any text, no *particular* rules of reading are universal: Different texts call upon different sets of procedures, just as putting together a bicycle and installing an internal modem require different tools and different skills. But rules do tend to come in clusters; that is, texts that call for Rule A often call for Rule B as well. Texts with apocalyptic configurations often call on the rules of signification that ask us to see the religious connotations of words. The Rule of Magnetic Opposition is often found in texts where we are asked to pay attention to the ways in which characters double each other, in particular the ways in which their names echo each other phonetically, as the names of the hero (Marlowe) and villain (Mars) do in Raymond Chandler's *The Big Sleep*. Indeed, I have argued elsewhere (Rabinowitz, 1987/1997) that genre is best understood not as a group of texts that share textual features but rather as a collection of texts that call on similar sets of rules, that invite similar interpretive strategies.

Many traditional accounts of genre have recognized (even founded themselves on) a connection between genre and configuration. But genre, in my sense, is tied to rules in the other three categories as well. The rules of notice we are expected to apply to a naturalist novel—with its dense accumulation of socioenvironmental detail, much of which can be skimmed over—are quite different from those called forth by one of Shakespeare's tragedies, which demand more attention to detail, especially linguistic detail. Certain words take on religious connotations in Christian allegories—but not necessarily in secular thrillers.

From this perspective (and this is another point where my argument comes close to Hirsch's [1967] *Validity in Interpretation*), genre distinctions become central to literary interpretation. Specifically, knowledge of genre is a prerequisite to authorial reading. In order to participate as part of the authorial audience, a reader needs to know (explicitly or implicitly) the genre of the text in question.

Two caveats are in order. First, a rule may be relevant to the interpretation of a text even when the text undermines it. As I suggested above, this is clearest in the case of configuration. Even when an actual reader applies the appropriate rules of configuration, it does not follow that the specific text will in fact trace out the expected trajectory. Chandler's *The Big Sleep*, for instance, asks us to apply detective-story rules of configuration (including the rule that we should expect the detective to triumph over the villain), only to turn our expectations on their heads: The villain remains untouched at the end. Something similar happens to a romance rule of configuration in Harold Becker's 1996 political thriller *City Hall* (written by Bo Godman, Ken Lipper, Nicholas Pileggi, and Paul Schrader). Here we have a scene where the deputy mayor (played by John Cusack) travels to Buffalo with lawyer Marybeth Cogan (Bridget Fonda) in search of information; on the way back, the train is delayed, and there's a scene in a restaurant where the erotic tension between the two starts to crackle. That plot strand is unceremoniously snapped, and no romance follows. In both cases, however, rules of configuration are demanded, even though our expectations are frustrated. Indeed, our expectations could not be frustrated if the rules of configuration were not evoked. Similarly, Chester Himes's *Blind Man with a Pistol*, with its three intertwined plots, is a thriller, and that generic placement leads us to expect that the plots will be coherently merged. That coherence never comes, but the experience of failure is part of the intended effect. Here, it is the violation of rules of coherence that gives the novel its flavor.

Second, and more important, especially in a classroom setting, determining the genre and the rules in force for a given text would not be the end of a discussion but rather the beginning of one. There are still many important questions for the actual audience to answer. Is Chandler's decision to shift gears emotionally effective—or does it leave the reader with the feeling that the novel is simply awkward and poorly plotted? Does it have a political motivation as a critique of the conservatism of the detective-story genre? Is the shift in direction in *City Hall* a similar phenomenon—or does it produce a radically different effect? I have argued elsewhere (Rabinowitz, 1980) that Chandler's generic violation makes a strong political point; to my mind, *City Hall* merely exhibits Hollywood sloppiness. But I could well imagine a classroom debate in which both of those claims came under fire. Still, serious debates about such questions cannot take place without that initial generic placement. Without that first joining of the authorial audience, the rest of the questions do not even arise.

In sum, in order to read as authorial audience, you need to know the genre of a text. In order to know what rules of signification to call upon as they try to make sense of the imagery of Charlotte Perkins Gilman's "The Yellow Wallpaper," readers need to know whether or not to place the story in the genre of the ghost story. But there is a corollary to this principle: Readers who make different initial generic assumptions, because they apply different rules, may find that they are reading what appear to be different texts. As a consequence, as Dock, Allen, Palais, and Tracy (1996) have demonstrated, claims about the generic categories through which late-nineteenth-century readers read the text have significant consequences for any attempt to chart the politics of the reception history of Gilman's story.

The history of a text's reception, in other words, can often be understood at least partly as a history of shifting generic placements. William Savage (1992) has argued convincingly that the interpretation and evaluation of Chicago novelist Nelson Algren (most famous for *The Man with the Golden Arm*) were altered when the reading public—influenced by reviewers and by book jackets—started reading his books as popular trash rather than as serious extensions of the hard-boiled naturalist school; he further demonstrates that this shift was closely tied to shifts in the dominant literary-critical ideology brought about by the rise of McCarthyism. I observed something similar when teaching Jane Rule's richly poetic *Desert of the Heart* to first-year students. Those who bought the book in its gaudy, movie-tie-in version (complete with titillating photographs) read it simply "for the plot," assuming that it was junk reading and that the language consequently could not demand (or require) application of the kind of rules of signification they would apply to a writer such as Henry James or Edith Wharton.

Although Savage talks about "boundary texts"—specifically, texts that straddle the popular/serious distinction—in fact we'll interpret *any* text differently, depending on the genre we place it in and the subsequent strategies for reading we apply to it. I remember, as a seventh-grader, reading the recently published *Lolita* as an instance of the dirty-book genre. I consequently skimmed over all its literary references, which are simply not noticeable in that kind of text. Later on, as a young literary sophisticate, I learned to read the novel as an art-for-art's-sake manifesto. This generic placement illuminated many of the previously opaque details, but it encouraged me to apply interpretive procedures that reduced Lolita herself to a vehicle for discussion of such "higher concerns" as the nature of the sublime in the Western literary tradition (much as Conrad's Africans are turned into occasions for apostrophizing about the difficulties of narrative). Nowadays, *Lolita* tends to inhabit yet another genre, the exposé (although readers tend to split on whether Nabokov himself is the exposer or the exposed)—and readers tend to notice the patterns of abuse and to interpret them in sociopsychological, rather than "literary," terms. Humbert's union with Lolita is read not as a replay of Poe, but as a representation of a terrifyingly common form of sexual abuse.

Another example: For my students in the early 1970s, living in the shadow of the Vietnam War, *A Farewell to Arms* was obviously an "antiwar novel." They subsequently applied rules of notice that highlighted the descriptions of the pointless brutality of the war and rules of signification that turned Frederic Henry's jump into the river as a political rebirth. Catherine was merely part of the background. In the 1990s, my students are more apt to read the novel as a romance (although a romance they tend to read with suspicion, given prevalent perceptions of Hemingway as a "sexist"). Their rules of notice treat the relationship between Frederic and Catherine as the foreground, against a war that exists largely for local color; and while they still read the jump into the river as a symbolic rebirth, it's a rebirth into love and commitment.

The examples could be multiplied (for some detailed analyses of particular texts, see, for instance, Rabinowitz, 1989, 1994a), but the general principle seems to me clear. We do not read so much as *read as*—texts are always seen as instances of broader or narrower genres, and genre placement determines how they are read and, to a certain extent, what readers will find in them. Michael and I maintain, however, that these different generic placements do not all have the same status: It makes a difference how Gilman, Nabokov, and Hemingway wanted us to read their texts. Authorial reading always requires, then, more than finding a generic placement that works: It requires knowing the genre in which the authorial audience places the text.

THE GRIP OF FORM: RULE-GOVERNED WRITING

My stress on authorial reading and on what some would see as a limitation on the freedom of the reader could easily be misconstrued as a claim that authors, in contrast to readers, have full control over their texts. But one of the reasons I prefer the concept of authorial audience to the more familiar notion of authorial intention is that the former emphasizes a social/conventional dimension. And, as I've said, that dimension influences both reading *and* writing: There are consequently parallel limitations placed on authors as well. True, authors have a certain amount of control over the ways in which they use, and twist, conventions. But there are also very strong constraints on their activities. Michael's arguments about community in Chapter 2 have given me another way to conceptualize these constraints. Michael writes about the importance of common projects for the members of a classroom; and his ideas can be pushed a step further to the community of readers and authors. That is, rather than think about writing as an individual's act of pure creation (a way of thinking that encourages us to think of authors as "masters"), perhaps we should think of artists and audiences, too, as people who are engaged in a common project, one that requires prior agreements about the way the project is conducted. Genres, in this scheme, are the agreed-upon rules of conduct that make the activity possible.

Thus, just as readers have their interpretive freedom checked by the notion of the authorial audience, so do authors—genres are a powerful force. When an author does not play the game fairly, there is a good chance that his or her work will be deemed a failure—at least, until critics come up with some new generic placement within which it makes sense. One of my colleagues, the Romanian director Adrian Giurgea, once told me about an experience he had while in the hospital. He filled the time largely by reading thrillers, but he eventually came across one that so violated the rules of the genre, for no discernible reason, that he actually had a relapse of his hepatitis. An extreme reaction to generic failure, no doubt; but most readers and viewers respond with at least annoyance when a work doesn't follow the rules it seems to call upon.

I am not suggesting, of course, that artists cannot twist genres; on the contrary, almost any successful text will push generic patterns in one way or another. But genres are resilient and often resist an author's attempt to manipulate them. I'd like to pursue this idea, taking as my case in point Kathryn Bigelow's 1990 cinematic thriller, *Blue Steel*. The analysis that follows is somewhat more intricate than most of the others in this book, and this film—hardly a classic even of its genre—might not seem worth the effort. But *Blue Steel* is worth studying in detail here, for several reasons. First, I concluded Chapter 1 with a discussion of a classic of the high-art canon, *Heart of Darkness*. It therefore seems appropriate to look closely at a very different kind of text in order to stress that the theoretical claims about authorial reading fueling this book apply to popular art as well as to more canonical texts—and that our pedagogical arguments apply to classroom texts well beyond the classics. Besides serving as a token representative of popular culture, *Blue Steel* has the more specific advantage of clarifying the issues at stake: It is easier to see the operations of genre in works that rely on (and work against) formulaic genres, and *Blue Steel* takes on a number of standard generic patterns in an ingenious way. Most important, though, this analysis opens up for discussion two areas in which Michael and I do not quite agree: the question of how far to balance our readings toward the narrative audience and the question of the breadth of genres.

As we've said, Michael and I tend to feel differently about the importance of the reader's relationships to the characters in a text—Michael is more concerned than I am with the ethical imperative to treat characters with respect and somewhat less concerned with the transaction between author and reader. In the analysis that follows, I'd like to demonstrate some of the ways we can talk intelligently about the politics of the text even with primary emphasis on form and somewhat muted engagement on the level of the narrative audience. At the same time, I'd like to raise the issue of how fine a definition of a genre has to be in order for it to be useful as an analytic or pedagogical tool. The analysis that follows suggests that we often need to make fairly subtle discriminations; in Chapter 4, Michael argues that broader categories—although still less broad than the categories "narrative" or "drama" favored by many anthologies — are in fact more useful in the classroom.

The plot of *Blue Steel* centers around rookie cop Megan Turner (played by Jamie Lee Curtis) and the psychotic serial killer whose attraction to her—indeed, obsession with her—has been triggered by watching her kill an armed robber in a supermarket. Having stolen the robber's pistol, the villain has been acting out his passion by randomly gunning down people, using bullets on which he has meticulously etched her name. The first climax comes when Megan has to make a key choice. She has just discovered, in a twisted seduction scene, that her commodities-trader boyfriend Eugene Hunt (Ron Silver) is in fact the killer. As she starts to arrest him, Eugene makes an ardent appeal to her sinister side. Granted, it's a confused appeal. But for all this ambiguity, there's no doubt that he's inviting her to dig deeply into her psyche and explore the evil that he insists they share. He knows her, he tells her, better than she knows herself.

Megan starts to call for reinforcements—but hesitates; and especially since we are less than halfway through the film, we may well expect her to abandon her resolve. That's because the film invokes the Rule of Magnetic Opposition, which generates the authorial audience's expectations that Megan Turner will be true to her name and turn to her evil side in *Blue Steel*. This rule is called up in a number of ways.

First, there are intertextual cues. The title can reasonably be read as a reference to *Blue Velvet*, a classic exemplification of the Rule of Magnetic Opposition; and those who know Bigelow's later film *Point Break*, assuredly a Magnetic Opposition film, may be tempted to read that film's structure into the earlier one, too. Second, the first major scene of the film shows us a role-playing exercise (although we don't find out that that's what it is until it's finished) in which Megan is "shot" by an abused woman who is trying to protect her abuser. This reversal prepares us for a film in which women will in fact be taken over by their attraction to violence and abuse. Third, as I've said, the Rule of Magnetic Opposition is often signaled by the use of doubles. And there are reasons to read Megan and Eugene as doubles—including the slight phonetic echo in their names. Then, too, the film relies heavily on the metaphorical play between costume and psychological state, which serves as a conventional warning that we can never be sure of the "true" psychological nature of our heroine. When in official dress—and toward the beginning of the film we have a striking scene of her putting on her uniform—Megan looks quite different, and she acts quite differently, too. Her nonuniformed persona seems odd, confused, unable to cope with the world—in particular, with "normal" middle-class romance, which is always undermined by her gender-inappropriate profession. And since the seduction scene plays heavily on the essential item of her costume—her gun—our sense of possible revelation is heightened. Finally, and perhaps most important, Megan says and does things that can reasonably be interpreted as evidence of a certain mean streak. She is asked several times why she has decided to become a cop. The first time, she replies that she wants to "kill people," the second time that she likes to slam people up against walls. And indeed, it is because he believes that he has witnessed this supposed mean streak that Eugene falls in love—if that's the right phrase—with her.

In *Blue Steel*, however, the expectations so strongly set up by this rule of configuration are reversed. That hesitation in Megan's call is but another tease to the audience—it's simply that she does not know Eugene's apartment number. But otherwise, she's firm: She brings in the police, and a new plot pattern is launched. Some viewers have criticized this as an anticlimactic, even incoherent, moment, a sign that the film is unsure of its own genre—or simply badly made. In fact, however, it can be read as serving a crucial ideological function. For under the right circumstances, such a violation of rules of configuration can serve as what I call "generic refusal"—the explicit recognition and rejection of widespread generic patterns.

Generic refusal is not the same thing as generic ambiguity: this is not a situation where we cannot figure out the genre (as in *The Turn of the Screw* or Doris Lessing's *Briefing for a Descent into Hell*) or where a work seems to fall into several genres at once (as is arguably the case with *Pulp Fiction*). It is, rather, a definite slap in the face: a moment where a work clearly announces generic intent to the authorial audience and then ostentatiously refuses to follow through.

Generic refusal tends, among other things, to break the illusion of our participation as narrative audience and highlight the authorial level. In *Blue Steel*, the anticlimactic swerve specifically highlights the conventionality of the Rule of Magnetic Opposition. It thus nourishes resistance by making us aware of what we are tacitly accepting when we engage this particular interpretive strategy, especially in works where the magnetism operates between an attractively evil male and a seducible female. For even when, as in such films as Lou Diamond Phillips's *Dangerous Touch*, we sympathize with the woman as she ultimately extricates herself from the brutal relationship, the convention has the potential to nurture a rape-and-abuse culture by putting the reader or viewer, as narrative audience, in a position of positing the desire for abuse as a "natural" part of the female psyche. As a consequence, the Rule of Magnetic Opposition can contribute, among other things, to a construction of a masculinity centering around a "bad boys have more fun" ideology. And in ostentatiously refusing to maneuver us into that position, *Blue Steel* invites us to resist the ideological force of so many superficially similar thrillers.

Or so I originally felt when I watched the film. But as I've suggested,

I've become increasingly aware of what I call the grip of form: Genres have more tenacity than we often believe, and they often take their revenge on authors who are unfaithful to them. And, certainly, something very curious happens in this film: Megan never once, never for a moment, betrays the slightest interest in what Eugene has to offer. Yet by the time we're finished with the dreamily bloody final confrontation, where she chases and finally kills her nemesis, endlessly shooting bullets into his seemingly unstoppable body, it seems, in a sense, that Eugene has gotten precisely what he has wanted all along and that, in a curious way, he's been proven right. Indeed, Maria Garcia (1990) has gone so far as to claim that "Megan has the same instincts—and is as unstable—as the man she's out to get" (p. 366). How has generic refusal turned into what might be called generic "re-fusal"—that is, the insertion of a new fuse that reactivates the generic circuits that had previously been blown?

No doubt there are economic industry demands: Big-budget thrillers require spectacle if they are to succeed at the box office. But there are also at least two theoretical reasons that cast some illumination beyond *Blue Steel*, and even beyond mass-market film. First, generic refusal always involves what we might call generic enchaining: Unless you are willing to risk generic incoherence (and as I've said, many have read *Blue Steel* in that way; see Kauffmann, 1990), refusing one genre necessarily involves consenting to another that lies nearby. That is, in order to read a text as an instance of generic refusal—as an intended critique of the ideology behind certain conventions—it is necessary to be able to see its generic delinquency as one element in some larger coherence; and the rules of coherence with which one makes sense of it must come from some alternative genre, some contiguous genre that can replace the one refused. Thus, it's possible to read *Romeo and Juliet* as generic refusal of comedy, but only by employing the patterns of tragedy to make its generic refusal visible as such. Or—to use the text that really inaugurated my thinking on generic refusal—it's possible to read *The Big Sleep* as generic refusal of the classical detective story, but only by seeing it through, say, an Oedipal pattern of personal guilt. That's especially true when one is dealing with genres founded on the Rule of Magnetic Opposition, since that rule, if refused, must be refused fairly early in a work: To turn away from the attraction of evil only at the end (as happens, say, in *Dangerous Touch*) is still to admit the existence and the power and even the endurance of that attraction (otherwise, it couldn't generate the film) and to assert merely that the protagonist has made a rational choice to resist it—something quite different from what happens in *Blue Steel*.

The alternative genre, I suspect, has to have at least two characteristics. First, it needs to be familiar to the authorial audience—and especially in a mass-market film, this need imposes serious limitations. Second, and more important, the genre to which you shift has to be, as I've suggested, contiguous. That is, there have to be some shared points of contact between the genres, something analogous to what happens in common-practice musical modulation that uses a pivot chord shared by both keys. Thus Suzanne Moore (1990) may be correct when she says "Bigelow *likes* to take an established genre and bend it into something altogether different" (p. 30, emphasis added); but it is not apparent that she, or anyone, can succeed. Genres can be bent—but *not* into something "altogether different." And the inability to be "altogether different" is where the problems become increasingly vexing for artists, especially popular artists, who are trying to make a political point using this kind of strategy. The contiguous genres have their own ideological demands, and, as a consequence, you often find yourself not so much resisting the ideological pressures as merely displacing them. That's what happens in *Thelma and Louise* (a film of choice for narrative theorists in the early 1990s), and it's certainly one of the things that trips up *Blue Steel*, which actually moves in a three-part chain.

Let me chart the links briefly. After the climactic moment when Megan refuses the seduction and calls the police, Eugene is arrested. He is released through the intercession of his lawyer, however, and we settle down for a different kind of movie, moving from a rookie-cop film calling on the Rule of Magnetic Opposition to a tough procedural cat-and-mouser where the lines between good guys and bad guys are clearly drawn. But there are problematic ideological undercurrents to this genre, too. For if we apply the rules of reading appropriate to that genre, Megan would be read as a victim who must be "rescued." And since she's a woman, and the police force is primarily male, that would raise new problems for Bigelow. What has she gained if, in order to get her viewers to construct Megan as a woman with no tolerance for abuse, she has had to encourage them to construct her as weak and lacking self-reliance?

So, in what we might call an enchained refusal (in fact, as we'll see, the refusal turns out to be *literally* "enchained"), Bigelow turns down the invitations of that second genre, too. Bigelow highlights the ideological problems of this second genre by putting Megan in the hands of the aptly named Nick Mann, a detective who not only provides the expected romantic interest but also insists on "protecting" her by watching her every move—a combination voyeur/lover whose concern for her thus becomes double edged. It's Mann's failure to trust Megan that makes her decide that she has to act independently of the authorities; and in a crucial scene, she chains him—with her handcuffs—to the steering wheel of his car so she can confront Eugene without domineering male protection.

But this rebellion throws Megan into yet *another* genre: the renegade-cop genre. Indeed, David Denby (1990) titled his unfriendly review "Dirty Harriet" (p. 76). And that genre, unfortunately, reintroduces the Rule of Magnetic Opposition: In that genre, tough, independent cops and detectives, whether Clint Eastwood or Philip Marlowe, are invited to be read as people who walk very close to the line that separates them from the evil they are supposedly battling. As a consequence, when we watch the final scene, we're apt to forget about the earlier generic refusal. Indeed, once we are in the renegade-cop genre, there is almost no way to film the ending so that it won't confirm precisely what the film, earlier on, seemed to be intent on denying. The new genre, in effect, preinterprets the ending. If Megan appears to be triumphant, that will only confirm the pleasure she takes in the kill. If—as in the film Bigelow actually made, where the final shot shows her completely drained, numb—she appears worn out by the event, it will be read by the authorial audience as a kind of postorgasmic exhaustion.

That is, Bigelow seems to have gone out of her way to avoid any images that might suggest that Megan experiences pleasure in this final shoot-out. But because reading as authorial audience is a conventional activity, and because the conventions here come from the authorial audience's experience with other renegade-cop films, we are apt to read the final scene *through* them, and we're apt to interpret her final collapse as a kind of verification of Eugene's claims about her psyche. She is but his double, and when he ceases to exist, she's got nothing left of herself.

The problem of the ending is only one of the problems created by the generic enchaining. In addition, there is, as I've said, a second consequence with interesting theoretical ramifications illuminated by Bigelow's generic difficulties—something I would like to call, following the imagery of the film, "generic recoil." To put it briefly: Switching genres is not the same as changing planes at O'Hare. Or, to use a different image, an author cannot choose the ending of a text in the same way that you can choose a dessert in a restaurant. For generic enchaining influences not only where you are going but also *where you have been*, in ways that may not always be possible to map out in advance. If genres are collections of rules that readers are accustomed to find together, one does not always have the power to pick and choose which rules one wants to enlist. Refusing some rules involves a more complex realignment that changes other rules as well and that may recast what has already happened.

I am not limiting myself here simply to rules of coherence: Choosing new rules of coherence inevitably, of course, has an impact on the entire work. Nor am I talking simply about the way your interpretation of a text is apt to change in rereading (a subject to which I return in Chapter 5).

Beyond that, chaining genres has a recoil effect on other interpretive procedures even the first time through.

Consider two examples of how this works with respect to rules of signification in *Blue Steel*. First, in the crucial scene in the supermarket, Megan not only shoots the perpetrator—she empties all of her bullets into him. In the original genre—at that point, all that we've got is a rookie-cop film—we are apt to read that excess as a sign of her fear, anxiety, inexperience. But once the film slides over to the renegade-cop genre, the recoil effect pushes us to reinterpret it, rather, as a sign of the accuracy of Eugene's interpretation of Megan. That is, according to the rules of this new genre, that early scene really does reveal her sadistic side. Denby (1990), in fact, claims that this scene, one of the few in the film that he enjoyed, shows her "fear and excitement" (p. 76). The second example is even more striking, given the film's presumably feminist agenda—that, at least, is how I've interpreted Bigelow's claim that "I like to make films that are provocative, that can rattle your cage" (quoted in Schickel, 1991, p. 75; for a different perspective, see Acker, 1992). In a sequence in the middle of the film, Megan handcuffs her father and starts to bring him into the station for abusing her mother. When he breaks down in tears, however, she decides not to arrest him. In the cat-and-mouse procedural, which is the dominant genre at the moment, this can be legitimately read as representing Megan's reasonable ambivalence: Although she has no sympathy for abuse, he is, after all, her father. But renegade-cop films often feature a scene where the cop lets a villain escape because the cop recognizes some kind of mirror relationship between them; and once we've found ourselves in this genre, we are apt to put this scene in that slot and reinterpret it accordingly.

What conclusions can we draw from this analysis of *Blue Steel*? Although many critics these days seem willing to universalize from minute particulars, I'm not ready to generalize about the possibilities of generic refusal and generic enchaining from a single case—particularly such an off-beat case. Yet the generic complication of *Blue Steel* does seem a cautionary tale, not only for authors and filmmakers but also for genre critics, teachers, and readers more generally. And my arguments have significant consequences for classroom practice.

First, there are consequences with regard to the texts we teach. One reason that many of my students—at least at the college level—have trouble talking about genre in class is that they have been trained to believe that discussion of popular and mass-market texts and films is somehow inappropriate or unsophisticated. I would argue, in contrast, that study of genre has to start with those works where the workings of genre are most evident—and that, in many cases, this means looking carefully and seriously at noncanonical, even formulaic, texts. Let me stress that I believe this to be true whether or not you "believe in the canon"—that is, whether or not you believe it is important for teachers to instil in their students an appreciation for the texts that have come to be associated with high culture. For even if you believe that a literature teacher's job is to prepare students, say, to read Joyce and Faulkner, you can't perform that task without first teaching them to recognize the formulaic generic building-blocks that canonical authors use to construct their texts.

Second, there are consequences with regard to the way we teach genre. If we want our students to be careful readers, alert not only to what texts can "mean" but also to the manipulative power they have over both their readers and their authors, we need to start training our students to think, more astutely than they do now, about what genre is and how it operates. And that means we have to recognize that genres interlock in intricate ways that are more complex than our theoretical apparatus sometimes admits. More specifically, we need to think of genres less as distinct categories than as dynamic and overlapping fields where a single change can have unanticipated effects. And we have to remember that those effects matter, not only interpretively, but ethically and politically as well.

Third, there are consequences with regard to the attitude we take toward texts, both in terms of respect and in terms of resistance. To begin with respect: Recognizing the ways in which authors, as well as readers, are subject to social constraints can help students learn to be patient with older texts. If students know, for instance, the nature of the readers for whom Dickens's novels were written—and if they know the generic constraints that Dickens consequently wrote within—they can better understand, and appreciate, what might otherwise appear to be authorial excess. Recognizing social constraints on authors can also help them learn to be respectful of the craft involved in noncanonical texts and texts that come from different cultures. This is especially important when students are working with multicultural anthologies that juxtapose texts from different cultures—that hold up, say, the *Federalist Papers* and a Native American chant from the same period. Such juxtapositions can easily backfire unless students learn to ask about the generic demands made on the producers of the less canonical text. And asking about the generic expectations of the authorial audience can do more than simply increase our appreciation of the craft involved in a particular work. It can also bring other readers—readers far different in time and culture—into the classroom as well.

But recognition of generic constraints—like any self-conscious awareness of the way a text works—can facilitate resistance, as well. The bloody ending of *Blue Steel* is problematic for many viewers, especially those who believe that it represents, at some level, Bigelow's lurid attraction to the violence of the genre in which she ends up. Recognition of the constraints increases our respect for her position, but it does not require accepting the terms of the move. In fact, I believe that generic analysis of the sort I have set out here, by sharpening our awareness of the givens we are being asked to accept, has the potential to strengthen our resistance to the trajectory of the film. Similarly, generic awareness might help an atheist reader resist the sweep of *Crime and Punishment* as it transforms itself from a psychological thriller to a novel of Christian redemption—or help a socially conservative reader resist the generic swerve of *The Big Sleep*. To put it in other terms, understanding the generic currents beneath a text does not impose any politics in particular, but it does help make certain kinds of political discussions possible in the first place.

PLAYING BY THE RULES

Michael W. Smith

MY DAUGHTERS (a 5-year-old and a 6-year old) currently have three favorite games: Baby Booper, Mean Brother, and Heart Attack. Although I'm not privy to all the details, I know that Baby Booper requires Rachel, the younger, to crawl around and mess things up, after which she is scolded by Catherine, Mean Brother requires both to put on dress-up dresses and harumph about Mean Brother's indiscretions in what sounds like British accents, and Heart Attack requires their spreading a comforter on the floor of Rachel's room and tackling and wrestling with each other.

I suppose that talking about my kids' playing may seem like a non sequitur. But I think that my girls' play suggests a crucial point against which Peter's discussion of the rules of reading literature must be read: Play depends on shared rules. And, as Vygotsky (1978) points out in *Mind in Society,* so does pleasure: "Ordinarily a child experiences subordination to rules in the renunciation of something he wants, but [in play] subordination to a rule and renunciation of action on immediate impulse are the means to maximum pleasure" (p. 99).

My argument in this chapter is that if we value our students' getting the maximum pleasure from both their reading of literature and their talking about literature with others, we have to help them understand the kind of rules that Peter talks about in Chapter 3. In Margaret Meek's words, we need to share the "list of secret things that all accomplished readers know, yet never talk about" (cited in Thomson 1987, p. 109). I recognize that some people may see the kind of teaching I propose here as privileging teachers in a way that is at odds with the democratic vision we've been presenting. I close the chapter by explaining why I think that view is wrong.

THE SARDUCCI TEST

Comic Don Novello's Father Guido Sarducci used to be a popular visitor on "Saturday Night Live." One of his routines has provided me an important tool for thinking about my teaching. The good Father offered a modest proposal for a Five-Minute University. It was his idea that society could save a whole lot of money and students a whole lot of time if a course could teach only what the students would remember 5 years later. Spanish 101, for example, would become "¿Como está usted?" Under his plan an entire college education would take only 5 minutes. I started to think about what the Five-Minute High School version of my literature course would be, and I was afraid that it would be a list of works and vague statements of what they were about.

It bothered me. I went back to work on my Ph.D. in large measure to think about what I could do about it. What I wanted to do was find a way to teach students something that would matter across texts. Peter's discussion of rules of reading has helped me understand the extent to which readers' ability to play with texts depends upon their knowledge of rules. I have come to believe, therefore, that what I should aspire to in a Five-Minute University version of my course is an understanding of rules, of powerful ways of reading that would help students play with and take pleasure from a variety of texts.

As a teacher, then, I had to ask two critical questions: What kinds of rules matter and what kinds of rules are useful to teach? On the surface, these questions may seem to be the same, but Peter's explanation of the importance of genre suggests why they are not and in so doing offers a powerful critique of the way literature is traditionally taught. As I have argued elsewhere (Smagorinsky & Smith, 1992), much literature instruction is informed by what I call a belief in general knowledge, that is, the belief that reading one literary text prepares students to read another. In such a view, teachers of literature either wouldn't have to teach any rules (students do know how to read, after all) or they would only have to teach the general kinds of rules that Peter spins out in his initial discussion of rules of notice, signification, configuration, and coherence. However, as Peter points out, even the rules that seem to be the most broadly applicable (e.g., pay attention to titles) don't necessarily obtain across genres (think of the poetry of Emily Dickinson). At the same time, the subtle shifts in expectation that inform Peter's interpretation and critique of *Blue Steel* aren't useful for teachers, for slicing genres so thinly would involve teaching a virtually limitless number of rules that have very limited application. It seems to me, therefore, that teachers should search out a middle ground by identifying relatively broad genres that invite the application of similar interpretive strategies. As an example, I want to share work that I've done on helping students understand the ways experienced readers reconstruct the irony of stories with unreliable narrators and to explain how the model I used to generate the instruction might be applicable in other contexts.

SHARING OUR SECRETS: RECONSTRUCTING IRONIC MEANINGS

A story to start: A couple of years ago I was at a barbecue at a friend's house where I noticed that Sean, his 6-year-old son, had gotten extremely dirty playing in the garden. So I said to Sean, "Your dad'll have to hose you off before you go into the house." Quick as a flash, he stripped naked and called out, "OK, Dad, I'm ready."

I think that this incident can be explained in terms of our discussion of literary reading. It seems to me that what happened was that there was a game being played in which one of the participants didn't know the rules. Sean didn't recognize that I was being ironic, and so he gave a literal interpretation to my words. And it was funny. We laughed with Sean. We laughed with Woody on "Cheers," who habitually made similar mistakes. But such mistakes may not be so funny for our students, for they may deny them the chance to experience the unique and powerful way of knowing that literature provides. One of my favorite books of recent years is Ishiguro's *The Remains of the Day,* a novel in which a British butler reflects on his life as he takes a short trip to the nearby countryside. Through his reflections I learned of a man who had given up everything, most poignantly his relationship with his father and the possibility of love, because his perception of service to his master precluded fully developing other relationships. I saw this man struggle with the awareness that his master was a Nazi sympathizer and therefore unworthy of such devotion. Finally, I saw him evaluate his current position with a new master and decide that his failure must have had its root in not trying hard enough. When I finished the book, I wanted to cry (OK, maybe I did cry) because a man I had come to care about had failed to learn a lesson that to me was so plain. For me *The Remains of the Day* was one of those books that, in Josipovici's words, "can sink so deep that it alters our lives, and we know . . . that its reverberations will never cease to be felt until the day of our death" (quoted in Meek, 1983, p. 218). It is because literature has provided me with such experiences that I became a teacher. I suspect that many teachers come to teaching for a similar reason. But a reader could not have this experience unless he or she knew how to understand unreliable narrators, an ability that I'm afraid numbers among those secret things that experienced readers seldom share.

To share our secrets we must first recognize what they are, and that's not so easy, for, as Linda Flower (1987) puts it, much of our knowledge about language and literature is "happily tacit" (p. 5). That's why we have to be grateful to people such as Wayne Booth, whose work on irony (1974) and modes of narration (1983b) inspired the unit I will be discussing, and Peter, who have worked to make our tacit knowledge visible. But it's important to recognize that neither Booth nor Peter was handed tablets from above that outlined rules for reading. Rather, their ideas are the result of self-studies. It seems to me, therefore, that it's important for teachers to study their own reading behavior. Peter's argument about genre suggests that the narrower the focus, the easier such study will be.

I've narrowed the focus to the study of texts with unreliable narrators. As you read the following little story I composed, I'd like you attend to how you go about making sense of it.

> Of course, I'm upset. Anyone would be. She leaves me for no reason. To take up with that slime. I break into a sweat whenever I think about it. And I think about it. Always. I was so good to her. Three, four, five phone calls a day. Flowers twice a week. And all this after only one date. What more could any woman ask? Now I sit in my car outside her door, watching, waiting, hoping to catch even a glimpse of her. But she's with him. I know that she is. It makes me sweat just to think about it.

Does the author share the narrator's view that the woman left the narrator for no good reason? I hope it's clear that the answer is no. I worked to create a narrator who is unbalanced, as evidenced by his breaking into a sweat and watching the woman's house. I included the flowers and the phone calls after only one date to reveal that he is obsessed. My little story, then, is not one of a man who was wronged but rather of a woman who is being harassed.

Such a reconstruction requires an authorial reading. In the first place, I counted on readers' recognizing that I deliberately distanced myself from my narrator. This guy is obsessed. I certainly wouldn't want readers to identify such a person with me. Authors may distance themselves in other ways, among them by making their narrators immoral, inexperienced, inconsistent, self-interested, or uneducated. Second, I counted on readers' searching out the facts of the situation. In this case, while readers certainly question the speaker's interpretation of events, they are likely to believe certain things about his story: the calls, the flowers, the fact that he's sitting in the car watching and waiting. Finally, I counted on readers' applying their knowledge of the world to interpret what that means and to understand the harassment the woman faces—and maybe even fear for her safety.

Unfortunately, our students tend not to make these sorts of reconstructions. Indeed, I've found (Smith, 1991a) that students tend not to adjust their style of response to meet the demands of a text. What I'm proposing, therefore, is that teachers should design instruction to give students directed practice in strategies experienced readers use to do authorial readings of different kinds of texts, a goal I work to achieve in the unit on unreliable narrators that I now describe.

The unit (see Smith, 1991b) begins by having students generate criteria for evaluating the reliability of narrators through a discussion of cartoons and little monologues like the one above. I've included two additional monologues that I've used to give a sense of the kind of discussion that might result from such an introduction:

"THEY GOT IT IN FOR ME"

Oh, man, these teachers. I mean, they got it in for me. Four different teachers send me to the dean in the same month. It must be a conspiracy. And, I tell you, I don't deserve it. Nope. This is just another classic case of discrimination.

"TAKE WHAT HAPPENED TO JANE"

Sometimes teachers can be unfair. Take what happened to Jane this afternoon in English. Jane worked so hard on her paper. I was there in the library with her. She finished it last week and asked me to read it. It was, quite frankly, better than mine. Jane had always done solid work, but this was exceptional. She told me that she wanted her final high school project to be a memorable one. It certainly was. When I told her that I thought her work was better than mine, she blushed. She said, "You always get the highest mark in the class, though. And you're the editor of the paper. And you won that writing contest last year. You're just saying that." I reminded her that this was the only time I had ever said it, even though I had read many of her papers over the years. To tell you the truth, it bothered me a little that her paper was better. I was certainly happy for Jane, but I've enjoyed getting praised for doing the best work. This afternoon we got the papers back—two days ahead of schedule. I received my usual A, but I couldn't be happy about it. Jane received her usual B. I saw a tear fall down on the title page. It smeared the grade and the brief sentence beneath it, the only marks on the paper. After class I went up to Mr. Smith's desk. "Something wrong, Margaret?" he asked. I asked whether he would consider rereading Jane's paper. I told him that I had read it and that I thought it was an exceptional work. He seemed to come unhinged at my request. He started shouting that it wasn't my place to accuse him of being careless. I tried to tell him that I had no such thought, that I realized with so many papers to grade teachers cannot spend too long with any one paper. I seem to have

offended him deeply. He shouted again that he had taken exceptional care with everyone's paper and that I had no right to question his dedication. Now I have a week of detention for my "insub-
ordination." I feel so sorry for Jane. She deserved a better mark.
She really did.

A comparison of these two monologues helps students develop criteria for evaluating the reliability of narrators. In these cases, for example,
the issue of self-interest is key. The first narrator clearly has his or her
interest in mind, while the second narrator pleads the case of a friend.
These monologues also reveal the importance of determining the facts
that are beyond dispute. In the first case it's important that the narrator
had been sent to the dean by four different teachers. There are more details in the second story, but the one that I've found resonates with most
teachers is that the papers got back ahead of schedule. Of course, these
details are only telling if we apply our knowledge of the world to them.

What does such an introduction do? In the first place, it helps students identify the strategies they use. Instead of seeing the strategies as
another thing that the teacher is making them do, they recognize that
they, in fact, make use of those strategies in their lives. This is especially
important because, as Garner (1990) notes, children and adults are unlikely to use strategies that demand time and effort unless they believe
that the strategies will be effective.

Once students have been introduced to the concept of unreliable narrators and to the strategies experienced readers use to recognize them
and to reconstruct their judgments, they should be ready to apply these
strategies to their reading of stories. However, because the strategies are
new, it's unreasonable to expect that students will be able to apply them
before they have received guided practice in doing so. To give them that
guided practice, I suggest having them discuss a series of stories with the
aid of questions that highlight the narrator's characteristics, the steps of
reconstructing the narrator's meaning, and the narrator's judgments that
may need reconstruction. But there's a risk to such pointed questions. We
don't want discussions of literature to become recitation sessions. I try,
therefore, to identify questions that both highlight the strategies that students use and engage students in the important issues of the stories. If
students are to use the strategies, they have to feel a reason to do so. That
means we have to devise experiences that make it clear that the strategies
are a means to an important and enjoyable end, the grappling with the
underlying issues that makes us lovers of literature.

Ultimately, however, we want students to exert their own textual
power. Consequently, the instruction continues by asking students to de-

velop and debate their interpretations of stories without the benefit of a teacher's questions. Finally, because there is no better way to have students exert their textual power than making them authors, I conclude the unit by asking students to create their own unreliable narrators.

The model of instruction I'm suggesting, then, has these steps:

1. Analyze the genre-specific strategies students need to have meaningful transactions with a particular kind of literature.
2. Introduce those strategies so that students recognize their importance.
3. Give students directed practice in applying the strategies toward some significant end.
4. Move students to independent application of the strategies.

Of course, this model is only useful if it can be applied to other kinds of literature. I think that it can. David Anderson (1988), for example, created a unit of instruction around interpretive strategies experienced readers use to understand drama. Basing his instruction on Martin Esslin's (1987) semiotic analysis of drama, Anderson helped students learn to make inferences about plays on the basis of five sources of implication: front matter, set directions, technical directions, dialogue, and stage directions. Students practiced making inferences about each source of implication in prereading activities that highlighted how much they could learn if they attended to that source of implication. They then applied what they had learned to reading a series of one-act plays.

A look at the way one student responded to "The Liar" both before and after the unit on unreliable narrators suggests the potential effects of the instructional model. "The Liar" is a story of a minister's family, narrated by a young girl who is the best friend of the minister's daughter. The narrator explains how much she likes playing at the minister's house, for the minister's wife has tea parties with the girls as though she were one of them. The narrator describes the minister's house, focusing especially on the vinegar cruets the minister's wife collects, one of which is her "special tea-time favorite." According to the narrator, the liar in the story is the minister's son, who complains of how difficult it is to live with his family and tells of the "sins" his mother has committed. Through the course of the story, readers are invited to understand that the son is not a liar at all, that the minister's strictness made life difficult for his family and caused his wife to seek solace in something stronger than vinegar. The narrator's father, a less religious man who is a model of love, provides a counterpoint to the minister.

Although the student was a "good" reader, at least according to her standardized test scores, the final remarks of her think-aloud protocol indicate the problems she had with the story:

> What the hell was this story about? I mean, it sounds like, every one who's in this preacher or minister's family is like, some kind of awful sinner who's damned and is gonna go to hell. I'm sorry this story, er, didn't even make sense. Something about these people totally sinning, and now they're damned sinners. They sound awfully psycho to me.

In the first place, this student does not have the strategies she needs to understand "The Liar." She seems to suspect that something is amiss in the family ("They sound awfully psycho to me"), but instead of pursuing her suspicion, she relied on the narrator's and other characters' interpretations of the story's events. She blames the story for not making sense, blames it for not making the connections she failed to make. In the terms we have offered previously, she fails to respect the conventions the author invoked.

After she received the instruction, this is how she concluded her think-aloud:

> Why do they put such a high title, minister's son, I mean so what? Cause he's a normal person like every one else. He's not any better. I mean, if anything it sounds like he's [the minister's] worse. He sounds like the strict dictator over the entire family. But, this, sounds like one of those families, one of these stories that takes place like, way back when, but still has like, a modern sort of insight into it, I mean it's showing that those, all those you know, God-fearing families aren't all what they're cracked up to be. But, sort of cynical . . . story.

Her critique suggests that she began to trust her own assessment of the characters and that she was no longer thrown off by the narrator's judgments. Moreover, she feels the authority she needs to pass judgment on the story. Her concluding remarks display the kind of contentious talking back to texts that Peter discusses in Chapter 1. Because she is better able to recognize and respect the conventional invitation the author offers, she is able to assert her resistance to a view of the world she doesn't admire.

The instructional model I'm suggesting here is different from that in most textbooks in at least two important ways. In the first place, it challenges the usefulness of many of the genre divisions used in secondary school curricula. Although Anderson (1988) and Esslin (1987) have persuaded me of the usefulness of thinking of drama as a genre because of the semiotic significance of features shared by most modern dramatic works (Peter's remarks in the previous chapter establish that he remains unconvinced), other traditional divisions don't fare as well. If we apply Peter's definition from Chapter 3 ("genre is best understood not as a group of texts that share textual features but rather as a collection of texts that call on similar sets of rules, that invite similar interpretive strategies"), the utility of poetry as a genre is called into question. Although Dickinson and Whitman both wrote poetry and although they're often placed next to each other in American literature anthologies, I don't think that they invite many of the same reading strategies. (Reading Whitman with, say, Ginsberg, would be a different matter.) The instruction that I explain above was designed to help students recognize a particular kind of invitation and apply a particular set of strategies.

In addition, the approach I outline above moves the discussion of literary terms from memorizing and applying definitions to the application of complex strategies. Textbooks generally address point of view by providing definitions of first-person point of view, limited third-person point of view, and omniscient or third-person point of view and by asking such questions as "What is the point of view of this story?" That approach seems to me to be extremely reductive. It's easy to recognize the pronoun that the narrator uses. But understanding the relationship between the author and the narrator is a complicated enterprise. Even though I've been thinking and writing about how readers determine the reliability of first-person narrators for some time now, I don't think I have a clear sense about how Richard Ford feels about Frank Bascombe, the narrator of *The Sportswriter* and *Independence Day*.

Because the unit depends upon the activity of students, I think it's student-centered. However, it's very different from some curricula calling themselves student-centered. Although I applaud our movement away from fragmentation and toward holistic activities, I agree with Courtney Cazden (1992) "that immersion in rich literacy environments is necessary but not sufficient" (p. ix) and that "as people of any age learn to read and write, they need help in focusing attention on specific features of written language; they need deliberate, well-planned help in attending to parts as well as wholes" (p. ix). Sharing what we know about how we read is one way to do just that.

INTERPRETIVE STRATEGIES AND DEMOCRATIC TEACHING

I'm aware that many teachers and theorists might be suspicious of instruction centered around interpretive strategies. Indeed, in one of the very thoughtful reviews of the prospectus Peter and I sent to Teachers College Press the reviewer was concerned that our discussion of rules of reading and how teachers might share them "reifies the undemocratic classroom that [we] argue so vehemently against." It seems important, therefore, to explain why Peter and I don't share this concern.

In the first place, we are not suggesting that novices be made to copy experts but, on the contrary, that teachers help students understand what it is that experts do (which is quite different). We do not believe that such teaching results in authoritarian classrooms. Lisa Delpit (1988) helps explain why in her article "The Silenced Dialogue: Power and Pedagogy in Educating Other People's Children." She delineates five aspects of power in her discussion, two of which seem to be central to my argument here: (1) "Those with power are frequently least aware of—or least willing to acknowledge—its existence. Those with less power are often most aware of its existence," and (2) "If you are not already a participant in the culture of power, being told explicitly the rules of that culture makes acquiring power easier" (p. 282). Although we recognize that teachers can be fallible, can learn from their students, and can share experiences, we also believe that they also know more than their students, otherwise they wouldn't be teachers. This "more" may not come in the form of knowledge of correct interpretations. Rather we think it comes in the form of knowledge of interpretive practice. In any case, democracy in a classroom setting—an unequal situation to begin with—cannot involve pretending that student/teacher knowledge distinctions do not exist.

In the second place, we think that helping students understand the strategies that experienced readers bring to texts helps promote the kind of democratic discourse I talk about in Chapter 2. I'll explore this argument in three related lines of reasoning.

First, it seems to me that the model of instruction I outline in this chapter challenges the relationship students and teachers tend to have with the literature they discuss in class. James Marshall's studies (Marshall et al., 1995, chapter 3) strongly suggest that discussions of literature in school tend to fall into particular patterns, patterns that are so entrenched that they carry the weight of generic expectations (cf. Bakhtin, 1986) and so constrain the behavior of participants. For example, in school discussions of literature, teachers regain the floor after each student turn and tend to use these turns to elaborate on students' remarks, weaving them into an interpretive framework that the teachers are constructing.

I believe that this practice evolved for two reasons: (1) Teachers teach texts that students find difficult, and (2) teachers have regarded their goal as teaching particular readings instead of teaching ways of reading. Both of these practices seem to me to work to make students submissive (see Smith, 1992b, for a more complete discussion of this term) to the texts they read in school. However, as I explain above, I would suggest that the texts teachers use to help students identify the interpretive strategies they use to understand particular genres should not be canonical literary texts, but rather should be texts students feel more in control of: texts such as cartoons, songs, and brief monologues. The preliminary work that students do in a unit should do more than help them understand a set of interpretive strategies. By using these kinds of texts, teachers are saying to students that they are challenging the old rules, that students need not be submissive to the texts or to their teachers' reading of those texts.

Further, putting strategies at the center of the curriculum frees teachers from the responsibility of pursuing a particular interpretation. Marshall's interviews with the teachers he studied suggest that the teachers' desires to initiate student-centered discussions were undermined by their belief that discussions needed to "get somewhere." What I'm suggesting here is that somewhere does not have to be a shared interpretation. Hillocks (1989) has found, in fact, that in a classroom in which developing interpretive strategies is the central aim, students control the direction of the discussion and the teacher's primary role is to encourage students to explain how they go about their journey rather than to make certain that everyone arrives at the same destination.

This emphasis sets me apart from Peter, who feels, I think, a greater obligation to help students critique idiosyncratic readings and to come to a defensible interpretation of particular texts, a difference I'll attribute to the influence of Father Sarducci. When I ask myself what students will remember in 5 years, I'm hopeful that they'll remember to question the reliability of narrators. I'm hopeful that they'll remember how the discussion of those narrators engaged them with others in meaningful ways. But I'm much less sanguine than Peter that they'll remember the details of particular interpretations.

Second, instruction in interpretive strategies has the potential to help teachers overcome the difficulty of what I've come to think of as taking away a student's reading, a difficulty I encountered most often when I cared about the politics of the text we were discussing in class. I know I'm not alone in this difficulty. Sarah Allen and I have worked together to understand the factors that affect the discussions in her class. We began our work together by analyzing how her eighth-graders talked about Angelou's *I Know Why the Caged Bird Sings*. As I note in Chapter 2, Sarah found that those discussions featured talk that she especially admired, talk characterized by students' collaborating to come to grip with important ethical issues in the text. However, Sarah was concerned that the free-wheeling collaborative exchanges so common in the discussion of *Caged Bird* did not carry over into the class's discussion of the next major text they read, *Jane Eyre*.

As we talked together about why this might be true, it became clear to both of us that one major factor that could account for the difference is that Sarah has a much clearer agenda in mind for the discussion of *Jane Eyre*. She wants her students to experience the kind of feminist reading suggested by Gilbert and Gubar (1979). She noted that her stake in a particular reading caused her to direct the discussion in ways that she does not direct the discussion of *Caged Bird*. In my view, the issue extends beyond the way teachers manage discussions. I would argue that Sarah has to direct discussion because her students don't notice the kinds of details that suggest a feminist interpretation. Noticing those kinds of details would require that students position themselves against Jane or at least question her judgments instead of identifying with her. But if students don't do this *as* they are reading, they can't do it in subsequent discussions. Consequently, in order to help students to come to a feminist reading, Sarah has to take away the romantic reading her students were constructing as they read.

Reading research in selective attention may help clarify my point. For instance, Anderson and Pichert (1978) found that readers playing the role of a burglar were more likely to recall the kind and location of valuables in a house while those playing the role of prospective home buyers were more likely to recall that the house had spacious grounds. It seems to me, then, that instruction in unreliable narrators of the sort I describe in this chapter would increase students' ability to work together to construct the kind of understanding that Sarah is seeking. Teachers choose to teach texts for a variety of reasons. We need to recognize that one important reason is because we care about the political points a text makes or about the points we can use a text to make. We also need to recognize the attendant difficulties that come when we have a clear agenda. I think that instruction in interpretive strategies minimizes some of those difficulties.

Recognizing that we may have a political agenda when we teach a text doesn't mean that I'm endorsing the kind of Institutional Reading that Peter critiques in Chapter 3. Unlike Institutional Readings that can exist almost independently from a text, the kind of feminist reading that Sarah wants her students to experience requires resistance to an authorial reading, a point Peter develops in Chapter 1. Consequently, the suggestion that teachers teach strategies for resistance before students read a text doesn't undercut the suggestion that they teach strategies that allow an authorial reading. As I argue in Chapter 2, this has important implications for the democratic character of discussions. In the first place, when students do an authorial reading, they can use that reading to resist the authority of the teacher, in effect resisting the teacher's resistance. Further, the notion of a common project depends upon the belief that healthy democratic communities "possess members whose unique functions . . . complement one another" (Fishman, 1993, p. 319). The Procrustean Institutional Readings that Peter critiques do not provide that complementarity because they tend to ignore the narrative audience where complementarity is most often realized.

Third, by sharing the secrets of our expertise we open up conversation to students who consider themselves inexpert. Fred Hamel amended the unit of instruction I describe in this chapter for his lower-track eleventh-graders. We report the results of his work at much greater length elsewhere (Hamel & Smith, 1997), but a brief excerpt of a discussion Fred had with his students about *The Adventures of Huckleberry Finn* suggests the potential power that teaching interpretive strategies can have for students who are alienated from school and from literature.

The excerpt that follows occured halfway into a 30-minute discussion, which included eight active participants. The discussion focused on whether Huck or Tom was the more reliable interpreter of events:

TEACHER: OK. [Student 1 is] going to read the text.
STUDENT 1: All right. It goes, Tom said, uh, "If I warn't so ignorant, but had read a book called *Don Quixote,* I would know without asking." And "he said it was all done by enchantment" or something.
TEACHER: Yeah.
STUDENT 1: Well—
TEACHER: So that proves that—
STUDENT 1: Well—
TEACHER: —that proves that Huck is ignorant.
STUDENT 1: Well, yeah, it just says that, but, I mean—all, all Huck was doing was just like seeing if Tom was telling the truth. He was like asking a bunch of questions to make sure, you know, all right, is he lying? Is this one of Tom's lies, or something like that? And then, um, how do you know that just because you read something out of a book, you know—well, what if they're wrong?
TEACHER: So you don't like the fact that Tom—I mean, Tom knows what he's talking about, because he takes the stuff from the books.

STUDENT 2: The books he's reading are the fiction.
STUDENT 3: He lies.
STUDENT 4: All right, here—
TEACHER: Wait. Wait. What do you mean, he "lies." Give me the—
STUDENT 3: It says right here. "So then I judged that all that stuff
    was only just one of Tom Sawyer's lies."

What Fred found most striking about this conversation is the way
his students freely disagreed with his position. It was especially significant to Fred that student 3, one of his least engaged readers, was willing
to take this risk. Fred explains why he thought the instruction encouraged
such risk-taking as follows:

> Not only have students gained authority vis-à-vis the text as they
> critically assess the status of both Huck and Tom, but they also ex-
> perience more authority in the classroom itself. Students are not
> passive recipients of my expertise about the novel, nor are they
> brief respondents to a series of questions that reflect my concerns
> for the chapter, both common patterns in discussions of literature.
> Rather, students are applying an interpretive strategy that they
> have gradually developed over a number of weeks, and in this dis-
> cussion they interact to construct and support their own complex
> inferences about character motives and experiences.

If Fred is right, student 3's engagement supports Vygotsky's argument
that rules allow pleasure, for it was his knowledge of interpretive strategies that allowed him to read and discuss with authority. As such, it challenges Peter's contention that the knowledge of interpretive strategies
ought to proceed the pleasure that literature can bring. For some students, at least, the pleasure lies in the feeling of power that comes from
knowing the rules.

I want to stress that a reader's knowing and respecting the rules
doesn't lead to passivity. Rather, it is what allows active reading and what
provides the possibility for subsequent resistance. In the case of unreliable narrators, respecting the rules necessitates resistance to characters.
As the student's comments on "The Liar" demonstrate, respecting the
rules is what enabled resistance to the worldview the author expected of
the audience. Moreover, recognizing the rules enables resistance to authors who break them. This resistance might be on aesthetic grounds, as
in my book club's discussion of whether the narrator of Pete Dexter's *The
Paperboy* would ever offer the kind of generalization that ends the book
or whether the final line is an intrusion in the author's voice. But the

resistance might be political as well. In the previous chapter Peter talks about naturalist novels, with their "dense accumulation of socio-environmental detail." Although, as Peter points out, readers may not have to attend to any specific detail in a naturalistic novel, rules of coherence for a naturalistic novel have it that any generalization ought to come as a consequence of the accumulation of those details. When Richard Wright breaks those rules in the trial scene in *Native Son* by having Bigger's lawyer offer explicit commentary on those details, I think he's breaking the very rules he invokes. My resistance comes from my belief that Wright was afraid that the details didn't add up to the political generalizations he wanted his authorial audience to come away with.

Peter and Father Sarducci have forced me to rethink my goals for teaching literature. Whereas I once emphasized encouraging students to have meaningful transactions with particular texts, I've come to believe that this goal is best achieved in service of a larger goal: helping students develop meaningful *ways* for reading particular *kinds* of texts. This seems to me to be a fundamental departure both from the way I had taught and from other progressive alternatives to the way I had taught.

The distinction between readings and ways of reading is an important one. It depends, however, upon a distinction that makes an even more radical challenge to the way literature is traditionally taught: the distinction between reading and re-reading. In the next chapter Peter explores that distinction and argues that failing to recognize it both makes it difficult for teachers to teach how they read and makes it difficult for students to pay characters the kind of ethical respect they deserve.

"A THOUSAND TIMES AND NEVER LIKE": RE-READING FOR CLASS

Peter J. Rabinowitz

LIKE MOST LITERATURE TEACHERS, at least at the college level, I've heard (and even told) scandalized anecdotes about students who refuse to take a course because *Hamlet* is on the reading list and they've "already read *Hamlet*." And as I point out in Chapter 3, I'm no stranger to that sudden chill that seizes us when a student asks a question about a significant detail in a book we're teaching (say, Thea Kronborg's response to Tolstoy in *The Song of the Lark*) and we find that we didn't even notice it, much less register its importance. Like most teachers, when that happens I resolve to re-read the text more carefully the next time I teach it. Given the polemical drift of this chapter, it's probably prudent to begin by admitting—even proclaiming—that both my shock at a student's philistine belief that "once is enough" and my own pledge to re-read more carefully in the future are entirely commendable. Commitment to re-reading is, after all, like the commitment to close reading, one of the few remaining principles that's shared by almost everyone in the increasingly fractured world of literary studies. And rightly so. The experience that Michael's student had re-reading "The Liar" shows us how re-reading, especially in the light of new knowledge, can often correct gross misunderstanding of a text. Re-reading can also enrich texts we do understand: Whether our personal canons take their ammunition from John Milton or *Gone with the Wind* or Toni Morrison or *I Am the Cheese*, the texts we value are not exhausted the first time through. And yet, first principles are always suspect, and it's worth asking ourselves the price—particularly the pedagogical price—of this unswerving loyalty. Is re-reading always a good thing?

Obviously, my answer here is going to be that, like any global interpretive strategy, re-reading is not always appropriate. I've argued elsewhere (Rabinowitz, 1992) that even so widespread and apparently neutral a technique as close reading privileges certain kinds of interpretations and certain kinds of texts. For instance, canonizing close reading as an interpretive technique trains readers to favor "figurative writing over the realistic portrayal of material social conditions, deep meaning over surface meaning, form over content, the elite over the popular, and indirect expression over direct" (p. 233). In this chapter, I would like to make a similar claim about re-reading. Specifically, I would like to propose that the way we treat re-reading (specifically, the re-reading of novels) privileges certain reading strategies over others and that, in so doing, it can confuse our classroom practice: It makes it hard for us to know either what we *are* teaching or what we *should be* teaching, and it consequently widens the gap between students and teachers. Specifically, as I will be showing in this chapter, it increases our frustrating difficulties in helping students come to share our secrets (as Michael so aptly puts it in Chapter 4)—in helping them get from where they are to where we are. That leaves the pedagogical disjunction that Gerald Graff (e.g., 1992) has rightly been warning us against. But before I can make these polemical leaps, I need a running start. So let me begin by enunciating a limitation and a distinction that will underlie my argument.

READING AGAINST MEMORY

First, the limitation. Some of the New Critics were fond of defining "literature," at least in part, in terms of a binary opposition to "science." Cleanth Brooks (1947), for instance, claimed that science uses a different kind of language from poetry, a preformed language based on notation rather than a newly minted language arising out of paradox. In our contemporary theory-driven climate, the suspiciously self-evident common sense that fueled that opposition seems increasingly essentialist and increasingly suspect. Still, even if "science" and "literature" are neither essential nor stable categories, they do, especially at the high school and early college level, mold our perceptions and hence our activities. That is, no matter what the status of the categories, we read whatever it is that we *take to be* literature differently from whatever it is we take to be nonliterature, especially science, where, as Judith Langer (1989) has pointed out, students will read "to narrow in on increasingly more specific meaning" (p. 18). So let me emphasize that my claim here applies only to the re-reading of literary texts—in particular, fictional narratives.

As for my distinction: Since I'm going to be talking specifically about re-reading, I need to clear the ground by distinguishing three kinds of re-reading experiences and focusing in on one of them. Granted, they are not easily separable in practice, for any given act of re-reading may include elements of all three. Still, they are separable in theory, and the distinctions among them pay significant analytic dividends.

First, there's the re-reading that consists of repetition of pleasurable experience. Young children, of course, re-read (or are re-read to) in this way more tenaciously than most adults do: They consume the same texts over and over again, not because they expect to uncover hitherto hidden incestuous dynamics among the Berenstain Bears, but rather because they enjoy the comfort of the familiar. But there's reason to believe that even academically trained adults sometimes re-read in this way as well, although—and the reasons for this might be the subject of a chapter in itself—they probably do so more often with films and reruns of "I Love Lucy" than with canonical, high-art novels.

But, of course, re-reading does not always produce mere repetition. As we get older, our perspectives—our values, our desires, our aesthetic tastes—change, and familiar books can come to seem disturbingly new. If the first kind of re-reading experience might be summed up as the *Casablanca* phenomenon, this second might well be dubbed the "Young Mme. de Rênal" syndrome. When I first read Stendhal's *The Red and the Black,* Mme. de Rênal appeared to me (as she did to her young lover, Julien Sorel) as a mysterious "older woman" (what Bayard Sartoris, in Faulkner's [1938] *The Unvanquished,* calls "the eternal and symbolical thirty to a young man" [p. 264]); now she seems like just another confused, repressed postadolescent. It's this kind of re-reading that Adrienne Rich (1972) called "re-vision" and that Wayne C. Booth was writing about when he discussed his rethinking of Rabelais in *The Company We Keep* (1988, chap. 12). It's this kind of re-reading that led to my discomfort when I realized the medical implications of the Catholicism presented in *A Canticle for Leibowitz.* And it's this kind of re-reading that allows Joan Williams (1982), "having raised two active boys a year and a half apart," to admire Caroline Compson in a way that she could not when she first read *The Sound and the Fury* at the age of 19 (p. 403). Valuable and important as it is, this kind of re-reading is, paradoxically, only minimally connected with having read the text before; that is, most of Booth's discomfort with Rabelais (although not his discomfort with himself) would be there even if he had read him for the first time as a feminist male in his 50s.

In this chapter, I want to accentuate a third kind of re-reading, what I call "reading against memory." One need not share Harold Bloom's (1973) extreme vision of the poetic tradition as a bloody combat between fathers and sons to recognize that all literary texts take on their meanings in part *intertextually*—that is, because of the grid against which they are read, the prior texts they copy, contradict, dally with. Even that headline about Hamilton and Utica College that I mentioned in Chapter 3 makes sense only against a backdrop of other, similar headlines. But our increasing concern with intertextuality should not blind us to another, parallel source of literary meaning: On a second or subsequent reading, at least, the meaning of a novel is just as much a result of what we could call "intratextuality"—the ways it copies, contradicts, dallies with not a prior text but our *memory* of the prior reading(s) of the *same* text. Bayard evokes this kind of repetition in *The Unvanquished*, in a passage that is ostensibly about kissing his war-hardened and incest-driven stepmother (his "symbolical thirty") but is also readily applicable to reading:

> Again it was like it had been before. No. Twice, a thousand times and never like— . . . each time both cumulative and retroactive, immitigably unrepetitive, each wherein remembering excludes experience, each wherein experience antedates remembering. (Faulkner, 1938, p. 264)

Reading against memory changes the text, not because we are older or wiser or ideologically purer but simply because we've read it before and know (or think we know) what's coming. It is to this activity, reading against memory, that I will be referring when I discuss re-reading in the rest of this chapter.

FIRST LOVE, SECOND READING

Re-reading in this sense is different *in kind* from first reading. That is, it's not simply a richer or deeper or more sophisticated reading, but a substantially different kind of activity. Specifically, reading against memory tends both to apply different interpretive operations to the details of the plot and to treat those details in a different order, since the re-reader, unlike the first reader, is not bound by the chronology of the text. To put it more fancifully, if reading is a perplexing walk, full of stumbles and confusions and wrong turns, through an unfamiliar forest, reading against memory is the production of a Park Service map that abstracts from the events of the first reading—transcending the order in which they occurred—to show the proper trails.

My notion of a perplexing walk is not the same as the "inferential walks" that Umberto Eco (1979) speaks about in *The Role of the Reader*. Inferential walks are reasoned conclusions drawn from partial evidence given in a text. For instance, in Turgenev's (1860/1968) novella *First Love*, the narrator falls in love with a young neighbor, Zinaida, only to discover that she is having an affair with his father. The affair eventually ends, partly because of pressure from his mother; but, the narrator tells us,

A few days before [my father's] death he received a letter from Moscow which upset him greatly. He went to beg some favour from my mother and, I was told, he even wept. . . . My mother, after his death, sent a considerable sum of money to Moscow. (pp. 214–215)

We later learn, from a local gossip, that "there were consequences" of the affair that made it difficult for Zinaida to find a husband (p. 215). The conclusion that she has gotten pregnant is the result of an inferential walk. That relatively straightforward process of inferring is quite different from the kind of floundering that a reader is apt to engage in, earlier in the novel, when she or he tries to figure out which of the characters introduced at Zinaida's party are likely to be important to the plot, which secondary.

Nor, in comparing reading to a "perplexing walk," am I making the same point that Judith Langer (1989) is making when she discusses "changing stances" (p. 6). Langer points out, in particular, four such stances in which student readers, at least, engage—and there is no doubt that her schema represents an important process. But my perplexing walk is not a stroll from one fairly static stance to another; for even *within* some of her stances, the reader's perspective, as she demonstrates, is in a state of flux.

Precision in our discussion is made even more difficult by a fairly widespread rhetorical practice: The word *reading* is often used, loosely, to refer in fact to reading against memory. Indeed, re-readers often find it difficult to distinguish between the two even when they are aware of the distinction, because it's harder than we think to reconstruct, after re-reading, those initial operations. Thus, for instance, when James Cox (1986) tried to "posit . . . a fair description of a first reading" of Faulkner's *The Sound and the Fury,* he readily recognized that to "encounter" the novel "is, first of all, to be lost." He nonetheless "project[ed] a 'better' reading" than his actual first reading because he drew "upon [his] experience of teaching the book" (p. 5). It would be hard to imagine how he could do anything else.

Now some texts seem to require reading against memory by their very structure. In Nabokov's *Lolita,* for instance—at least if you are reading it as high art rather than as a dirty book (see Chapter 3)—all sorts of apparently irrelevant details, like the titles of the plays given in the brief biography of Quilty in the beginning of the novel, turn out, *in retrospect,* to be important. Indeed, even the first pages of the novel demand re-reading; for although the novel begins with the crucial announcement of Lolita's death in childbirth, you can't recognize the event for what it is the first time around, since it's only at the *end* of the book that we learn her married name. Lermontov's *A Hero of Our Time*, a major influence on Nabokov, engages in similar techniques: It is only when we get to the final section that we have the information necessary to read the opening of the novel intelligently.

But how common is it for novels to demand reading against memory? Cleanth Brooks (1947), in *The Well Wrought Urn*, explicitly proposed that the way we have "learned to read Donne and the moderns" should serve as a model for reading the poets who came between them (p. 193). And while our increased sensitivity to the ideology of theory has made us rightly wary of that kind of gesture, I suspect that even today, we do something similar. Even if we don't teach *Lolita* itself (and I doubt it's a staple in even the most chic high school English classes), we normalize the kind of reading that *Lolita* demands, assuming that students ought to learn to read other texts the way we've taught them to read that one.

I, THE READER: COHERENT AND CONFIGURATIONAL ENDINGS

Although I'm a committed pluralist, I'm not sure that, until fairly recently, I would have felt that there was anything especially wrong with teaching students to read against memory. After all, unlike certain other normalized reading techniques—say, J. Hillis Miller's (1979) dogmatic claim that the "center of our discipline . . . is expertise in the handling of figurative language" and his insistence that our fundamental task in the "teaching of reading" is inevitably "the teaching of the interpretation of tropes" (p. 13)—reading against memory doesn't close anything off. It doesn't commit you to read like a formalist or like a feminist or like a New Historicist or like a Bakhtinian. Regardless of how you situate yourself politically or theoretically, reading against memory is simply common sense. Isn't it?

Well, several years ago I had a classroom experience that gave me pause. I was teaching a first-year college course called "Literature and Ethics." Since, as I argued at the end of Chapter 3, we can often learn a lot about the nature of genre by looking at formulaic texts, I was illustrating some of the ways in which sexual ideology can be covertly transmitted through generic patterns by having my students read a novel in which the formulas are especially crisp: Mickey Spillane's *I, the Jury*. Few were surprised by the ending. I was pleased to see that one or two knew how it would turn out because of their intertextual expertise. Having read (or seen) *The Maltese Falcon* and *The Big Sleep* among others, they knew that any woman who directs her sexual energy toward a hard-boiled detective is a prime suspect. But I was alarmed when several others (indeed, about half the class) admitted that, out of a curiosity bred from a low tolerance for suspense, they had read the ending while still in the middle of the novel.

In fact, one student, "Philip," had actually read the ending *first*. His justification tripped me up. This was a "literature course," he said, and he therefore knew that when he came to class, he'd be expected to know what details were important and how they fit together; as he himself put it on his self-evaluation, he knew (or thought he knew) that he'd be asked "a lot of questions along the lines of 'Don't you think that the symbolism on page XY relates well to the inner struggle on VW?'" But he also knew that in a detective novel, there's no possible way to figure out what details are important except in terms of the ending. He felt, therefore, that he couldn't begin to do what would be expected unless he read the novel twice—but like most first-year students, he didn't have time to do so. He concluded that the next best thing was to read the ending first so he'd have what he needed to sort out the textual elements properly. In a sense, then, he short-circuited the first reading—or, to put it more paradoxically, he re-read the novel the first time through.

I say that Philip's response tripped me up—and it did so because we found ourselves in positions of fundamental incompatibility. From my perspective, he'd missed the whole point of the book. In fact, since I was, at the time, in the middle of re-reading Wayne Booth's *The Company We Keep*, I went so far as to suggest that he'd been ethically irresponsible and went on to harangue the class on the moral responsibility of getting the maximum authorially sanctioned pleasure they could out of the texts they read. But from Philip's perspective, I was making no sense: He took seriously what he'd been taught in "literature courses" (including, unfortunately, mine) and, implicitly recognizing the central importance of reading against memory, had done his best. Why did I chastise him? Shouldn't he be *rewarded* for his strong sense of intellectual responsibility?

How could I respond? I might, of course, have pointed out that *I, the Jury* is not *Lolita*—and that, specifically with regard to Philip's reading process, the two novels have very different kinds of endings, what I call configurational endings and coherent endings. Configuration, as I suggest in Chapter 3, is the interpretive activity by which, *during the act of reading,* a reader assembles the emerging details of a text into larger patterns. It's the application, for instance, of specific strategies that stem from our general recognition of the *predictive* nature of events in novels, the recognition that in art (unlike life) there is a controlling force over the shape of events and that one can reasonably assume that the future will *in some recognizable way* be prefigured in the present. Application of rules of configuration, for instance, allows us to assume that, because in the opening chapter of *I, The Jury,* Mike Hammer pledges to shoot the killer of his buddy Jack Williams "with a .45 slug in the gut, just a little below the belly button," the novel will climax in just such an event (Spillane, 1947, p. 8). More generally, it's through the application of rules of configuration that readers develop expectations and ultimately achieve a sense of completion. Configurational endings are found in those sorts of novels (detective stories are perhaps the foremost example) that invite you to read *toward* the end.

Coherence, in contrast, is the process by which a reader makes *retroactive* sense of an *already completed* text. It arises from a general (if often implicit) axiom—what Northrop Frye (1963) once insisted supported "the primary understanding of any work of literature" (p. 63). According to this axiom, any serious and worthwhile work of literature is in fact unified, and both apparent patterns *and* apparent breaks and inconsistencies can be assumed to bear significant meaning. Using this principle, we are able to generalize broad themes from local meanings and to convert apparent incongruities into metaphors or ironies. And coherent endings are those found in books that invite you, even require you, to read back *from* the ending—as *Lolita* or *Crime and Punishment* or *The Sound and the Fury* or Cormier's *I am the Cheese* do. To be sure, the distinction is not a sharp one. The differences really lie along a continuum, with differences of emphasis. Still, there are differences in the ways books end. The famous closing paragraph of *The Great Gatsby* ("So we beat on, boats against the current, borne back ceaselessly into the past" [Fitzgerald, 1925, p. 182]) provides coherence to the text but does not fulfill any configurational imperative. The union of James Bond and Pussy Galore at the end of Ian Fleming's *Goldfinger* provides closure by filling out the pattern demanded by the genre but does little to help us wrap up the thematics of the novel as a whole. Why was Philip so literarily dense that he couldn't see the difference?

That answer might appease my critical conscience if I could summon up a stronger belief than I have in the stability of texts. But many times, texts do not clearly and unambiguously "invite" us, much less "require" us, to read one way or the other. And even when they do, Michael's observations in Chapter 4 about the ways students sometimes refuse to adjust their reading strategies to different texts remind us that invitations and even imperious demands can be misconstrued or refused.

To be sure, not every interpretive strategy "works" with every novel. Sometimes the brute facts of a text resist a certain kind of reading, just as certain parts of a swingset or gas grill resist attempts to assemble them in a particular way. I once had a student—an excellent one, in fact—who insisted on applying to *Hamlet* rules of signification more appropriate to detective stories. Specifically, she tried to apply the rule that no unverified

claims by a character can be trusted, especially when details of a death
are at stake; and she concluded that Gertrude had, in fact, murdered
Ophelia by pushing her into the water. She soon realized, of course, that
the play was simply not working. But much as it would ease our jobs as
teachers, I don't think we can say that this instance of textual resistance
is a paradigm case. While it is true that you cannot read any text any way
you want to, texts are in fact more resilient than we often pretend they
are, and they often submit to multiple, contradictory readings. This does
not mean that all of those readings are correct. Just because you've man-
aged to get all the bicycle pieces attached together does not mean that
you've assembled the bike; and just because all the pieces of a text hold
together does not mean that you've correctly determined the nature of
the authorial audience. In other words, you can't use the *fact* of complete
assembly, by itself, as proof you've done it the right way.

   In fact, with respect to the dichotomy that I have been discussing,
most novels can be read either way—with the assumption that their
endings are either configurational or coherent. Even a text as simple-
mindedly banal as *I, the Jury* is subject to this double perspective: Certainly, besides fulfilling a configurational promise, Hammer's act of shooting the killer *in the belly* has a retrospective, cohering quality as well when
it's linked to our discovery that Charlotte is in fact the killer. For in combination with Charlotte's professionalism and her other betrayals of what
Spillane sees as her appropriate gender role, this attack on her womb
provides an especially appropriate punishment.

   That is, the distinction (or continuum) between configurational and
coherent endings isn't a distinction between different kinds of endings as
much as it is a distinction between different ways of thinking about endings. And our academic practice, which canonizes novels like *Crime and
Punishment* that respond especially well to thinking coherently, encourages students to think one way and not the other. Our commitment to re-
reading is concretized in our general unwillingness to distinguish the two
and to use the term *reading* when we're really talking about reading
against memory; and this commitment cannot be considered simply common sense—it's a theoretically loaded practice. We therefore need to ask
ourselves more carefully: What's lost by cajoling our students into thinking that reading against memory is the best, the most "intellectually responsible" way to read?

   There are, I think, at least two primary negative consequences: First,
it encourages us to teach the wrong things to our students by introducing
unquestioned hierarchies of value into our classrooms; second, it makes
us inefficient in teaching what we *do* teach. Let me take each of these
in turn.

THE UNVANQUISHED: HIERARCHIES OF VALUE

First, the privileging of re-reading introduces covert systems of value into our practice. I'd like to point to two of the ways in which this happens. First, as I've said, when we stress reading against memory, activities of coherence take precedence over activities of configuration. Now, in a sense, that's nothing new: Whether it was called "unity" or "resolution," coherence was always the prime virtue for the New Critics, and, as Arthur Applebee (1989a) has pointed out, even as late as 1989, New Criticism remained the dominant critical school in high school education (e.g., p. 37). Reading against memory therefore serves to shore up a set of evaluative principles that were already in place. But principles of value do not gain validity simply by hanging around, so it's worth asking ourselves: Just what is this hierarchy and what does it imply?

The hierarchy is, of course, not simple, and there are many ways of articulating it. For instance, it might be seen as the priority of the lyrical over the narrative. Certainly, in re-reading a novel, the story usually becomes less important, while patterns of imagery begin to move into the foreground. More generally, whether we're teaching a poem or a story, our preference for reading against memory encourages us to think of it in terms of its total pattern, rather than in terms of what James Phelan (1989) calls its progression.

Granted, there are exceptions. Readers of *The Sound and the Fury* may well find that the story becomes *more* visible the second time through. Especially in the first two sections, there's virtually no way, on first reading, that you can develop any large-scale expectations—and therefore there may well be a tendency for readers simply to take what comes and to appreciate the novel as a series of isolated moments. But I suspect that happens very rarely. More often than not, reading against memory encourages the priority of static notions of form (like Cleanth Brooks's, 1947) over dynamic notions of form (like, say, Kenneth Burke's, 1924/ 1968). Likewise, it encourages the priority of figurative language over plot; or, to use Judith Langer's (1989) terms, the priority of the stance of "Stepping Out and Objectifying the Experience" over the stance of "Being Out and Stepping In"; or, to use Michael's terms, the priority of readings that stress "the shaping principle of a text" over "story-driven" readings that "emphasize . . . plot, character, and event" (Smith, 1992c, p. 156). According to some apocryphal but extremely attractive stories, Mozart was able to hear an entire symphony "at once"; and whether or not he really could, that architectural model often seems to serve as a corollary for the way we ought to read.

And some readers actually do read quite happily this way. For instance, when she was in grade school, my daughter Rachel read (or was read to)—and watched videos—with almost no interest in progression, almost no desire for completion, for finding how things were going to come out. Much as she enjoyed the opening chapters of *Mrs. Frisby and the Rats of NIMH*, she evinced no strong desire for the last chapters, and her preferred way of watching *Three Men and a Baby* (which we had made the unfortunate error of taping) was to jump around, not only among favorite scenes but among favorite commercials as well. For her, the movie was coherent—you couldn't, for instance, substitute scenes from some different movie, for everything fit an overarching conception; but that coherence had virtually nothing to do with the order of presentation. Despite the pleasure it gave her, however, I see no reason why this hierarchy, generalized to texts and readers at large, is anything but arbitrary.

Indeed, the hierarchy is more problematic still, for our stress on re-reading does more than devalue certain reading activities—it helps make them invisible. That is, our privileging of re-reading goes further than supporting coherence at the expense of configuration—it makes it doubly difficult for readers to explore and question this habit because it obscures the precise nature of the difference. That's because coherence is so often presented as if it actually *were* configuration. More specifically, facts that readers are unlikely to notice on first reading—much less likely to draw appropriate conclusions from—are often treated, in retrospect, as if they were examples of what teachers love to call "foreshadowing." To return, for a moment, to *I, The Jury:* Charlotte's treacherous straddling of gender lines is, for instance, unsubtly implicit in her name—Charlotte *Manning*—and I've had few student readers who failed to make the connection when, in the closing pages, Mike Hammer accuses her of losing "the social instinct of a woman—that of being dependent upon a man" (Spillane, 1947, p. 167). But it's not really an example of foreshadowing at all, since virtually no one is likely to glimpse the direction of the ending when her name is introduced. And to present the reader's recognition of the significance of the name as if it involved the same interpretive strategies as foreshadowing does simply *mystifies* the act of reading.

At the same time that re-reading privileges coherence over configuration, Michael's prodding has reminded me that it also encourages the type of misreading I earlier called Blimberism, muting our involvement with the narrative audience. That's because the act of holding a work up to itself—the act of looking at the formal ingenuity of its coherence rather than being carried along by the perplexing flow of the plot—stresses design at the expense of dramatic force and makes us more aware of the artiness of the novels we read at the expense of whatever realism they might have intended. Reading *Lolita* for the first time, we are apt to be caught up in questions about what will happen to Lolita. Reading against memory makes us more aware of the intricate artiness of the work as a whole. To put it another way, reading against memory (in contrast to many *Casablanca* rereadings) tends to stress our relationship with authors at the expense of whatever relationships we might develop with the characters. With some novels, under some circumstances, that's obviously appropriate. But as a general rule, especially a covert (and hence unquestioned) one, it makes our students less flexible in their interactions with the texts they read. I am sure that reading against memory was at the heart of the readings of Conrad that I discuss in Chapter 1.

CLOUDING THE CLASSROOM

It's possible, of course, to rebut my first complaint against the unquestioned privileging of reading against memory—that is, its covert hierarchies—by claiming that the hierarchies are in fact valid: that coherence *is* more important than configuration, that sophisticated reading plays down the narrative audience, and that even at the high school level we should, in fact, be teaching those values that reading against memory promotes. Even if one granted those objections, however, I'd make a second claim—that reading against memory interferes with the classroom because it makes teaching whatever it is that we do teach more difficult, both by debasing student experience and by making it more difficult to teach our students how to read in the first place.

Note that when I talk about student experience, I'm not talking primarily about the kind of passionate "thinking about experience" that Robert E. Probst (1988, p. 25), taking his cue from Gardner, rightly points out has often been ignored in formalist classrooms: I'm talking even more about the intellectual experience of trying to make sense out of a text. Michael's experiences teaching about unreliable narrators, described in Chapter 4, persuasively support the notion that in order to teach reading well, we need to teach students the rules that govern the practice. As he points out, this does not require handing down dicta from on high. Rather, it requires sharing a set of skills. But on the whole, that seems to happen rarely in our classrooms. Arthur Applebee (1989a) points out that even in schools with a reputation for excellent English programs, teachers "lacked a vocabulary to talk about the process of literary understanding, or about the instructional techniques that might support such a process" (p. 37). And I'd argue that the silent preference for reading against memory only makes this bad situation worse, especially in high school courses and undergraduate courses for nonmajors.

In order to see why the stress on re-reading devalues student experience and makes it difficult to teach them, we need to recognize not only that reading is substantially different from re-reading but also that these differences are both horizontal and vertical. In a particular classroom situation, re-reading is not simply a chronological stage that comes, horizontally, after first reading. Rather, these two sets of strategies are represented vertically by two *different* people at a given moment, two different people who are inevitably in a power relationship with each another. That is, in class, it is for the most part the teacher who has re-read the book and who provides the perspective of reading against memory; especially in high school and undergraduate courses, students, for the most part, will be talking about or listening to lectures about texts that they have read (at most) once. To the extent that our class discussions and lectures center on our *re*-reading experiences, whether or not they are rhetorically presented as if they were simply the experience of the text, they center on teacher experiences that are substantially different from those that our students have engaged in.

Now the fact that teachers and students are different people, and that they're engaged in different activities, is not necessarily destructive. But this acidic combination of factors eats away at the classroom in two interlocking ways: by demeaning student experience and by setting up a barrier to communication. First, as so often happens, differences *in kind*, especially when they are tied to differences in authority, are readily alchemized into differences in value. Even those of us who like to think of ourselves as democratic teachers and who try to validate our students' experiences often find ourselves falling into what Warwick Wadlington (1987) aptly calls the "profession's impulse to arrogate legitimate reading to itself" (p. 36). For instance, the initial act of reading inevitably involves expectations that aren't met, predictions that don't work out, details that are missed, patterns that aren't completed. As I've said, it is a perplexing walk. That sense of dislocation—with its consequent surprises—is among the *fundamental* experiences the first time through a text, especially a complex one. But it's precisely that sense of dislocation that's erased with the map of re-reading. That is, the foiled expectations are reduced, from the perspective of the re-reader, to *false starts*—and what is essential to the reading experience is converted into mere error. Thus the very vitality of the student's first reading is trivialized.

But it's not only that we trivialize what our students do; by privileging reading against memory, we also subvert our ability to teach our students how to do what they do better. In large part that's because, as I've said before, when we appear to be talking about reading, we're often talking in fact about re-reading. As a result, our students never see clearly the difference between the two and hence never learn how to get from where they are to where we are. To put it in Judith Langer's (1989) terms: The last of her four stances, "Stepping Out and Objectifying the Experience," is precisely the kind of stance that is encouraged by reading against memory; but because we don't distinguish clearly enough between reading and re-reading, we encourage our students to *mimic* that stance from the start, without really teaching them how to get there. To view the phenomenon through another lens: If we return to a distinction I made earlier, it can be seen that the map produced by the re-reader is more like reading as a product than reading as a process. No wonder, then, that the coalescing of reading and re-reading tends to confuse the way we go about testing our students—either as a way of measuring them as receivers (the traditional testing situation) or of measuring us as teachers (as Michael does in his research concerning the effectiveness of the teaching of interpretive strategies). On occasion, for instance, Michael has used, as his measure, student response on particular tests. But those tests center on questions to which the teacher inevitably knows the answers beforehand, and the success of a teaching methodology is thus measured by how well a student meets predetermined standards—for instance, how well a student finds irony that the teacher knows to be there, or discovers the truth about someone whom the teacher knows already to be an unreliable narrator. In a sense, then, we're not examining the student's reading abilities—the perplexing walk—at all, but rather his or her ability to *end up* in the right place, his or her ability to replicate the stance of the re-reader. The race has been replaced by the act of crossing the finish line.

Let me stress something I've said before: It's not always a bad thing simply to give our students knowledge, to convey information, or even to help them learn to find the true map of new texts. But how universally can this serve as a model? Without distinguishing carefully between reading and re-reading, how can we hope to distinguish between teaching techniques and teaching interpretations?

Imagine, for instance, a cooking class where the students had done the mixing and baking but only the teacher had actually eaten the results. The teacher would, of course, be able to provide specific recommendations—by telling them, for instance, to add another square of chocolate the next time they make these brownies. And the students might, in fact, be able to put that wisdom to practical use. But they'd never learn how to improve on their own, because the teacher has, in a sense, cheated: His or her advice came not from an analysis of the conditions in which the students found themselves, but rather from a reflection on those conditions from a perspective outside the students' experience.

We could solve this last problem, perhaps, by requiring our students not simply to bake, but to eat as well: not simply to read, but to re-read, too—for instance, by organizing courses or curricula where repetition of texts is built in as part of the normal process. And I think that would be a good idea. But even if we can manage to teach our students how to read against memory, we ought to precede that by teaching them to read intelligently and sensitively the first time through (which is all that most of them will be doing once they graduate). In terms of teaching strategies, my argument would tend to support the position that one should teach interpretive strategies explicitly rather than tacitly, for such an approach permits you to teach reading without directing interpretations. In terms of research about teaching effectiveness, it would certainly support the notion that we should look at protocols of actual reading experiences rather than answers on tests of interpretive results. But to do the actual teaching, we need, in some way, to get back to where our students are— to blunder along *with them* through a text rather than to stand in some other place entirely and urge them onward and upward.

How might this happen? I'm sure there are lots of ways—but at least one that's apparently worked has been developed by Mary Beth Shaddy and Steven Bickmore, high school teachers in Anchorage, Alaska, and West Jordan, Utah. Each year, they read, with their classes, a serial novel that they've never read before—and they read it installment by installment, over the whole year, so that at any point, they're in the same position that their students are. That approach takes a lot of courage—a willingness to be as much in the dark about the details of a particular text as your students, and a willingness to be proven profoundly wrong as you grope through it. But it seems to me an act of intellectual comradeship that's well worth the risk.

You might wonder, by the way, what happened to my student Philip, whose experiences with Mickey Spillane started my thinking on this topic. He finished the semester with his same unflagging good spirits— and he'll probably never be aware of the impact he's had on me. He did, however, write the following in his end-of-the-semester self-evaluation: "I can say, with complete honesty, that I read all of the readings from beginning to end (or with the case of *I, the Jury,* from end to beginning to end)."

A BALANCING ACT

Michael W. Smith

I USED TO TORTURE my students with *The Scarlet Letter*. That's ironic because I loved the book. Every semester I taught it, I re-read it, and the book rewarded every re-reading. I'd come away with a more complete understanding of how well-crafted it was. And, of course, I wanted to share my insights with my students.

On about the tenth or eleventh reading, I discovered a hat motif (the "steeple-crowned" hats of the Puritan men, the contrast between the "skull-cap" of the Reverend John Wilson and the feather in Governor Bellingham's hat, and so on). Hard to believe I had missed it for so long. So among the lists my students were keeping in their notes was a list of hats.

We spent about 4 weeks working on the book, weeks that became increasingly full as the number of details I regarded as important increased. I panicked when my department bought a new edition of the book, though the old ones were falling apart. The page numbers were different. I remember working out an algorithm to calculate where important passages would be in the new edition. When that became unwieldy, I meticulously copied my notes and my marginalia.

I worked hard. I was enthusiastic. I wanted to give my students textual power by modeling what could be done in a close reading. I tried to engage them in the discussion of symbols and motifs that made *The Scarlet Letter* so rich for me. They hated it. They didn't care about hats. They (those that read the book, anyway) were interested in a different kind of question: "Why the hell didn't she leave if they treated her that way?" "How could she be interested in such a wimp as Dimmesdale?" "How could she have married that Chillingworth in the first place?" But we didn't talk much about those kinds of questions. They didn't come up in most classes; my students were aware of what was important, at least to me.

So I quit teaching the book. I knew something was wrong with the way I was teaching, but I couldn't articulate what it was. Maybe that's why I knew I couldn't keep myself from repeating my mistakes. Peter's explanation of reading against memory has given me insight into the problem. Instead of helping my students become better readers, I had promulgated, in Thomas Newkirk's (1984) words, the myth of the "inspired reading" (p. 756). My activities and questions had to result in my students' questioning their own abilities as readers ("Why didn't I notice the hats?"). More importantly, they kept us from discussing the truly important issues of the novel.

Although the way I taught *The Scarlet Letter* illustrates the potential problems of teaching a book one has read many times to students who are reading it for the first time, it's probably too easy a target. It's even easy for me to poke fun at what I did. What I'd like to do instead is look carefully at how Peter's ideas have affected the way I think about how I taught *To Kill a Mockingbird*, teaching of which I was prouder. Teaching to which my students responded well. Teaching that I shared with colleagues in a presentation at the annual meeting of the National Council of Teachers of English (NCTE) and that I have used as a model in methods classes. Teaching that is, as a consequence, more painful to examine critically.

A BRIEF DESCRIPTION OF THE UNIT

My teaching of *To Kill a Mockingbird* was informed by both logistical and theoretical concerns. I had always found it difficult to teach a novel as students were reading it. I was reluctant to assign more than 20 to 30 pages of reading; reading that much each night was a struggle for a number of my students. On the other hand, other students would have finished whatever novel we were reading by the next day, and I was constantly worried that they would "spoil" the novel for others by revealing what would happen. But even if everyone read only the assigned pages each night, I found it difficult to teach a novel as the class was reading it. Our discussions of each night's reading, whether they were held in small groups or large ones, would rarely take up the entire period. So during the last minutes of class I would ask my students to read. There were two problems here: Many students wouldn't accept my invitation, especially if there were only 10 minutes or so left of class. And I always felt that I was somehow shirking my duty as a teacher if I was giving them so much "free time."

In addition, I realized that many of my students had never read a text the length of *To Kill a Mockingbird*. I theorized that reading a novel required readers to be able to identify the salient themes and then to integrate those themes in a coherent statement of the whole. I thought that if I alerted my students to important issues in the text through class discussions of songs, poems, and short stories while they were reading the novel at home, they would be much more likely to attend to those issues as they read. In our subsequent discussions of the novel, we could then talk about how these issues are developed and how they are related.

I'll be discussing my teaching of *To Kill a Mockingbird* at some length. Applebee (1989b) found that it is one of the most commonly taught novels in high schools, so I trust that most readers will be familiar with it. For those of you who aren't, a brief summary of the book follows.

Harper Lee's (1960/1962) *To Kill a Mockingbird* is set in Maycomb, Alabama, during the 1930s. The novel centers on the experiences of the Finch family: Atticus, a widowed lawyer; his son, Jem; and his daughter Scout, the narrator. The novel has two parts. One focuses on Jem, Scout, and their friend Dill's attempts to make Boo Radley, a recluse who is the object of many rumors and much scapegoating, come out of his house. The other centers on Atticus's defense of Tom Robinson, an upstanding African American unjustly accused of raping Mayella Ewell, the oldest daughter of Bob Ewell, the head of a White family that had, in Atticus's words, been the "disgrace of Maycomb for three generations" (p. 35). During the course of the trial, Atticus's defense of Tom Robinson makes it clear that Tom had been resisting Mayella's attempt at seduction, that Mayella is the victim of incest, and that Mayella's bruises were the result of a beating by her father. Although the jury finds Tom Robinson guilty, it deliberates far longer than customary when the testimony of a White person and the testimony of a Black person conflict. Tom is subsequently killed in an escape attempt. Bob Ewell, who, according to Atticus, had had his "last shred of credibility" (p. 221) destroyed in the trial, stalks Jem and Scout. Boo Radley, who, we are led to believe, had been living vicariously through the children's activities, saves Jem and Scout from Bob Ewell's vicious attack. Scout walks Boo home, and when she returns says to her father, "Atticus, he was real nice." Atticus's response closes the novel: "Most people are, Scout, when you finally see them" (p. 284)

To prepare students to read the book, we talked about four themes: the Southern mind, the family, growing up, and the outsider. We read Faulkner's "A Rose for Emily" and listened to Neil Young's "Southern Man" and discussed how the characters in these texts manifested a sense of history, sense of place, and resistance to change and what happened as a consequence. We read Roethke's "My Papa's Waltz" and Hayden's "Those Winter Sundays" and discussed how stereotypes of what makes a good family aren't always valid and how family members show love in subtle ways. We read a number of stories about growing up and worked to develop a definition of maturity. And we asked three key questions about the outsiders about whom we read: Why is the person an outsider? What is the outsider's reaction to being an outsider? How could the ostracism end?

In our discussions of the novel, we focused on how these themes played out. But that's not all we did. We made maps of the street on which they lived. We wrote an issue of the local paper. We rewrote the trial scene as a play and performed it. Groups of students taught sections of the text. My students were actively engaged with the text throughout the unit.

What I remember most about the unit was the last day or so when I helped students put everything we had been doing together. In brief, I think Lee invites her audience to believe that children are naturally good but that they are corrupted by a prejudiced society, a society that will ostracize and even sacrifice its African American members in order to maintain a racist status quo. If change is to occur, therefore, children must grow up in families that teach them to try to see things from other people's perspectives, especially those who are outsiders, to, in Atticus's words, "climb into [their] skin and walk around in it" (p. 34). I think the book is ultimately optimistic. Although Tom Robinson dies, the children do stand in Boo Radley's shoes and in so doing bring him back into society if only for a moment, which leaves readers with some hope for the future. I elaborated this interpretation as we discussed the small-group work students did on the following questions, the last of many small-group discussions they had during the unit:

1. What characters have been associated with mockingbirds? Explain the evidence that links these characters to mockingbirds.
2. Why does Lee divide her novel into two parts?
3. What happens to Tom? Why? How do the kids finally feel about Boo? How is what ultimately happens to Boo different from what ultimately happens to Tom?
4. Jem and Scout are different from most of the townspeople. How are they different? What accounts for their differences?
5. On p. 282, Scout says that "Jem and I would get grown, but there wasn't much else for us to learn, except possibly algebra." How have the kids grown up?
6. Atticus said that "it seems that only children weep." What does he mean? Does Harper Lee think that Jem and Scout will change for the worse? Defend your answer.
7. A scout is a person who goes in front of an army. Jem is short for

Jeremy, a variant of Jeremiah. In the Bible, Jeremiah is a prophet. Why did Harper Lee choose these names?

When my students left this discussion, they seemed to have a greater appreciation for the novel. I'd hear, "Wow. You think she really meant all that?"

RETHINKING

When I first heard the talk on which Peter's chapter is based, I began to doubt the quality of my unit. An uncomfortable feeling to be sure. I had worked so hard on it, and changing it would, of course, mean more hard work. Moreover, I had really enjoyed teaching it. But I had to figure out exactly what was bothering me. The easy answer would be that I forced a particular authorial reading on my students. But that's not it exactly. I didn't really force a reading on my students. Rather, I created a context in which only one was available. (I admit that I still think it's a damn good one.) Moreover, my reading really didn't undermine the authorial readings my students were developing, for very few students ever worked to develop a reading of coherence. To be sure, my students made inferences about specific details, and they had plenty of emotional responses to the events of the novel. But, for the most part, they didn't work to put them together. As the final set of questions suggest, I think that doing an authorial reading of *To Kill a Mockingbird* involves using the structure of the novel as a way to do that putting together.

So what's the problem? My instruction helped students get something, a coherent interpretation of the text, that they were unlikely to get on their own. Further, because of the preparatory work we did together, they participated in the construction of that interpretation. In some sense, through our reading and discussion of the stories, poems, and songs in terms of the four themes I had identified as important, we developed an intertextual grid against which to read the novel, one that approximated the intratextual grid I had as someone who had read the novel many times. That is, when I (re)read the sentence "Being Southerners, it was a source of shame to some members of the family that we had no recorded ancestors on either side of the Battle of Hastings" (p. 8), I regarded it as important because it's an early and clear articulation of attitudes that are at the center of the conflict of the novel and of my interpretation of that conflict. My students might recognize that the sentence was important because it betrayed an attitude similar to that of Miss Emily Grierson in "A Rose for Emily"—and look at the trouble it got her into. So although

I guided my students into a synthesis of details, unlike the questions about foreshadowing to which Peter refers, I had prepared them to recognize what details might be important as they read for the first time.

It's not just that students could only participate in the construction of the interpretation rather than truly discuss that interpretation. (See Peter's distinction between participation and discussion in Chapter 1.) After all, I wanted to model a way of reading that students could apply to other novels. I wanted to help students recognize the importance both of looking for the salient themes and of looking for ways to integrate those themes. So we talked about the four themes I had identified and we talked about how to integrate them, in this case through the analysis of a symbol and a consideration of what Harper Lee wanted her audience to make of her choice to divide the novel into two parts. In fact, in our discussion we talked about a number of the rules of signification that Peter explained in Chapter 5, though we didn't name them and though my explanations were neither as succinct nor as good.

It's not just that my instruction did not recognize the uncertainty and dislocation that are an essential part of first readings, at least of most first readings, an uncertainty that Peter compares to a perplexing walk though an unfamiliar and confusing forest. At least I tried to give them the map before they undertook their journey so that their experience could be more like mine. Further, I tried to share the techniques I used to make the map.

I no longer think that "the novel" is a useful genre division. I no longer think that authorial readings require the kind of neatness for which I was searching and to which I guided my students. But what bothers me most about my teaching is the ethical implications of my privileging reading against memory.

I do not agree with Peter that reading against memory makes it more difficult to teach our students *how to read* in the first place. In fact, I'd argue that it was Wayne Booth's proficiency in reading against memory that allowed him to devote the mental attention he needed to identify and articulate the strategies he employs to understand irony (see my discussion of Booth in Chapter 4) and that it was Peter's proficiency in reading against memory that allowed him to devote the mental attention he needed to identify and articulate his rules of coherence and configuration. However, Peter has convinced me that in privileging reading against memory, the kind of reading that allowed me to construct my interpretation, I privileged our relationship with the author over our relationship with the characters. I've come to think that that's too great a price to pay, a point I'd like to make by focusing on the brief encounter Scout and Dill have with a minor character in the novel, Dolphus Raymond.

Readers are introduced to Dolphus Raymond during the trial scene. People are gathering to enter the courthouse. Dolphus Raymond, whom the children know as the town drunk, is the only White person sitting with the Black townspeople. Jem explains that Raymond has a "colored woman" and "all sorts of mixed chillun" (p. 163). During the course of the trial Dill is so upset by the scornful cross-examination of Tom Robinson that Scout takes him from the trial. As they leave, they see Dolphus Raymond, who offers Dill a drink from the bottle he carries in a sack—it turns out to be Coca-Cola. When the children ask him about his pretense, he explains:

> "Why do I pretend? Well it's very simple. . . . Some folks don't—like the way I live. Now I could say the hell with 'em, I don't care if they don't like it. I do say I don't care if they don't like it, right enough—but I don't say the hell with 'em, see. . . .
>
> "I try to give 'em a reason, you see. It helps folks if they can latch onto a reason. When I come to town, which is seldom, if I weave a little and drink out of this sack, folks can say Dolphus Raymond's in the clutches of whiskey—that's why he won't change his ways. He can't help himself, that's why he lives the way he does. . . .
>
> "It ain't honest but it's mighty helpful to folks. Secretly, Miss Finch, I'm not much of a drinker, but you see they could never, never understand that I live like I do because that's the way I want to live." (p. 203)

When Scout asks him why he shared his pretense, he explains, "Because you're children and you can understand it . . . and because I heard that one—. . . Things haven't caught up to that one's instinct yet" (p. 203).

This brief episode was a key to my interpretation of the novel, for I think it establishes that Lee wants her audience to believe that children are naturally good, the idea that allowed me to unite our discussion of the four themes into a unified statement of the whole. But because of the hindsight that Peter's ideas provide and because my life is different now, I have a different response to this episode. My wife and I have adopted two biracial daughters. I don't want to be helpful to racists. I don't want them to be comfortable in their lack of understanding. I want people to challenge bigotry so that my daughters will confront less of it. When I read of the biracial girl who sued the principal of her high school (a high school that had one prom for African American students and another for Whites) for calling her a mistake her parents had made, I admired her courage and applauded her effort. Now I wonder why Dolphus Raymond was content to do so little. He was from a prominent family. Perhaps Tom Robinson wouldn't have been convicted if more people had spoken out.

Maybe I'm overreacting. Maybe I'm bringing a 1990s point of view into a 1930s setting. Maybe I don't understand the risk that any challenges to the traditional order entailed. What worries me, though, is that my unit didn't have a place for discussing such issues. My students never heard my feelings about the moral choices Dolphus Raymond or the other characters made. I believe that we didn't talk about them because I treated Dolphus Raymond as a tool Harper Lee was using to develop an idea rather than as a human being about whom I ought to care and with whom I could dispute. That is, we didn't talk about those issues because I was so intent on playing the authorial audience that I lost sight of playing the narrative audience.

Peter's distinction between readings of coherence and readings of configuration helped me understand what's at stake in privileging students' relationship with the author over their relationship with the characters. Not only does such privileging make it less likely that students will grapple with the ethics of the choices that the characters make, but, as I argue in Chapter 2, it also makes it less likely that they will be able to resist the author. Challenging the choice that Dolphus Raymond made would raise questions we could ask of Lee as well, questions such as whether her optimism has been justified by history. Challenging the choice that Dolphus Raymond made could also raise questions that students could ask of me, questions such as why a story told from a White person's perspective was the most commonly read novel about racism in American schools.

Research by Pat Enciso (1992) and Jeff Wilhelm (1997) has given me another way to understand what informed my teaching. They both studied students' response to literature through the use of symbolic story representations. To do a symbolic story representation, students make realistic or symbolic cutouts of the characters in a story and use them to represent major scenes. As part of those representations, Enciso and Wilhelm asked students to make cutouts to represent themselves as readers and to use those cutouts to illustrate how they experienced the story world. By using this technique, Enciso and Wilhelm gained insight into where students were when they read. For example, some students adopted the perspective of a character. Others were an unseen presence in the midst of the action, acting, in Enciso's words, as a spy. Their work caused me to ask myself where I was when I experienced *To Kill a Mockingbird* as I re-read it. And the answer is behind a teacher's desk.

That's a significant realization. I thought that I was sharing myself as a reader by structuring a unit to help my students experience my interpretation of a novel. But I realize that in doing so I ignored much of what drew me to the novel in the first place—my emotional engagement in the lives of the characters. Moreover, my re-reading of the texts that I was teaching began to affect how I positioned myself when I read a text for the first time, at least a text that I might consider teaching. Too often I kept my distance from the characters and looked for the structural elements that could help me construct a reading of coherence.

I read quite differently when I read a novel for my book club. Part of our discussions always focuses on which characters we admire and which characters we despise. That's not to say that we don't work to construct a reading of coherence; most often we do. We always profit from the effort, both because it helps us understand the perspective of another and because it often provides another springboard for the discussion of the ethical and political issues the author raises. My literary training helps me contribute to those discussions, and that's one of the reasons I value it. But in our book club discussions we somehow manage both to share our experience of the dramatic force of the novels we read and to work to understand their design. In my classes, I'm afraid I lost that balance. I'm afraid that my efforts to help students construct a reading of coherence made it far less likely that we would ever share what we experienced as we read.

SO WHAT TO DO?

Peter suggests that teachers read serialized novels together with their students, installment by installment. A great idea, I think, but one that doesn't fully address the problem. Reading a serialized novel together would likely increase our emphasis on readings of configuration and our attention to understanding and critiquing the moral choices characters make, especially if we enter the project determined to step out from behind our desks when we read. It would also push us to explain the reading strategies we are using to make our predictions and to develop and test our interpretive hypotheses because we would have to defend them in terms of the utility of our strategies rather than on our knowledge of how the text continues.

But, of course, most teachers will still have to teach texts that they've read many times because they are a required part of the curriculum. We could simply be content to offer students two kinds of experiences. However, if we recognize that the experience our students have as they read a text is both valuable and different from the experience we have as we re-read, and if we believe that what we do when we re-read has merit, all of our instruction should seek a balance between honoring a student's experience and educating it. I believe that we can strike that balance if we both encourage students to document and share their experience of reading and create contexts that encourage students to do readings of coherence.

Documenting and Sharing Students' Experience of Reading

Now that I understand that what my students and I discussed in class was informed by my reading against memory and that reading against memory and first reading are substantially different activities, I realize more fully the importance of having students keep journals that document the experience they had as they read. I know that's not a very radical suggestion. But I think it's important to note that it's a suggestion that challenges some types of journals.

Because I believe students will profit if all of the members of the class share what they experience as members of the narrative audience, I would use prompts that encourage students to document that experience, something on the order of "In your journal, I'd like you to focus on how you respond to one or more of the characters you encounter. How would you describe what the character is going through? What thoughts and feelings do you have about the character and the choices he or she is making?" The suggestion to use journals in this way is grounded in a different theoretical perspective than are most suggestions to do journal writing. Probst's (1992a) work exploring the pedagogical implications of Louise Rosenblatt's writing once again provides a case in point. As I note in Chapter 2, Probst contrasts Rosenblatt's transactional theory with the theories of the New Critics, who argue that literary texts are autonomous and that the reader/critic's role is to uncover the meaning that resides in the text. Probst bases his suggestion that teachers use journals on the argument that reading is a constructive act and if readers are different, their readings must be different as well.

However, as Peter and I argue throughout the book, we are persuaded that literary reading is socially rather than personally constructed. Moreover, as I explain in Chapter 2, I'm uncomfortable with some of the ethical implications of making individual students' experiences and psychology the focus of a class. Although that doesn't mean I think journals ought not play an important role in literature classrooms, it does mean that I turn to a different source of support to justify their use. Instead of highlighting the distinction between the personal and the public, Peter's work has helped me understand the significance of the difference between what Rosenblatt calls the evocation and the response, a temporal distinction that I believe receives too little attention.

Rosenblatt (1985) notes that the term *response* is problematic because

> the term is used rather loosely to cover two processes—both the aesthetic relationship to the text and our response to the work we are evoking. Hence,

I prefer to speak of, first, *the evocation*—what we sense as the structured experience corresponding to the text—and second, *the response* to the evocation. In our transaction with Dickens' text, *Great Expectations*, for example, we evoke the characters of Pip and Joe. We participate in their relationship and, at the same time, we respond with our approval or disapproval to their words and actions. We see parallels in our own lives; perhaps we savor the vividness of imagery or linguistic exuberance. All of these processes may be going on at the same time. Later reflections on the transaction can be seen as an effort (a) to recapture, to reenact the evocation, and (b) to organize and elaborate our ongoing response to it. (pp. 39–40)

Rosenblatt hints at the differences that are apt to mark the evocation and the response, differences that Peter elaborates both in the distinction he draws between readings of configuration and readings of coherence and in the distinction he draws between the narrative and authorial audience. But Probst (1992a) seems to me to conflate the evocation and the response in arguing that "one text, read by thirty students, will yield thirty poems" (p. 59). Rosenblatt and Peter have convinced me that each reader is likely to do different things with a text at different times. One text, read by 30 students, therefore, will likely yield 60 or more poems. The primary function of the journal, it seems to me, is to document the evocation so that, in Rosenblatt's words, it can be recaptured. Without such documentation, even teachers who put students' interpretations at the center of their classrooms are likely to focus on the ways that students organize and elaborate their ongoing responses to their evocations.

The difference in grounding is important. As I note above, I believe students will profit if all the members of the class share what they experience as members of the narrative audience. As I argue in Chapter 2, this kind of sharing is one of the major benefits of talking about literature. But if we regard these responses as manifestations of the uniqueness of individual readers, class members are likely to listen to them uncritically. They will be much less likely to push for articulation and to challenge assumptions that they believe are poorly grounded or unfair to the characters or to the text. I neglected the opportunity to have a discussion with my students about how Dolphus Raymond responded to the racism of his society. That discussion could have led to a consideration of the comfort and cost of taking a morally superior position to people of other times and other cultures. It could have led to a greater understanding of the personal risk involved in making change. It could have led to a more careful scrutiny of others who seem on the surface to have a more appealing attitude toward race relations. But none of these discussions could have ensued if my students simply regarded my response as a function of my adopting two biracial children.

Although students can use journals to document their experience as the narrative audience, journals do not require that students articulate how they read. If we believe that part of our jobs is to teach students how to read, then writing and discussing journals cannot be enough. In Chapter 4 I argue that we should devise instruction in which we share our secrets. The research of Enciso (1992) and Wilhelm (1997) suggests how much students can profit if we encourage them to share their own secrets, as a closer look at Wilhelm's study reveals.

Wilhelm (1997) brought symbolic story representations to the very center of his class. Once students began to include themselves in their representations, they could share with each other some very sophisticated understandings of the way they read. Students began to identify and talk about who and where they were in the world of the story and to share when and how they created particular types of experiences and meanings. Some students began to elaborate on the assignment by including cutouts to represent the author, major concepts, previous readings, and real-life experiences. Sharing their symbolic story representations led to some dramatic exchanges, such as this one between Jon, a reluctant reader, and Ron, an active and committed one:

> JON: I can't believe you do all that stuff when you read! Holy crap, I'm not doing . . . like nothing . . . compared to you!
> RON: I can't believe you don't do something. If you don't, you're not reading, man. . . . It's gotta be like wrestling, or watching a movie or playing a video game. . . . You've got to like . . . *be* there! (Wilhelm, 1997, p. 49)

Wilhelm's students became serious researchers into, and amazingly eloquent speakers about, their reading. Even though I disagree with Peter's contention that reading against memory makes it less likely that we can share the strategies we employ as readers, I realize that the strategies on which I focused as a teacher were centered on what Peter calls the "intellectual experience of trying to make sense out of a text." Wilhelm's students did a far better job than I could of sharing the strategies that allowed their passionate involvement in a story world.

Creating Contexts to Encourage Readings of Coherence

Peter's chapter challenges the unquestioned privileging of readings of coherence and his challenge has led me to rethink what I did as a teacher and what I do as a teacher educator. Peter's ideas have forced me to think about ways that teachers can demonstrate that they value students' transactions with literature. When teachers have students share their journal entries and their symbolic story representations, they make that demonstration.

However, Peter's challenge has not caused me to reject the benefits that can come from constructing readings of coherence, benefits that we consider in Chapters 1 and 2. And I recognize that my knowledge of literary reading usually made me better able than my students to construct this kind of reading. In fact, although reading against memory certainly allows me to fine-tune my readings, I'm usually able to develop a reading of coherence as I'm reading a text for the first time (though I'll admit that when I read some stories, I resist any kind of intellectualization lest it spoil my emotional engagement). The question, therefore, becomes: How can I help my students develop the literary knowledge they need to construct readings of coherence without undermining my efforts to engage them in sharing their experience as readers?

Unfortunately, the unit I designed for *To Kill a Mockingbird* does not provide an answer. For all its strengths, my efforts to share my interpretation with my students made it far less likely that we would have meaningful exchanges of what we experienced as we read. As I reflect upon it now, I've come to believe that my unit was flawed because it was opus-oriented. The unit prepared students to come to a particular reading of a particular text. My stake in that reading, therefore, was so great that I lost sight of what else the novel could provide. I think my students would have profited more if I had devised instruction that engaged them in understanding that constructing readings of coherence, far from being the province of an intellectual elite, is something that all readers can do and can benefit from, and if I had helped them develop reading strategies that they could readily transfer across texts.

One way to encourage students to do readings of coherence is to pair texts that take different positions on important issues and to focus discussion on how the works speak to each other and on students' evaluation of the morality of the positions they take. This kind of organization would have the additional benefit of bringing the discussions of readings of coherence more in line with the discussions of students' readings of configuration. Although discussions of students' readings of configuration would focus on characters and discussion of readings of coherence would focus on the work as a whole, each would center in large measure on the ethical implications of what the students are reading. Finally, such an organization demonstrates to students that we take the idea of resistance seriously; it will be far easier for students to resist authors when they see that authors resist each other.

Another way teachers could encourage students to do readings of coherence is to engage them in declaring their positions on the issues a text raises before they read (cf. Smagorinsky, McCann, & Kern, 1987). For example, before reading *To Kill a Mockingbird,* students could agree or disagree with statements such as "One person can change a society." If a class had discussed this question before reading, students would be more likely to note and put together the details in the novel that suggest Lee's position on this issue. Using an opinionnaire in this fashion has the additional benefit of making a critical examination of Lee's ideology far more likely, since teachers could encourage those students who took opposition to this statement to explain why they believe that Lee's vision is flawed. As I note above, Wilhelm's (1997) research has persuaded me that I undervalued my students' capabilities. Maybe if students expect that they will be asked to construct a reading of coherence, they'll develop the strategies they need to do so.

Despite my growing confidence in students' abilities, I still believe that teachers can help them develop interpretive strategies more quickly than they would develop them on their own. In Chapter 4, I focus on the study of genre as a way to identify appropriate strategies to teach. Another possible approach is to focus on particular discourse conventions that are used across genres. For example, in teaching *To Kill a Mockingbird*, I could have given students practice in identifying and interpreting symbols. Before reading the novel, we could have read and discussed a story such as "The Butterfly" by James Hanley (1961). In that story Cassidy, a boy of 15 who attends a Catholic boarding school, misses Mass one day because he and a friend are so intently studying the life that abounds in the hedges that they fail to hear the bell that calls them in. For this transgression he is punished by Brother Timothy, who locks Cassidy in a room until he can give a satisfactory explanation for his behavior. Brother Timothy will not accept the simple truth; he sees Cassidy's refusal to offer another explanation as defiance and vows to break down the "steel wall" (p. 117) of his silence. Cassidy's only solace in his confinement is the joy that he takes in the caterpillar that he has brought from the hedges, storing it in a tiny box filled with moss. He is moved by the beauty of the caterpillar. He thinks: "And one day it would turn into a beautiful butterfly. How marvellous" (p. 119). Brother Timothy returns to the room and finds Cassidy examining the caterpillar. He grabs the box, turns out the caterpillar, and crushes out its life. The story ends with Cassidy's bursting into tears.

In reading and discussing that story, students would begin to apply strategies they could use to help them understand other symbols. For example, they would begin to develop an understanding of the rules that allow readers to notice symbols, rules such as "Pay attention to what seems to be undue attention to trivial details" (a student of mine once termed it "weird authorial behavior"). They would also begin to develop an understanding of how to apply rules of signification for those symbols, for example, identifying salient similarities, drawing inferences on the basis of the details, and so on. Beach (1985) explains why this kind of preparation is useful:

> As suggested by sociolinguists, social psychologists, ethnographers, and now writing researchers and others, one learns or gains "competence" in particular types of discourse conventions through discourse experiences. The fact that readers are continually acquiring discourse and literary experiences suggests that the potential or capacity for the "fullest response" or understanding of a work is related to a reader's level of development in these experiences. (p. 105)

A more elaborate unit could be modeled on one found in the Euclid English Demonstration Center's Project English materials (1964). This unit begins by introducing symbolism through the use of fables and parables and culminates in having groups of students teach symbolic poems to the class.

Both the activities designed to encourage students to document and share their experience of reading and those that are designed to encourage students to do readings of coherence would make it far more likely that students would be able to move beyond participation to discussion. If I had encouraged my students to document the experience they had as they were reading *To Kill a Mockingbird*, I think it would have been far more likely that we would have explored our relationship with the characters' moral choices. If I had engaged my students in understanding how to do readings of coherence rather than focusing on the product of my re-reading, we could have had a freer exchange about our various responses to playing the authorial audience.

Peter's argument has caused me to question what had been my unquestioned privileging of reading against memory. I'll admit that upon doing so, my first inclination was to rid my teaching of any legacy of that privilege. But I would have been falling into the trap that Rosenblatt (1993) describes in a recent article descrying the dualistic habits of mind that persist in our field. The balance between encouraging readings of configuration and readings of coherence may be delicate, but I believe that we can strike it.

At least we should try. Our relationships both with authors and with characters are important. But like most relationships, they can be difficult to establish and to maintain, especially as our reading becomes more and more diverse. In Chapter 7, I will explore the ways in which authorial reading can help overcome some of those difficulties. But as Peter will explain in Chapter 8, he worries that I'm too optimistic and that I fail to recognize that some efforts to establish relationships may, in fact, damage texts.

MULTICULTURAL LITERATURE AND THE PEDAGOGY OF PERSONAL EXPERIENCE

Michael W. Smith

THE SUMMER BEFORE my first year in high school, my dad gave me his copy of *Manchild in the Promised Land*, Claude Brown's memoir of coming of age in Harlem. He had just finished reading it. "Here," he said. "Read this. It's something you should know about." And then a pause. "Don't tell your mother I gave it to you."

I'd never read a book like it before. It was one of the first adult books I ever read. The graphic language and descriptions of violence and sex were a far cry from what I was used to. But it was much more than that. I was 13. I suppose I, too, was coming of age. Yet the struggles to overcome racism and poverty that Brown endured in his life and detailed in his writing are a far cry from anything I had ever experienced.

My dad didn't give me the book because it could help me understand what was going on in my life. He gave it to me in the hope that reading it would help me begin to understand a life much different from my own. His gift is one of the touchstones I think of when I think about how I became what I am.

The argument of this chapter is that an emphasis on the personality of the reader, an emphasis that is at the heart of many reader-centered theories and pedagogies, might have the effect of denying students similar gifts. I'm aware that on the surface this argument may seem inconsistent with those I offer elsewhere in this book. In Chapter 2 I contend that playing the narrative audience allows readers to bring their personal experience to texts in ways that can challenge traditional hierarchies and go on to argue that the common project of authorial reading can create a context in which other readers can regard those personal experiences as important resources. In Chapter 4 I explain how reconstructing irony requires readers to apply their personal experience. In Chapter 6 I talk about how my quarrel with Dolphus Raymond is informed by my family situation. In each instance, however, I call for life experience to be applied in the service of authorial reading or after an authorial reading has been

done. In this chapter I'll explore the potential consequences of an emphasis on the personality of the reader that's unconstrained by the goal of
doing an authorial reading. I will argue that such an emphasis interferes
with literature's capacity to help readers develop an ethical respect for
others, one of the primary goals of multicultural curricula.

THE PERSONALITY OF THE READER AND THE READING
OF LITERATURE

I argue in Chapter 2 that "What does this mean to me?" is the central
question that flows from reader-response criticism. As Peter points out
in Chapter 1, David Bleich (1975) has gone so far as to argue that "the
role of personality in response is the most fundamental fact of criticism"
(p. 4). But as Peter also points out in that chapter, we've been trying to
avoid using the most extreme position to caricature the theories we're
writing against. To consider the consequences of an emphasis on the personality of the reader, then, I'll turn to two more moderate theorists who
have exerted more influence on teachers in part because of their modera-
tion: Louise Rosenblatt and Wolfgang Iser.
    Rosenblatt (1985) has worked to articulate a balance between "no-
tions of the passive reader acted on by the text, or the passive text acted
on by the reader" (p. 40). She puts it this way in *The Reader, the Text, the
Poem: The Transactional Theory of the Literary Work* (1978):

> First, the text is a stimulus activating elements of the reader's past experi-
> ence—his experience both with literature and with life. Second, the text
> serves as a blueprint, a guide for the selecting, rejecting, and ordering of
> what is being called forth; the text regulates what shall be held in the fore-
> front of the reader's attention. (p. 11)

Iser (1978) makes a similar argument: "The text mobilizes the subjective knowledge present in all kinds of readers and directs it to one particular end. However varied this knowledge may be, the reader's subjective
contribution is controlled by the given framework" (p. 145).
    Rosenblatt and Iser argue that the text regulates or controls what is
called forth by readers. However, neither theorist offers clear grounds for
rejecting what is called forth. My studies of inexperienced readers suggest why offering those grounds is so important. Consider, for example,
the think-aloud protocol of a ninth-grade girl responding to John Collier's
story "The Chaser" (the italicized portions are the remarks she made as
she was reading):

Alan Austen, as nervous as a kitten, went up a certain dark and creaky stairs in the neighborhood of Pell Street, and peered about for a long time on the dim landing before he found the name he wanted written obscurely on one of the doors. *Reminds me of, we have stairs in our house that go down to our cellar that are really . . . creaky!*

Um, he pushed open this door, as he had been told to, and found himself in a tiny room, which contained no furniture but a plain kitchen table, a rocking chair, and an ordinary chair. *Reminds me of something I saw on TV last night.* On one of the dirty, buff-colored walls were a couple of shelves, containing in all perhaps . . . a dozen bottles and jars. *The shelves remind me of, trying to remember the word "shelves" in Spanish!*

Her protocol suggests that this reader asked of even the most trivial details "What does this mean to me?" and that the text "called forth" or "mobilized" superficial associations in response to that question. The problem, then, is what to do. If "a text, once it leaves its author's hands, is simply paper and ink until the reader evokes from it a literary work" (Rosenblatt, 1978, p. ix), the reader (or teacher) doesn't have any grounds to critique an evocation, even when it centers on such trivial associations as this reader made. Rosenblatt (1994) does offer Dewey's notion of warranted assertability to counter charges of extreme relativism. However, she also points out that warranted assertability depends on "shared criteria concerning methods of investigation and kinds of evidence" (p. 1078), and her theory doesn't suggest how to develop those shared criteria. Indeed, in that same article she explains that while a theoretical model may help us think about reading, "we cannot evade the realization that there are actually only innumerable separate transactions between readers and texts" (p. 1057).

I think it's important for readers and teachers to have a theoretical model that allows them to critique readings. Not long after my dad gave me *Manchild in the Promised Land,* he overheard my telling a friend about "a dirty part." "I'm disappointed in you," he said. I felt terrible because I had violated a covenant. Peter's conception of the authorial audience has helped me understand that I violated a covenant not only with my dad but also with the author. Claude Brown didn't expect his audience to read about the sexual experiences he had at a young age in order to be titillated. Rather, he expected his audience to see these experiences as evidence of his living in a world that made him grow up much too fast. It's only because my father critiqued my reading and reminded me to meet those expectations that the book had the effect on me it did.

Maybe things are different in schools. Maybe a discussion of the text with other readers would have been enough to help the reader of "The Chaser" and me recognize that others were having more meaningful transactions with the texts we were reading. However, discussion would seem much less likely to help when the associations are more deeply felt. Peter provides an intriguing example in Chapter 3 when he talks about Alex from *A Clockwork Orange.* If Alex asks "What does this mean to me?" when he reads "all about the scourging and the crowning with thorns and then the cross veshch" in the Gospels, his answer of the enjoyment he gets from imagining "helping in and even taking charge of the tol-chocking and the nailing in" (Burgess, 1988, p. 92) follows. We may be dismayed, but we have to admit that the Gospels *are* about scourging and crowning with thorns. Alex's mention of them certainly falls within the "blueprint" the text provides, so a discussion isn't likely to provide a corrective for Alex's reading. However, if Alex asks "What would this mean for the audience the author was writing for and how do I feel about that?" at the very least a discussion could force him to recognize that his response is at odds with the authorial audience's. I'm not saying that a text, no matter how powerful, is likely to transform a reader like Alex. I am saying that unless he reads authorially, no text has a chance to transform him.

Returning to "The Liar," the story I used in my discussion in Chapter 4 of the potential effects of instruction in interpretive strategies, provides another example. Consider the final remarks that a ninth-grade boy made about the story:

> The um . . . I think every minister's son . . . should follow the ex-amples of his father, and become like his father. And if he doesn't follow examples like his father, and does what God wouldn't want him to do, um he should . . . be damned to hell for life I guess. And everybody . . . should just, not bother, bother with him. If he ain't gonna follow uh, these good examples his father set, and if his, if his father did, don't set good examples and he's a preacher, he shouldn't be a preacher any longer either. Thank you.

The story apparently activates beliefs that were already fully pre-pared in his mind. He uses the story as an occasion for making a speech about these beliefs, as evidenced by the "thank you." His prior beliefs seem likely to keep him from noticing the details that might make him question the actions of the minister and his wife. In so doing, they may have kept him from actually reading the text, at least as a number of critics define that term. Scholes (1985a) puts it this way: "The supposed skill of reading is actually based upon a knowledge of the codes that were operative in the composition of any given text and the historical situation in which it was composed" (p. 21). But it's not hard to understand why the student's beliefs were "called forth" or "mobilized." After all, the proper conduct of a minister and a minister's son is at least in part what the story is about. Though the student's beliefs interfere with his reading, they seem well within the blueprint or framework of the text. The theories of Rosenblatt and Iser, therefore, offer little help in explaining why the student should have at least provisionally put those beliefs aside.

I want to stress that I am not critiquing the student's beliefs. A student might read the story well, understand it as authorial audience, and still make a very similar speech. In fact, I held out the resistance of the student I discussed in Chapter 4 to what she saw as the story's cynicism as a positive consequence of the instruction. However, as I argue in Chapter 2, such a speech would be far more likely to get a hearing in a classroom when it could be seen as part of the common project of doing an authorial reading of the text or of critiquing an authorial reading. Objecting to a text on religious grounds is a risky business in schools. If those objections can be seen to be grounded in an idiosyncratic reading, it allows those objections to be easily dismissed.

Using one's personal experience uncritically seems to me to have especially worrisome consequences for many texts that are termed multicultural. (Although I use the term *multicultural*, both Peter and I are uncomfortable with it. In the first place, using it does not allow us to make a distinction between texts in which a variety of cultures are represented and those in which only one nonmajority culture is represented. In the second place, the term does not recognize that an author from a nonmajority culture may write a text and deliberately exclude readers from other cultures from the authorial audience of that text, an argument that Peter will develop in the next chapter.) Treating others with an ethical respect (see my discussion of Giroux in Chapter 2), it seems to us, means living with the discomfort of knowing that although you can empathize with the experience of others, although you ought to try to imagine it, at least some of the time, you won't be able to know it. As Gwendolyn Brooks has written:

> There is indeed a new black today.... And he is understood by *no* white; not the wise white nor the Schooled white nor the Kind white. (Quoted in Dilg, 1995, p. 22; emphasis in original)

Peter and I have talked about a variety of kinds of resistance: to authors, to teachers, to characters, to classmates. Here we add two more: Sometimes, we think, readers must resist equating their politics, ethics, and so on, uncritically with that of the author, and they must resist equating their experience uncritically with that of the characters about whom they are reading.

Toni Morrison's *Beloved* (1987) provides a striking example of the necessity of such resistance. Let's imagine what would happen if I applied the interpretive strategies of the two students I discussed above to the chapter that describes Sethe's killing her daughter so that she cannot be returned to slavery. If I read like the reader who was responding to "The Chaser," the discussion of the beatings Sethe received might make me recall the one time my father spanked me. If I read like the young man who responded to "The Liar," my belief that it is wrong to kill except in cases of self-defense might cause me to condemn Sethe. In both cases, what I would do is turn away from Sethe. And if I did, I would no longer have to face the horror of the scene.

However, if I believe that Toni Morrison is part of the literary transaction, if I play the authorial audience, I have to ask whether she wants her audience to equate their experience with what Sethe has gone through. And I have to be prepared to hear no for an answer. If I cannot hear that answer, if I uncritically use my experience as the way to understand Sethe, I'm acting like one of the men who provoked and witnessed the scene:

> What she go and do that for? On account of a beating? Hell, he'd been beat a million times and he was white. Once it hurt so bad and made him so mad he'd smashed the well bucket. Another time he took it out on [the dog]—a few tossed rocks was all. But no beating ever made him . . . I mean no way he could have . . . What she go and do that for? (p. 150)

Further, if I recognize that an essential part of doing an authorial reading is playing the narrative audience, I won't dismiss Sethe through the application of moral principles evolved in a world less horrible than Sethe's. I'll always keep her humanity in mind. I'll try to imagine as best I can what she must have been going through. I'll be moved by her pain. If I don't, I'm acting like another of the men who came to take Sethe back into slavery, a man who draws this lesson from the scene: "You just can't mishandle creatures and expect success" (p. 150).

Morrison's novel seems to me to be different in important ways from the texts that Peter will discuss in the next chapter, texts designed to keep part of the actual audience from getting it. I think that I "got" *Beloved*, at least to some extent. I was moved by Sethe's plight. At the same time, I was aware that nothing I could conjure from my own experience would let me say "I understand what she must be going through." In fact, I think that my ongoing awareness that Morrison wanted me to be conscious of the inadequacy of my experience and beliefs in gaining an understanding is one of the most educative aspects of my reading *Beloved*. This awareness forced me to try to imagine the situation in Sethe's terms and not my own. Recognizing the inadequacy of my experiences and beliefs forced me to cultivate my capacity for ethical respect in a way that simply applying my own experience could not.

This is not to say that readers ought not use their personal experience in their reading. But it's important to be aware of how one uses that experience. Villanueva (1996) makes this point when he distinguishes between saying "I understand your pain from having had a splinter once" and saying "I understand your pain because I had a splinter once." In the first case, the speaker is articulating the experience on which the speaker is drawing in order to understand. In the second case, the speaker casts all pain as being equal.

It is also not to say that readers ought to endorse every choice a character makes. As I argue in Chapter 2 in my discussion of Eli's response to *A Canticle for Leibowitz*, resistance that follows respect requires readers to articulate and defend their own beliefs in ways that have the capacity to strengthen their understanding of their own ethical frameworks.

THE PEDAGOGY OF PERSONAL EXPERIENCE

And, of course, people are interested only in themselves. If a story is not about the hearer, he will not listen. And here I make a rule—a great and lasting story is about everyone or it will not last. The strange and the foreign is not interesting—only the deeply personal and familiar. (Steinbeck, 1952/ 1992 p. 276)

The above rule that Lee offers Samuel in Steinbeck's *East of Eden* is consonant, it seems to me, with the emphasis on the personality of the reader found in even moderate response theorists like Rosenblatt and Iser. What I want to explore now is its pedagogical corollary, a corollary that goes something like this: Teachers must select stories that are about their students or must teach them in such a way as to make them about their students if they want their students to be interested. I'm afraid that that corollary has effects that are at odds with a fundamental goal for teaching multicultural literature.

Selecting Texts

As I note in Chapter 2, Robert Probst offers a powerful critique of text-based pedagogies that in his view inevitably lead to selecting the kind of texts from which many, if not most, young readers will be alienated. (Probst also talks about how those texts are and could be taught. More on that later.) By building on the ideas of Rosenblatt, he suggests that curricula could be developed around the transactions that are likely to ensue between students and the texts teachers select. More specifically, he argues that "If we could learn enough about adolescent psychology, we might be able to develop a literature curriculum that would promote reflection upon one's own experiences" (1992a, p. 76).

On the surface, this seems to be a sensible recommendation. And indeed, as Probst argues, it may be a sensible way to approach teaching canonical texts. However, one potentially negative impact of Probst's suggestion is that multicultural issues would be either ignored or introduced through a middle-class European American lens. In Chapter 6 I note that my students and I failed to think together about why *To Kill a Mockingbird,* a story told from a White perspective, was the most commonly read novel about race in American schools and to explain some of the reasons behind that failure. Here's another reason: My students were comfortable reading the novel. We got to talk about race relations, an issue that I feel is crucial. But I didn't have to answer the kind of question that I was met with when I taught a unit on African American literature: "Why are we always reading about them?"

We can see a similar dynamic play out in popular culture. In the *Philadelphia Inquirer* on the morning I drafted this paragraph, there was a review of Joel Schumacher's film adaptation of John Grisham's *A Time to Kill.* After noting that the film is long, critic Desmond Ryan notes, "More damagingly, *A Time to Kill* follows the example of many apartheid films in portraying the wrongs done to a black family from the perspective of a white liberal" (July 24, 1996, sec. C, p. 1). In fact, Ryan reports that the "final, eloquent" speech to the all-White jury was delivered by the White attorney who represented the African American man on trial for the murder of the two White men who had brutally raped and abused his 10-year-old daughter. In the novel, the defendant delivered this speech. Why the change? Why do we see the film story of Steven Biko, the Black South African opponent of apartheid who was murdered by police, through the eyes of a White journalist who befriends him in Richard Attenborough's *Cry Freedom*? It seems to me that studios and directors are making the same assumptions about the White audience that they need to make a profit on their films that I made of my students: "If a story is not about the hearer, he or she will not listen."

Publishing houses that produce literature anthologies appear to make similar assumptions even when they select multicultural texts. I'd like to consider the poetry of Gwendolyn Brooks as an example. Brooks's case began to interest me when I was reading around in my *Norton An-*

thology of Modern Poetry and happened upon Don L. Lee's (now Haki Madhubuti) "Gwendolyn Brooks." In that poem, Lee (1973) disputes the characterization made by a "whi-te" critic that Brooks is a "credit to the negro race" (p. 1377), that is, that she is safe. Lee's poem made me think about how my view of Brooks had been conditioned by the poems that appeared in the high school literature anthologies I have taught from or examined. The McDougal, Littell American literature anthology from the "Responding to Literature" series (Johnson, 1992) provides a case in point. It features only one poem by Brooks, "Life for my child is simple, and is good," a poem that originally appeared in 1949 in *Annie Allen*, the book for which she received the Pulitzer Prize for poetry. The title poem is a celebration of a child, who, like the speaker, "want[s] joy of undeep and unabiding things." The poem closes this way (G. Brooks, 1987a, p.120):

> Not that success, for him, is sure, infallible.
> But never has he been afraid to reach.
> His lesions are legion.
> But reaching is his rule.

Now I'm not saying that I don't like the poem. I do. But it seems to me that this selection makes it easy on the anthology's White readers because it doesn't force them to face the difficulties in understanding the "new Black today" and the reasons for those difficulties. Moreover, it freezes Brooks in time. It doesn't honor nearly 50 years of additional writing, writing I encountered not in school anthologies but in Brooks's 1987 anthology *Blacks*. Although the biographical sketch of Brooks notes that in her later years she began responding to "the social upheavals of the time," students don't see any of Brooks's anger or any of the powerful political critiques of White sensibilities that have increasingly marked her work. Students don't see stanzas like the one that closes "Young Afrikans" (G. Brooks, 1987c, p. 495):

> And they await,
> across the Changes and the spiraling dead,
> our Black revival, our Black vinegar,
> our hands, and our hot blood.

Or lines like these from "Music for Martyrs," a poem dedicated to the murdered Steven Biko, which speak directly against the ways that Whites responded to the oppression of Black South Africans (G. Brooks, 1987b, p. 50).

Now for the shapely American memorials.

....

The singings, the white lean lasses with streaming yellow hair.
Now for the organized nothings.
Now for the weep-words.

These lines are especially challenging for me when I think about Attenborough's film and how my teaching proceeded at least in part from a
similar impulse.

Maybe it's unfair to ask a broad-based anthology to represent completely all those included in it. But I don't think it's unfair to ask for a
careful consideration of the principles underlying the selections that are
made. The notion of the authorial audience challenges the pedagogy of
personal relevance by establishing the importance of seeing things
through a lens of another's making. As a consequence, Peter and I think
that it justifies selecting texts that call for students to keep their distance
and to question constantly whether the personal experiences, beliefs, and
standards of interpretation that they are applying are the ones that they
are called upon to employ. If multicultural literature is to challenge students' ethnocentricity, then they have to engage in looking at things, at
least provisionally, through new perspectives. In the next chapter Peter
provides evidence of the power of doing so in his students' comments on
the impact of reading Anzaldúa's *Borderlands/La Frontera*. But if teachers
select texts written by people of color because they are accessible to White
audiences, much of their power will be lost.

If trying on the perspectives of others is at the heart of reading, then
the importance of providing access to different perspectives necessarily
follows. Attention to diversity in a literature curriculum would mean not
only including works from writers of diverse races and ethnicities; it
would also mean trying to capture something of the diversity of perspectives in the writing within a racial and ethnic group. For example, because the perspective toward one's home language that Richard Rodriguez invites his readers to take in *Hunger of Memory* (1982) is radically at
odds with the perspective that Gloria Anzaldúa insists upon, honoring
diversity might mean reading them against each other. Seeking out diversity within groups has an additional advantage as well. As I noted in the
last chapter, encouraging students to resist authors will be far easier
when they see that authors resist each other.

An emphasis on personal relevance as a primary criteria for selecting
texts may also be counterproductive in contexts in which White readers
are not in the majority. My colleague Dorothy Strickland and I recently
worked with a group of teachers in a Literacy and Diversity Study Group.

The teachers all taught at one of two K–8 schools in one of New Jersey's special needs districts, districts designated by the state to receive "special funding" because a significant proportion of their students come from high poverty areas with a history of low achievement. The vast majority of their students were either African American or Latino. Twelve teachers participated in the study group: four African American women, one African American man, three European American women, three European American men, and one Latina woman.

One of our primary goals for the project was to help teachers learn about texts and teaching strategies that would help them foster an understanding of cultural diversity. Dorothy explained that goal in the grant application to the Turrell Fund that sought support for our work:

> Some multicultural education programs that purport to foster an understanding of cultural diversity actually focus on one culture— that of the predominant group within a school. Thus, African American students learn only about their own culture and Latino children only about theirs. The intent, of course, is to instill a sense of cultural pride in these children. Such a one-dimensional approach denies children the opportunity to broaden their understanding and appreciation of the cultures of others. In addition, many urban minority children live in areas where they have little opportunity for meaningful interaction with individuals outside their own cultural communities.

With support from the Turrell Fund, we met once a month for 10 months to talk about children's, adolescent, and adult literature written by men and women from a variety of races, ethnicities, and classes. Our goal was to help teachers adopt a truly multicultural approach. However, we now believe that an emphasis on personal experience may have interfered with achieving that goal.

As part of our work together, we asked the teachers in our group to consider whether they would select *Been to Yesterdays, Smoky Night,* or *The Whispering Cloth* if they could only teach one of the three books to their classes. *Been to Yesterdays* is a collection of poems by Lee Bennett Hopkins, a European American author. In the poems Hopkins reflects on both the trials (his parents' divorce, his mother's drinking, a hand-to-mouth existence) and comforts (his grandmother's love, his ambition to be a writer) he experienced growing up in the 1950's. *Smoky Night,* written by Eve Bunting and illustrated by David Diaz, chronicles the experiences of a young African American and his mother during the Los Angeles riots in the aftermath of the Rodney King verdict. It details how the boy witnesses looting, loses his home and cat, and comes to feel some kind of connection to the Korean grocer on his street who had experienced similar losses, someone of whom he had always been suspicious. *The Whispering Cloth*, written by Pegi Deitz Shea and illustrated by Anita Riggio, features an embroidered story cloth created by You Yang. It relates the story of You Yang, a young Hmong girl in a refugee camp in Thailand, who comes to tell her own story through an embroidered story cloth.

Been to Yesterdays was by far the most popular choice among both the African American and White teachers. The teachers who chose it did so because it has what one teacher called "a universal theme," that is, it has situations to which their students can immediately relate. As one teacher wrote: " I feel children can examine their own emotions and feelings through the words of Lee Bennett Hopkins." In the words of another: "I chose [*Been to Yesterdays*] because I feel that there are several situations described in the story which many of our students can identify with."

I'm not arguing that there is no place for having students read literature that is personally relevant. In fact, I think that doing so is especially important when students seldom if ever see their lives reflected in the stories that they read. But I do want to point out that such an emphasis makes it unlikely that *The Whispering Cloth* would ever be chosen. Moreover, if it were chosen, the emphasis on relevance could undermine what Peter, in his discussion of Blimberisms in Chapter 1, calls a serious mimetic interaction with human lives. For example, a teacher who emphasizes personal relevance might ask students to think about the range of ways in which they can tell their stories rather than to imagine the experiences and feelings of the Hmong girl.

Although our project had as a major aim helping teachers think about texts that would foster an understanding of cultural diversity, it did not fully achieve that goal. We think now that the primary reason for our failure is that the goal conflicted with our other major aim: to engage teachers in conversations about literature that would challenge the patterns of discourse that prevail in school discussions of literature (cf. Marshall, et al., 1995) and to model instructional strategies that would be helpful in making that challenge. In fact, we've come to believe that what we thought of as progressive instructional practices may actually have made serious mimetic interaction with the lives of others less likely.

Thinking About Instruction

Dorothy and I began our project with the belief that standardized tests and basal series exert much the same influence on classroom discussion that Probst (1992a) suggests the New Criticism has had on secondary schools. The belief in single, identifiable, right answers seems to lead inevitably to the domination of teachers who know what that right answer is and to the passivity of students who don't. In our discussions, therefore, we hoped to complicate matters by discussing issues of both meaning and significance (see Peter's discussion in Chapter 1 of how our understanding of these terms differs from Hirsch's) that would provoke an engaging interaction among a variety of perspectives. Although Dorothy and I were not teachers of the Literacy and Diversity Study Group, we did take on leadership roles. We selected the readings and we determined the instructional strategies that we wanted to model. Because we thought that one powerful way teachers can encourage active and engaged reading is to ask students to write response statements, we asked the teachers with whom we worked to write a response statement each month.

I think we were successful in promoting engaging discussions. However, the area of significance that seemed to carry the most weight was the personal significance that a story or passage had for individual readers. Peter Smagorinsky (Marshall, et al., 1995, chap. 4) explains how particular ways of talking become privileged in particular instructional settings. In our discussions, what became privileged were turns in which speakers explored how the texts related to their lives as can be seen from the following excerpts from two teachers' final written statements about their experience in the group:

> I particularly enjoyed our round-table discussions about the many books and pieces of literature because they led to lively talks about our personal experiences.

> At first, I kept feeling as if I were in a therapy group for teachers. Much of what we did in the beginning seemed to revolve around our own feelings and interpersonal relationships (family).

The following exchange comes from our discussion of a portion of *The Joy Luck Club*, by Amy Tan, which appeared as a story entitled "Two Kinds" in the McDougal, Littell *Multicultural Perspectives* anthology (Foote, Forst, Hynes-Berry, Johnson, Miller, & Perkins, 1992). The exchange suggests how privileging one kind of talk may have the consequence of silencing other kinds of talk. It begins with my second attempt to initiate discussion of what in the text may be culture-specific:

> MICHAEL: When I was reading, I was wondering about that stuff, about obedience, you know. . . . Is the conflict worse in this story

because being a Chinese daughter meant being an obedient daughter in a way that it might not across cultures?

S: I am amazed at the way my own kids behave. I remember my father, he spanked us very little. When we sat at the table—[the speaker's parents] were both teachers—and in [the speaker's home country] you go home to have lunch. Everybody goes home to have lunch, even if you're in high school and you go back to school in the afternoon. If I didn't like the food, and I would say I don't like it, he would just look at me and I would eat it. Never answered him back, never to my teachers. My children were born and raised here and they're very different. They're more open and opinionated. You know, they argue with me and they're very different. It's just, it's just a different culture. I have certain values from my culture, I'm not able to—

R: When my father gave me one look, that was it, but my mother, I could talk back to. And then she told him I wanted to run away from home.

K: And I think what you said was so true; it was the time. I never would think, even to this day I don't talk back to my mother and father, and it's not that I'm a goody-goody, but I just respect her. And if I have an opinion that's different from her, sometimes I keep it to myself because she takes it in a very like, you know, she takes it too personally. So I just don't want to deal with that, and I would just want to, you know, I won't go against her in any way. . . . They are still Mommy and Daddy to me and I would never, ever talk back to them. And with my daughter, like she said, it's different.

Perhaps the turns that followed my question could be read as saying, "No, the conflict isn't worse." But my experience in the discussion and my experience on reading the transcript is that they turned away from the story and from a consideration of the particular culture portrayed in the story to their personal experience. As I reflect on what happened, I think that the writing we asked the teachers to do may have contributed to that turning away.

Because Dorothy and I wanted to model a kind of teaching that was less teacher-centered than what is characteristically found in schools and because we were interested in finding out more about what the teachers we worked with were like as readers, for most of the sessions we simply asked them to write any kind of response to the reading that they wanted to. But we failed to recognize how our asking the group members to write that kind of response would privilege the sharing of personal experience.

Probst (1992a) explains that such free responses encourage readers to "respect their own readings" and to use the experience as a way "to articulate and investigate their own emotions and thoughts" (p. 65). Moreover, the responses gave each teacher a set piece to share. Rather than promoting interaction among group members, then, the writing seemed to encourage teachers to take extended turns that were not dependent on the turn that preceded them.

I know that our study group was not a classroom. However, it seems to me that the differences between the study group and classrooms only strengthens my argument about the potential effects of instruction that privileges personal experience. The teachers who volunteered for the study group were likely to have had an interest in multicultural literature and a predisposition to value reading that would let them learn about others. In addition, the teachers were much more experienced readers than are students, which would presumably make them less susceptible to the influence of instruction. Nonetheless, our sessions took on something of the character of the kind of "therapy session" that the book club member I quote in Chapter 2 said her club manages to avoid. The effect of instruction that emphasizes personal experience would likely be far more dramatic in a room full of inexperienced readers who may not share an interest in multicultural literature or a predisposition to value reading that teaches about other cultures.

Sharing personal experiences may be important. However, as I argue in Chapter 2, we're most likely to value what we learn about others when it helps us complete the common project of doing or critiquing an authorial reading. Moreover, I think that we have to recognize that personal sharing of the kind that occurred in our discussion of "Two Kinds" comes at a cost: the reduced likelihood of an imaginative engagement in the lives of others who are different from ourselves.

Ironically, Probst himself seems to recognize this cost when he writes of how literature can foster a knowledge of others. What's especially striking to me is that for Probst, knowledge of others is not knowledge of the characters about whom students are reading. Rather, it is knowledge of the other students in the class. He explains it this way: "One virtually inevitable result of concentrating upon individual responses to texts is that students will see similarities and differences within the classroom. They will notice that readers make sense of texts in different ways, that significance and meaning depend as much upon the reader as upon the text" (1992a, p. 65). He continues, "They might . . . be encouraged to see these differences as indications of the uniqueness of each reader, and as opportunities to learn something about others" (p. 66). I think that we have to recognize that at least in classrooms that are not themselves diverse—a condition that still exists in many schools, both suburban and urban—fostering this kind of knowledge will not achieve the goal of developing an ethical respect for those from other cultures. What's more, I think we have to recognize that even the most diverse class is not as diverse as the library.

Once again, I want to heed Peter's Chapter 1 warning to avoid the kind of easy inferences that come from oversimplifying the positions of others to set up a favorable contrast. I'm certainly in sympathy with Probst's calls to make literature instruction more humane by encouraging students to elaborate their responses and by treating those responses with dignity. However, I believe that such a strong emphasis on the pedagogy of personal experience runs the risk of homogenizing what students get to read and mitigates against experiencing the uncomfortable growth that can occur when they have to face a character whose life is much different from their own.

Richard Wright (1940/1966) makes a compelling case for the importance of this discomfort in his introduction to *Native Son*. He explains that he was spurred to create Bigger Thomas, a character who threatened both White and Black readers, because of the reception of *Uncle Tom's Children*—a book of short stories that he published before beginning *Native Son*. He explains:

> When the reviews of that book began to appear, I realized that I had made an awfully naive mistake. I found that I had written a book which even bankers' daughters could read and weep over and feel good about. I swore to myself that if I ever wrote another book, no one would weep over it; that it would be so hard and deep that they would have to face it without the consolation of tears. (p. xxvii)

If I understand Wright correctly, he's saying that *Uncle Tom's Children* allowed readers to appropriate the experiences of his characters through sensibilities that were already in place before readers began his book. But in order for a book to be transformative, it has to resist such appropriation. It has to force readers to accept it on its own terms.

Our task as teachers, therefore, is to devise instruction that helps students play the authorial audience and accept texts on their own terms while at the same time encouraging the kind of engagement that Probst seeks. Accepting this task as a central aim may result in rethinking the way we ground common instructional practices. For example, in the previous chapter I suggest using writing not as a way for readers to explore personal associations but rather as a way to document their engagement with characters as they play the narrative audience.

Doing so seemed to have an effect in the Literacy and Diversity Study Group. The only time we specified what the teachers should write in response to the text was when we read "Everyday Use," a story I summarize in Chapter 2. We asked teachers to track their understandings of the three main characters by identifying passages they found meaningful and explaining what they learned about the characters in those passages. Our discussion of "Everyday Use" had a much different feel than did our discussion of "Two Kinds," as the following exchange reveals:

M: So... she really did not have a strong appreciation of her culture because, I guess to me, what Alice Walker always repeats in a lot of her work is that the first and foremost appreciation of your culture begins with your mother. I mean, how can you appreciate or even act like you're going to appreciate your culture [unless] you have this respect for your mother? That doesn't make sense.

P: Well, I think that you have to first get to the point where you can find dignity in all kinds of work. And see it's easy to say now but when you have to—it takes a lot to appreciate your mother who's not doing what you think she should. Maybe not what someone else is doing.... You really have to grow to be able to see past that.... If you notice, the picture that was painted, everything on the outside was rough, but you had to go a little deeper in order to see other qualities of the mother....

D: What about, just picking up on that. I'm not using the exact words, but often people will use—You know, I never wanted to be like my mother but as I get older I find I'm my mother all over again. You know, words come out of my mouth that are things that my mother said. And I think for the men here probably the same thing with fathers. I'm just wondering about some other people, too. What does that mean to you in relationship to the story or to just life. I think there's a tension here with Dee. I think it's a tension that maybe goes beyond the story. When someone steps way outside of their culture that they've grown up in ..., they're drawn in two ways at once trying to find themselves.

A number of differences seem especially noteworthy here. The story was much more central to our conversation. In fact, the first speaker actually made Alice Walker a participant, which gave us a chance either to learn from her or to resist her. Dee's character was evaluated on her own terms, which, I have argued, is at the core of treating someone with respect. There was more give-and-take. In the first transcript, each turn related to the same initiating event, but they were not clearly related to one another. Such sequences call to mind spokes in a wheel. In contrast, in the second transcript, each turn built upon the previous turn, perhaps because we were working on the common project of understanding the characters.

I don't want to offer the journal prompt we used with "Everyday Use" as some kind of panacea. Our focus on the text brought with it an interesting problem: None of the White teachers participated in the exchange. When we talked about why, the White teachers noted that while they felt the discussion enriched their understanding of the story, they didn't feel that the personal experience they had gave them anything relevant to contribute. Projects can't be common unless everyone feels free to join in.

In Chapter 4 I argue for the importance of instruction in interpretive strategies. The argument of this chapter provides additional justification for such an approach. Recognizing that membership in the authorial audience requires more than a particular personal history suggests that teachers ought to devise instruction designed to give students something to contribute even (and maybe especially) when they recognize their personal experience is of little use. Literary knowledge of how characters are created, for example, could have been useful to our discussion of "Everyday Use." (See Smith, 1993, for a discussion of instruction designed to help develop that knowledge.)

Imagining the purpose of instruction as helping students play authorial audience and accept texts on their own terms may also cause a rethinking of other progressive instructional practices as well. Consider, for example, the use of drama. Rogers and O'Neill (1993) begin their discussion of drama this way:

> Besides being an imaginative alternative to more typical literature activities in the English classroom, drama is a powerful instructional tool. Drama provides an opportunity to transform classroom interaction patterns so that student talk becomes richer and students' responses become the center of the literary interpretive process. (p. 69)

This justification highlights students' responses. Consequently, it could lead to activities that take students away from the characters in and authors of the texts they are reading. For example, having students do a group improvisation about experiences in their lives that were evoked by a text seems to follow from the justification Rogers and O'Neill offer.

Other proponents of drama in the classroom ground their argument in a different way. Heathcote contends that in drama you "put yourself into other people's shoes and by using personal experience to help you understand their point of view you may discover more than you knew when you started" (quoted in Wilhelm, 1997, p. 100). Coupling this justification with an understanding of what it means to play the authorial audience would mean that teachers would not ask students to do improvisations that were inspired by a text but that centered on the students' lives. Rather, they would encourage students to use drama to imagine the lives of the characters about whom they were reading or to enact the sensibilities of the authors who created those characters. For example, students could take on the perspective of a character in a scene in which that perspective wasn't specified. In "Everyday Use," students could play Maggie as she listens to argumentative exchange between Dee/Wangero and Mama. Students could role-play a conversation among authors of various perspectives, for example, by having a "Meet the Press" or "Meetings of the Minds"–style discussion on the importance of one's African heritage between the Walker who wrote "Everyday Use" and the one who wrote *The Color Purple*. (See Wilhelm, 1997; Wilhelm & Edmiston, in press, for detailed suggestions of how to incorporate a wide variety of dramatic activities designed to achieve the goal of activating students' ethical imaginations.)

I'm not saying that Rogers and O'Neill would disapprove of such practices; I don't think they would. In fact, their discussion of the impact that drama had in the classroom they studied suggests that they see drama as a powerful way to help students enter a story world from the perspective of a literary character much different from themselves. Yet their emphasis remains on the way that drama can transform the politics of the classroom rather than on the potential for drama to promote an ethical respect for others.

My experience with the Literacy and Diversity Study Group taught me a very valuable lesson: We have to think about the theoretical bases for our instructional decisions or we might go astray. I don't think we ought to be content to devise instruction solely to promote the activity of the reader. I believe instead that we should seek ways to encourage students to engage actively with characters and authors while they sublimate their own experience. Doing so, it seems to me, is essential if students are to get the kind of gift that my father gave me.

"BETRAYING THE SENDER": THE RHETORIC AND ETHICS OF FRAGILE TEXTS

Peter J. Rabinowitz

IT WOULD BE POSSIBLE to read the first seven chapters of this book as a utopian call: If we pay attention to the processes of reading, we can help our students join the authorial audience. And if we can get our students to join the authorial audience, they can learn to share their experiences and join together in a productive and democratic discussion of their differences as actual readers without losing their engagement with the narrative audience. Specifically, such a practice, as Michael puts it in Chapter 6, can help us find that elusive "balance between honoring a student's experience and educating it." Furthermore, as Michael argues in Chapter 7, reading as authorial audience, which helps reduce the emphasis on the personality of the reader, can help students gain an ethical respect for others, even others well outside their usual circumstances. By bringing the author's voice into the conversation, authorial reading can help us understand and appreciate the lives of people —from different times, from different cultures—whose experiences have no other voice in the classroom. Even the most multicultural classroom, we would argue, is profoundly enriched by the addition of authorial voices.

But as the image of the "culture wars" reminds us, culture is an especially conflicted area these days. I fully agree with Michael's claim, following his description of the NPR discussion of *How the García Girls Lost Their Accents* (Chapter 2), that "authorial reading can ground truly progressive practice." And I fully agree that, say, an authorial reading of *Beloved* can improve us, ethically, by making us aware of how inadequate our own experiences and beliefs are when it comes to understanding the situation in which Sethe finds herself. Still, one of the aims of this book is to question the universal validity of such widely accepted practices as rereading; and it therefore seems only fair to question our own practices as well. Does reading as authorial audience always work to create proper respect for the text? Is it always appropriate?

RESISTING OURSELVES

In this chapter, I would like to turn the principle of resistance back on our own book, raising the possibility that our argument has been too optimistic, that there are certain circumstances under which authorial reading is, in fact, problematic. In particular, I want to question the image of "sharing" that runs through Michael's work, especially in Chapter 6. Michael believes "students will profit if all the members of the class share what they experienced as members of the narrative audience"—but is that always true? Can and should experiences as readers in fact always be shared? To my mind, the answer is no, and I would like to support this claim, and to complicate our model, by looking closely at a text that resists our theories.

SHARING SECRET JOKES: THE DOUBLE NARRATIVE OF *PASSING*

Let me ground my argument in a particular pedagogical problem. In the fall of 1992, I taught Nella Larsen's 1929 novel *Passing* in my course "Literature and Ethics." My aim was double. I wanted to expose my students to the carelessness of their reading; but I wanted, simultaneously, to dislodge them from their self-congratulatory liberalism, a liberalism more alert to racism than to homophobia. And I hoped to fulfill this twofold purpose by showing them that, in reading the novel from the perspective of race, as most of them did, they had defused much of its explosive power. Specifically, I treated *Passing* as an exemplification of its subject: a novel about lesbians passing as heterosexuals that passes as a novel about racial passing.

As an interpretation, I think that this reading of the novel was—and still is—reasonably sound. The story centers primarily on the rekindling of the relationship between two Black women: Clare Kendry Bellew (married to a White racist, John Bellew, who does not know she is Black) and her childhood friend Irene Westover Redfield (married to, but emotionally and sexually disengaged from, Brian, a prominent Black physician). And from the letter from Clare that opens the novel ("I . . . cannot help longing to be with you again, as I have never longed for anything before" [Larsen, 1929/1986, p. 145]) through Irene's recognition that Clare's beauty is a "torturing loveliness" that "had torn at [her] placid life" (p. 239), the novel hints at a "something else for which [Irene] could find no name" (p. 176), a "fascination, strange and compelling" (p. 161). This something else is "utterly beyond any experience or comprehension of hers" (p. 176)—and for decades, it was beyond the comprehension of most of Larsen's audience.

True, many early critics found something puzzling in the novel's psychological undercurrents. Thus, for instance, David Littlejohn (1966), speaking of both of Larsen's novels (*Quicksand* and *Passing*), pointed to "a certain nervous accuracy in their dramatizations of female psychology" (pp. 50–51). Michael Cooke (1984) noted that Irene and Clare "trigger depths in each other" (p. 66). And many insisted that this perplexing psychological strand was an aesthetic flaw (see, for instance, Bontemps [1972] and Singh [1975]). But more recent critics, such as Deborah McDowell (1986) and David L. Blackmore (1992), have made it clear that the novel has a homoerotic subtext (see also DuCille's [1993] "expansion" of McDowell's views). Blackmore argues, in fact, that *Passing* represents Brian's possible homosexuality as well as Irene's attraction to Clare. It is the lesbian relationship, however, that dominates the novel's thematics, and it is on this suppressed strand that I will be concentrating here.

Certainly, this strand is not beyond the grasp of sophisticated contemporary readers—at least those who, unlike Clare's husband, John, and even Irene's friend, the liberal White novelist Hugh Wentworth, have "learned the trick" of "tell[ing] the sheep from the goats" (p. 206). Part of my activity in class, then, consisted of teaching my students some tricks of close reading—and shocking them with the revelations that can come when heterosexist assumptions are abandoned.

Pedagogically, this strategy certainly worked—at least, for those students who had not read McDowell's (1986) introduction, which posits a similar (but, as we shall see, not quite identical) interpretation of *Passing* as a novel that "takes the form of the act it describes" (p. xxx). And yet, I felt a nagging dissatisfaction with my treatment of the text. It was not so much the Cleanth-Brooksian cast of my basic interpretive gesture, the way that my formulation (the novel exemplifies its subject) echoed Brooks's (1947) famous praise of Donne's "Canonization" as "an instance of the doctrine which it asserts" (p. 17). Nor did I suffer significant guilt about my position as a White, presumptively straight male interpreting a Black lesbian text: That kind of guilt by self-association ultimately leads, as Eve Kosofsky Sedgwick (1990) has argued, to the abandonment of reading and writing entirely (pp. 59–63). No, there was some other structural problem here, one that provoked the feeling that I had, in some way, tampered with a finely wrought text in such a way as to damage it. I am still not quite sure about the nature of this structural difficulty. But I would like to try to articulate my problems, as far as I can, here—problems that raise questions about our whole conception of what it is that we do as critics and teachers, especially in an increasingly multicultural environment.

When I suggest that the novel itself is passing—that it is an exemplification of its subject—what am I actually claiming? First of all, I am coalescing two kinds of passing. Granted, there are many typologies of passing.
Brody (1992), for instance, discusses the novel in terms of the distinction,
drawn from Jessie Fauset's *Plum Bun*, between "'play-acting'" and "'passing where a principle is involved'" (p. 1058); McLendon (1991) distinguishes between passing as a "state of mind" and passing as a "physical
act" (p. 158); and Wall (1986) makes a distinction between passing as a
"social phenomenon" and as a psychological one ("the loss of racial identity and the denial of self required of women who conform to restrictive
gender codes" [p. 105]). But for the purposes of this discussion, I'd like
to center on the distinction between what we might call "social passing"
and what I call "rhetorical passing." Social passing consists of adopting
a disguise in an attempt to trick or mislead people into thinking you are
something you are not: White, straight, Christian, aristocrat, whatever.
It doesn't require that anyone other than the person passing know the
truth—and, in fact, it works most efficiently when the secret is absolutely
secure. But the novel isn't really passing in that sense; rather, the novel as
a text exemplifies rhetorical passing (not to suggest, of course, that rhetoric is not "social"), an act that summons up a significantly more complex
relationship between passer and audience. That is, at least as it is the-
matized according to the rules of coherence operative in this novel, rhetorical passing is not simply a disguise, but a virtuoso tightrope performance, a flirtation with risk by flaunting your disguise in a context in
which you know that it will *fool only some people*—an act, in other words,
that has built into it the exhilarating possibility of exposure and destruction. This kind of passing is most clearly dramatized in the novel's crucial
tea-party scene. Here, Irene and Gertrude Martin, one of Clare's other
light-skinned Black friends, have to navigate a provocative conversation
with Clare's husband John, who is ignorant of their racial identities. It is
a conversation where the meaning of each utterance—even nonlinguistic
utterances like Gertrude's "queer little suppressed sound, a snort or a
giggle" (p. 172)—varies, depending on the relative positions and relative
knowledges of speaker and audience. And this complicated rhetorical
field produces complex and unsettling effects. On the one hand, it is a
harrowing experience, and yet— as Irene realizes—"it was rather a joke"
(p. 175). Apparently, Clare gets some perverse delight out of it; and Irene's
husband Brian later insists that the conversation must have been spiced
with pleasure for Irene, too, since "'you, my dear had all the advantage.
You know what his opinion of you was, while he—'" (p. 185).

   To talk of the novel as an instance of rhetorical passing, of course,
inevitably involves authorial intention: for, as I have defined it, rhetorical
passing is what speech act theorists, following J. L. Austin, call a perform-

ative. In contrast to "constatives" (statements that can be true or false), performatives are utterances "in which to *say* something is to *do* something" (Austin, 1955/1975, p. 12). Thus, for instance, saying "I bet" is not to make a statement "about something" but to perform the act of betting. And since, as Austin points out, "actions can only be performed by persons" (p. 60), performatives cannot be discussed without some consideration of intention. More important for my analysis, though, rhetorical passing involves not one but two audiences. It involves not an authorial and a narrative audience (as any fictional text will have), but two different authorial audiences, two assumed, intended, and *necessary* targets for the text. It requires one audience (what we might call the "gullible authorial audience") that is ignorant of the subtext and a second audience (the "discerning authorial audience") that not only understands the subtext but also realizes, and even relishes, the ignorance of the first audience. Rhetorical passing thus has close connections to those forms of "Signifyin(g)" that serve as "mode[s] of verbal masking" (Gates, 1988, p. 77).

In this regard, *Passing* is quite different from *Beloved*. It may be painful for a reader, especially a White reader, to try to join Morrison's authorial audience. It may even be, as James Phelan (1996) has argued, that the obstacles for the reader of *Beloved* involve not merely the difficult (a "recalcitrance that yields to our explanatory efforts") but also the stubborn ("recalcitrance that will not yield" [p. 178]). Even at the end, Phelan insists, the title character eludes him: "I still cannot—and do not want to—transform Beloved's stubbornness into a difficulty to solve, but I comprehend some of the reasons for that stubbornness" (p. 189). For Phelan, however, that stubbornness is part of the value of the text for the authorial audience. It is not a trick played on a gullible audience (like the secret subtext of *Passing*) but a serious attempt to communicate the radical disjuncture of slave experience.

To argue that *Passing* has these two authorial audiences, of course, is not to claim that one must read the novel simply as "about" race or "about" sexuality. Once they recognize the novel's lesbian strand, the members of the discerning authorial audience are apt to use rules of coherence to tie the two thematic levels together. They will thus be likely to interpret *Passing*, in the end, at least in part as a novel about what Judith Butler (1993) has aptly called "the interwoven vectors of sexuality and race" (p. 173). This interpretation, however, is only open to the reader who recognizes the lesbian elements in the novel to begin with. Furthermore, this act of interpretation does not alter what we might call the rhetorical constellation created by the text: the existence of two audiences, one of which delights in having "all the advantage" over the other. It is this double audience, and the kind of flaunting that it makes possible, that structurally distinguishes rhetorically passing texts from other complex texts that happen to have hidden meanings beneath the surface—whether that be the gay subtext of *Billy Budd*, for instance, or the political allegory of *The Wizard of Oz*.

This second, discerning authorial audience can be very small. When Alban Berg composed his *Lyric Suite* in 1926, he presented it to the world as if it were a string quartet without a program; but the work was simultaneously (and secretly) an elaborately coded musical evocation of a brief, but very intense, adulterous affair he had had with Hannah Fuchs-Robettin. Berg, however, apparently felt that the rhetorical act he was performing required that *someone,* even if only one person, know the truth, both about the meaning of the quartet and about the fact that other listeners did not. So he sent an annotated score to the only person who could be trusted both to understand and to keep the secret: Hannah herself. That the secret was eventually made public—although well after the deaths of the principals—reminds us of the risk involved even in what appear to be the most clandestine acts of passing. A somewhat larger, but still extremely limited, discerning authorial audience was involved many years ago in the case of a symphony written by a university musician who had been denied tenure. The symphony had a double message, allowing a few friends who had helped the composer during his tenure fight to share the exquisite pleasure of watching those who had axed him applaud politely (and uncomprehendingly) after listening to what was in fact a scathing musical critique of their own behavior and character. Jean Anhouilh's *Antigone,* originally performed in France during the German occupation, had a similar message for the knowledgeable underneath its classic exterior.

It's in regard to this double audience that my analysis departs from McDowell's. McDowell (1986) treats *Passing* as a traditional novel of revelation and then criticizes Larsen for failing to follow the lesbian subplot to the end, arguing that she "does the opposite of what she has promised" (p. xxxi). By my reading, though, the novel is not a flawed novel of revelation, not a *Good Soldier* gone AWOL, but, on the contrary, a cannily constructed exemplar of a very different genre. The novel certainly reveals, as Pamela L. Caughie (1992) puts it, Irene's "desire not to know" (p. 778): Larsen explicitly refers to "heights and depths of feeling that she, Irene Redfield, had never known. Indeed, never cared to know" (Larsen, 1929/1986, p. 195). But if "what is most striking about *Passing* are the many things that are *not* said, narrated, or verbalized" (Caughie, 1992, p. 780), that is because *Passing* also reveals (if that is the right word for it) Larsen's desire not to tell: not simply the desire, as Caughie suggests, to school her ignorant readers "in difference and indirection" (p. 788)—as I was schooling my own students—but rather the desire to shut them out entirely. (For yet another possible generic placement, see McLendon's [1991] suggestion that *Passing* is a novel of failed self-understanding.) It's probably futile to speculate on Larsen's motivations for her choices—although it's likely that she was responding, at least in part, to precisely those repressive, even violent social forces that are figured in Clare's death at the moment when her husband learns the truth of her racial origins. But whatever her motivations, Larsen worked within those constraints in an artistically viable way; and even if the cultural climate is less repressive today, it doesn't follow as a matter of course that we, as readers and critics, owe nothing to the artistic decisions she made in 1929.

What happens when we reveal the secret of this novel? Generally, we reconfigure the rhetorical constellation of the text—as we do, for instance, when we transcribe an oral account or publish a poem intended for manuscript circulation or record a piece of aleatoric music. But these reconfigurations are all quite different; to be more specific about the operations of this particular novel, we need to look at the details of the speaker/audience dynamics in rhetorical passing. This is tricky, though, for rhetorical passing turns out to belong to a special kind of speech act that is awkward to talk about. In *How to Do Things with Words*, Austin (1955/1975) makes the distinction between explicit and implicit performatives. Explicit performatives are those in which the illocutionary force is itself named in the act of utterance. When I say "I promise you that I won't be late," the phrase "I promise" explicitly distinguishes my speech act from, say, a prediction or a guess. Implicit performatives, in contrast, always leave something uncertain; if I simply say "The pizza will have anchovies on it," am I promising, threatening, or uttering a grim prognostication?

But rhetorical passing seems to belong to yet a third category, which—borrowing from a long tradition of not naming homosexuality, a tradition to which Larsen belongs—I'll call "unnameable speech acts." These are acts in which *not naming* the act in question is not only a possibility, but an *essential* part of the felicity conditions of successful performance—speech acts in which to name the act is simultaneously to nullify it. The principle behind unnameable speech acts is quite different from that governing Ann Banfield's (1982) notion of "unspeakable sentences." Banfield's concern is literary sentences (for instance, sentences of narratorless narration) that can be written but that do not occur in normal speech. Her category is really a matter of social practice: When uttered in conversation, unspeakable sentences may seem awkward, but they do not necessarily change their status as speech acts. The category of unnameable speech acts is, in contrast, determined by their very constitution as speech acts. Austin (1955/1975) touches on this problem—coincidentally, he uses the phrase "in passing" to describe his discussion—when he points out that not all performatives have explicit equivalents: "For example, we cannot say 'I imply that,' 'I insinuate,' &c" (p. 88). But the class is actually larger and more significant than Austin's cursory examination would suggest. Lying is a clear example: You cannot lie successfully if you announce that that's what you're doing. Bluffing, as poker players well know, is another unnameable speech act. So, more generally, are many acts that involve irony and hyperbole: an announcement that you're exaggerating (in contrast to an announcement that you're estimating) already undermines the act that you're performing. Likewise, you cannot begin a faculty motion—as a colleague of mine once proposed that we do—with the phrase, "The faculty hereby damns with faint praise . . ." Certain more poetic acts cannot be named without tempering their effectiveness, either; for instance, what Willa Cather (1936) once described as "the inexplicable presence of the thing not named, of the overtone divined by the ear but not heard by it, the verbal mood, the emotional aura of the fact or the thing or the deed, that gives high quality to the novel or the drama, as well as to poetry itself" (p. 50).

But because of its double authorial audience, rhetorical passing is even more intricate than such unnameable speech acts as lying or bluffing or damning with faint praise. Lying and bluffing require a speaker who knows the truth and an audience that does not; damning with faint praise requires that both the speaker and the audience not be fooled. But rhetorical passing requires a speaker and *two* audiences: one audience that's ignorant and another that knows the truth *and remains silent about it.*

It is this curious demand—that those who know what the work is doing need to refrain from speaking about it if the work is to fulfill its rhetorical aims—that makes Larsen's novel and other rhetorically passing narratives instances of a broader category, what I would like to call "fragile" texts, texts whose performative success requires the complicit silence of precisely those who know the most about them. And that paradoxical quality raises serious questions about at least three commonly held assumptions, questions that bring, in their wake, ethical entanglements for any teacher or critic wanting to take these texts on.

Granted, certain critical positions neatly detour around the ethical problems raised by textual fragility. For extreme adherents of what Steven Mailloux (1985) has called "readerly idealism" (theorists who believe that no textual facts are independent of the reader's interpretive procedures), that's because their theoretical commitments turn the problem into a nonproblem: All literary artifacts would be equally fragile. The problem is similarly moot, I suspect, for the firmest adherents of what he calls "textual realism," for whom texts exist fully on their own, for to believe that readers could mar texts would be to subscribe to some variant of the affective fallacy. But I suspect that most readers of this book fall uneasily somewhere between these conveniently conflict-free poles, and it is to those readers that I address these arguments.

CHALLENGING OUR ASSUMPTIONS

To begin with, my analysis of *Passing* challenges a cherished, if rarely articulated, theoretical principle that we might call the Doctrine of the Macho Text. There are two variants of this dogma, although, in the end, they amount to much the same thing. The first variant is the belief that significant texts are tough enough to handle whatever critical private eyes might dish out in the course of their investigations. Indeed, even those of us who are audience-oriented critics and who believe that readers in part construct the texts they read often have some implied image, as I did until recently, of a textual sturdiness sufficient to hold up against potential readerly demolition. For instance, behind my own metaphor of the text as unassembled gas grill was the assumption that if a reader messed up, the text could be taken apart again and sent back to the store for sale to someone else who would be better able to put it together. The second variant is the conviction that texts that *are* fragile belong to inferior genres and probably deserve whatever they get anyway. From this perspective, the canon consists not of those texts that have aged gracefully but of those that have withstood the critical third degree to which we subject them. What, after all, *are* the clearest instances of fragile texts? Some are morally suspect: plagiarisms, for instance (and it's a cruel coincidence that Larsen's own brief literary career ended when she was accused of plagiarizing a short story)—and frauds and fakes more generally. Who really feels any sense of responsibility toward *Naked Came the Stranger* or Marius Casadesus' fraudulent Mozart violin concerto? And fragile texts that are not morally suspect are often aesthetically suspect, members of despised genres like the classical detective story, texts whose fragility doesn't matter because they're disposable anyway.

Passing, however, is neither an immoral nor a trivial text—and it turns out to be even more fragile than most detective stories, much less *The Crying Game*, a film that, for whatever reasons, actually increased its box-office take after its secret became more widely known. A whodunit like *I, the Jury* (which, as I mentioned in Chapter 5, I had assigned in the same course) loses its fragility (along, unfortunately, with most of its rhetorical value) once it is read: It can thus be discussed without harm by readers who have already finished it. That is, although Spillane's novel, like rhetorically passing texts, requires a double vision, the rhetorical constellation that results from this duality is quite different. Instead of having two audiences comprised of different readers at the same time, we have a single group of readers who interpret the book differently at different times. Thus, like *Passing,* the novel depends for its effect, at least initially, on a gullible reader who misses the clues; if the actual reader is too discerning (either because he or she has been told the ending beforehand or because he or she is a sharper reader than the one Spillane was writing for or because, like Philip, he or she reads the ending first), the effect of the surprise ending is nullified. That effect also depends on the existence of a discerning reader who can look back at those clues and retrospectively recognize their meaning. But if it works as intended, Spillane's novel actually moves the reader from gullible to discerning in the process of reading.

It might seem that the detective story is not really special in this respect, since in most novels the authorial audience changes during the course of reading. But among the things that make *I, the Jury* different from, say, Proust's *Remembrance of Things Past* in this regard are (1) the degree to which the change in the authorial audience is simply a matter of increased knowledge about the facts of the text and (2) the extent to which the total emotional effect of the novel depends on this cognitive shift. While Proust, too, relies on the shock of discovery, the authorial audience's emotional and philosophical changes are far more important than any accumulation of data; and that shock is but one (small) element contributing to much larger and more complex effects, rather than the novel's primary aim. The novels lie, in other words, at almost opposite ends of the continuum between what Kenneth Burke (1924/1968) calls "suspense" and what he calls "eloquence."

To put it differently, *I, the Jury*'s fragility is temporally bound; the requirement that discerning readers remain silent about their knowledge is in force only when they are talking to people who have not yet read the novel.

Thus, once everyone in my class had finished *I, the Jury,* we could discuss it freely without threatening the text's post-reading rhetorical constellation. A more sophisticated detective story, like Chandler's *The Long Goodbye,* of course, posits initial readers who are less gullible than Spillane's—and it shapes out a more interesting trajectory as it moves them toward enlightenment. *The Long Goodbye*'s underlying structure, however, is similar, and as in Spillane's novel, the fragility vanishes once the novel is finished. But *Passing* remains fragile (perhaps more fragile

than ever) even after it is read: The novel maintains its delicate position-
ings of its multiple audiences past the end. As a consequence, letting
everyone in on what the novel calls "some secret joke"—a joke that even
Irene, the novel's central consciousness, doesn't ever quite get—destroys
precisely the intricate rhetorical negotiations the novel has been working
to achieve.

Second, my reading of *Passing* tests the limits of some favorite pluralist metaphors. It's common to claim that we can read texts through different lenses (a metaphor that supports the Doctrine of the Macho Text by
implying, in contrast to all that quantum mechanics has taught, that the
act of observation itself doesn't significantly alter the text in question), or
that we can read texts wearing different theoretical hats (which similarly
assumes that it is the reader, not the text, who changes), or (a metaphor
I used myself above) that we can look at texts from different perspectives.
But if we think instead of critical practice as a collection of old saws, then
we might come to some different conclusions about our activities: As
critics and teachers, we may not be viewing the text so much as hacking
it up. At the very least, the example of *Passing* urges us to consider the
possibility that some theoretical positions may be incompatible with
some texts—not because they don't expose the workings of the text, but
precisely because they *do* and, in so doing, inflict significant damage.

Third, *Passing* challenges the belief—one that Michael and I have implicitly maintained for most of this book—that teaching students to be
more self-conscious, more aware of what they are doing when they read
is always and necessarily a good thing. As long as we think of students
as more or less equivalent fungible goods, of course, then it's easy to
maintain the economic position that the more knowledge you create, the
better—that our job as teachers is to turn gullible readers into discerning
ones. But *Passing* reminds us that not every text puts all its readers (even
all the members of its authorial audience) in the same position. That is,
by providing one student with a key to the novel, we may be draining the
novel of the value it might hold for another student in the same class—its
supportive value to a closeted student, for instance, in its simultaneous
acknowledgment of her situation *and* its agreement to maintain the secret,
as well as its provision of a secret metaphor through which she might
talk about her situation without having to claim it or even name it. And
who am I to say what kinds of bonds the novel, as written, serves to foster
within the group of understanding readers?

In other words, to the extent that reading *Passing* is a complex rhetorical game that serves some social or psychological or aesthetic function
for actual readers who are capable of becoming members of the discerning authorial audience—to the extent, for instance, that the novel pro-

vides a certain kind of pleasure and support for a still-oppressed group—
then intervention in the rhetorical workings of that text has significant
practical (as opposed to theoretical) consequences for flesh-and-blood
readers. Blimberism, as Michael has argued compellingly, especially in
Chapter 6, cuts readers off from their moral engagement with the characters in a text by privileging their relations with authors. But in this case,
teaching our students to engage, as members of the discerning authorial
audience, on the narrative level may have an adverse impact on their
relation to other members of the actual audience—for instance, those closeted students. And it is hard to argue that respect for characters takes
priority over respect for other readers.

In suggesting that my analysis of *Passing* challenges the widespread
commitment to teaching students to be less gullible, of course, I do not
mean to imply that it supplies any easy alternative. Teaching the novel
in such a way as to keep its fragility intact is charged with ethical difficulties as well. For instance, the relationship between the novel's two authorial audiences is not symmetrical—specifically, the discerning authorial audience is in some sense profiting from (or at least gaining a certain
pleasure from) the ignorance of the gullible readers. Such a teaching strategy thus runs the risk of authorizing some students only by making others their dupes, and thereby creating an ethically problematic in-group
phenomenon. More troubling in the current cultural climate, it may run
the risk of encouraging closeted students to remain closeted, or at least
of muting a possible occasion for them to think differently about coming
out. Indeed, failure to illuminate the novel's lesbian strand may have the
dangerous consequence of psychologically undermining those students
who have recognized it by making them suspicious of their own perceptions. My aim here, in other words, is not to chart out a course of action
but rather to remind ourselves that fragile texts seem to make legitimate,
but competing, demands (including ethical demands) on teachers and
critics—and that one of these demands might be the demand of the text
for silence.

As I have suggested, none of this would matter much if *Passing* were
an isolated curio—a special genre with only one or two members. I don't
know how many texts are passing, but I do know that, more broadly,
there are lots of fragile texts, fragile in different ways perhaps, but sharing
the awkward quality that talking about them in certain ways controverts
their rhetorical intent: "serious" detective stories that don't disclose their
solutions (Robbe-Grillet's *Les Gommes*, Witold Gombrowicz's *Cosmos*, perhaps even *The Turn of the Screw*); African American spirituals; Mozart's
The Magic Flute, with its Masonic secrets; the Shostakovich symphonies
and many nineteenth- and twentieth-century Russian novels—indeed, all

works created with one eye on the censor and another on an initiated audience that gets much of its pleasure not only from reading the message but also from realizing that the censor has been tricked. And as the literary profession grows increasingly multicultural in its concerns, the potential pitfalls awaiting politically responsible critics are increasing. It is easy, as good liberals, to express outrage at the ways in which, say, British imperialists destroyed the integrity of ancient artifacts as they ripped them from their context and carted them off to the British Museum. As Gloria Anzaldúa (1987) puts it, "Ethnocentrism is the tyranny of Western aesthetics. An Indian mask in an American museum is transposed into an alien aesthetic system where what is missing is the presence of power invoked through performance ritual. It has become a conquered thing, a dead 'thing' separated from nature and, therefore, its power" (p. 68). But isn't it possible that we're doing something similar as we "interpret" colonial and postcolonial or other resistance texts, giving our students interpretive keys to cultures that have been trying to counter precisely the cultural forces that the American academy represents? It's one thing for readers to learn to resist texts; but what are we to do when the texts are specifically trying to resist us?

To give but one brief example: In my literary theory course I have taught Gloria Anzaldúa's *Borderlands*, a book written in a rich linguistic polyphony, moving, as she puts it, from "English to Castillian Spanish to the North Mexican dialect to Tex-Mex to a sprinkling of Nahuatl to a mixture of all of these" (1987, unnumbered page). Some of the non-English material is translated, but most of it is not. I could, perhaps, find someone to produce a translation and pass it out to the class—it would certainly make the book more intelligible to those of us without much knowledge of Spanish. But in dispelling ignorance in this way, I would simultaneously be appropriating a text explicitly constructed to resist such appropriation. Indeed, one of the things that makes *Borderlands as it stands* valuable for my class is that it empowers my Spanish-speaking students. As Julie Wolfe, one of my other students, put it,

> Not only is it a wonderful book, but I feel I was able to begin to understand some of the exclusion that goes on. I can't read Spanish . . . and I felt left out of those passages, but that could be how Chicanos . . . and Mexicans . . . feel when we say everything in English, refusing to listen to them because of different accents, or a few ungrammatical sentences. I . . . feel like I wasn't meant to understand those passages. She directed those passages at people who can and do understand what she wants them to.

Katie Winn, in one of my wife Nancy's classes, made a similar point with regard to Oscar Wilde's *Picture of Dorian Gray* during the same semester:

> The homosexual code in this book seems so obvious to me. Is this because of the class? My comp lit training? My awareness of the code since it's the '90s? I don't know. I said in class that I felt guilty recognizing the code. For some reason I feel as though Wilde would not want me, a heterosexual female, to be able to see it. Does my knowledge of their code uncloset them? Make them vulnerable? . . . Knowledge is power, especially when I'm in a position of power already. Perhaps I feel guilty about having both powers of knowing the code and having heterosexual privilege. [Thanks to both students for agreeing to have their private messages made public.]

In other words, it may be not only the struggle to understand but also the experience of failing to succeed in that struggle that provides the non-Spanish-speaking student with the most valuable reading experience. My analysis of *Borderlands* overlaps significantly with Reed Way Dasenbrock's (1987) critique of the calls for intelligibility in what he calls "implicitly multicultural" narratives (p. 10). But while Dasenbrock, too, recognizes that these texts are written for two simultaneous audiences, he doesn't see their connection in quite the way I do. Dasenbrock is largely concerned with the educational value of the work performed by the undiscerning authorial audience (what he sometimes calls the "monocultural reader," although of course the reader might well be conversant in several cultures and still not in the culture of the particular text in question). Although the text has a different value for the "multicultural reader," that value, in his analysis, does not depend on the existence of the undiscerning audience. My interest here is, rather, in the interaction of the two audiences and in the possible educational value of the transformation of power dynamics that such a book can create in the classroom.

And yet here, too, the ethical paradoxes mount up. So far, my argument has rested on the implicit assumption that the communities of discerning readers of the fragile texts in question are ethically positive, or at least neutral. But it's possible, as well, that a fragile text—say, *The Protocols of the Elders of Zion*, a manuscript forged by the tsarist secret police in order to justify anti-Semitism—may help nourish a sense of community that is in fact oppressive. And how can we decide what communities are worthy of our support?

CONCLUSION

So where does this leave teachers and critics? I certainly don't have any clear advice about how to determine which texts are fragile, much less about how to handle them. In the past I have taken a polemical stand against unswerving allegiance to close reading, and in this book I have questioned the value of re-reading. But I am not ready to take a position against public talk about reading entirely. I'm not sure I can even take what would seem an unobjectionable conservationist position against destroying fragile texts, for at least two reasons. First, there is a cognitive problem. As I've said, it's not easy to recognize fragile texts; and it may well be that we can't be sure which texts are fragile texts until we've shattered them. Even this chapter betrays Larsen's text; in fact, when I asked my research assistant, Christine Rosalia, to check the citations in an earlier version for accuracy, I suggested that she quickly read through the whole chapter first. She got to the end of the first paragraph and said, "Thanks! Now you've ruined the book for me."

But there is also an ethical dimension to the question. A conservationist stand would certainly respect the texts in question, but only by making it impossible for students to resist them—and as we have argued throughout this book, unquestioning respect is ethically suspect. It's not only fragile texts like *The Protocols of the Elders of Zion* that demand resistance: even *Passing*, a novel I greatly admire, demands (?) resistance from some people as well.

If readers only confronted such problems when reading fragile texts, then perhaps it would not be worth much attention. But I believe that the example of fragile texts serves as a broader caveat. In the end, there are no risk-free courses of action for teachers and critics, no way to guarantee that any discussion of a text, even if it begins with an authorial reading, will be bruise-free. I'm not even sure that avoiding bruises should be a goal. Some feelings ought to be bruised, ought to be challenged. But weighing what I take to be a positive discomfort like that of Nancy's student upon reading Wilde against the bruising a gay student might feel at yet another assertion of heterosexual privilege and power is an enormously complicated task. If we take seriously the possibility that art can improve us, we have to take seriously the possibility that our reading will maim us. But even if we can never eliminate the risks involved—in fact, especially if we can never eliminate the risks involved—it is still worth discussing how to articulate them and how to confront them responsibly. And the more we raise culturally charged questions in the classroom— the more we talk about issues of sexuality, ethnicity, and global politics— the more urgent the need for such discussion becomes.

In the end, then, this cautionary chapter does not really undercut the basic arguments of this book so much as force us to refine them. The central premise of our argument has been that the questions that most touch on the lives of our students—including risky questions about culturally charged issues—ought to be at the heart of our pedagogical practice; and the central argument has been that authorial reading is the best way to reach those goals. Authorial reading may not be a panacea to protect us from classroom discussions that hurt some of the participants, or even to protect texts from readers who hurt them; but in the end, it provides the best way that we know to get at those problems.

REFERENCES

Acker, A. (1992, March/April). Arts: Women behind the camera. *Ms.,2*, 64–67.

Addison, C. (1994). Once upon a time: A reader-response approach to prosody. *College English, 56*, 655–678.

Allen, S. (1995, November). *The languages of school.* Paper presented at the annual meeting of the National Council of Teachers of English, San Diego.

Anderson, D. T. (1988). *The effects of direct instruction in interpretive strategies on students' reading of drama.* Unpublished master's thesis, University of Chicago.

Anderson, R. C., & Pichert, J. W. (1978). Recall of previously unrecallable information following a shift in perspective. *Journal of Verbal Learning and Verbal Behavior, 17*, 1–12.

Anzaldúa, G. (1987). *Borderlands/La frontera: The new mestiza.* San Francisco: Aunt Lute Books.

Applebee, A. N. (1989a). *The teaching of literature in programs with reputations for excellence in English* (Report 1.1). Albany, NY: Center for Learning and Teaching of Literature.

Applebee, A. N. (1989b). *A study of book-length works taught in high school English courses* (Report 1.2). Albany, NY: Center for the Learning and Teaching of Literature.

Applebee, A. N. (1993). *Literature in the secondary school: Studies of curriculum and instruction in the United States.* Urbana, IL: National Council of Teachers of English.

Arac, J. (1994). An introductory texts and theory course. In D. F. Sadoff & W. E. Cain (Eds.), *Teaching contemporary theory to undergraduates* (pp. 169–178). New York: Modern Language Association.

Austen, J. (1933). *Sense and sensibility.* In R. W. Chapman (Ed.), *The novels of Jane Austen in five volumes* (3rd ed.; Vol. 3.) London: Oxford University Press. (Original work published 1811)

Austin, J. L. (1975). *How to do things with words* (2nd ed.; J. O. Urmson & M. Sbisà, Eds.). Cambridge, MA: Harvard University Press. (Original work published 1955)

Bakhtin, M. M. (1984). *Problems of Dostoevsky's poetics.* Minneapolis: University of Minnesota Press.

Bakhtin, M. M. (1986). *Speech genres and other late essays.* Austin: University of Texas Press.

Banfield, A. (1982). *Unspeakable sentences: Narration and representation in the language of fiction.* Boston: Routledge & Kegan Paul.

Barthes, R. (1974). *S/Z* (R. Miller, Trans.). New York: Hill & Wang. (Original work published 1970)

Barthes, R. (1977) The death of the author (S. Heath, Trans.). In *Image—music—text* (pp. 142–148). New York: Hill & Wang. (Original work published 1968)

Beach, R. (1985). Discourse conventions and researching response to literary dialogue. In C. Cooper (Ed.), *Researching response to literature and the teaching of literature: Points of departure* (pp. 103–127). Norwood, NJ: Ablex.

Beverley, J. (1993). *Against literature.* Minneapolis: University of Minnesota Press.

Blackmore, D. L. (1992). "That unreasonable restless feeling": The homosexual subtexts of Nella Larsen's *Passing. African American Review, 26*, 475–484.

Bleich, D. (1975). *Readings and feelings: An introduction to subjective criticism.* Urbana, IL: National Council of Teachers of English.

Bleich, D. (1978). *Subjective criticism.* Baltimore: Johns Hopkins University Press.

Bleich, D. (1988). *The double perspective: Language, literacy, and social relations.* New York: Oxford University Press.

Bloom, H. (1973). *The anxiety of influence; a theory of poetry.* New York: Oxford University Press.

Bontemps, A. (1972). *The Harlem renaissance remembered: Essays edited with a memoir.* New York: Dodd, Mead.

Booth, W. C. (1974). *A rhetoric of irony.* Chicago: University of Chicago Press.

Booth, W. C. (1983a). A new strategy for establishing a truly democratic criticism. *Daedalus, 112*, 193–214.

Booth, W. C. (1983b). *The rhetoric of fiction* (2nd ed.). Chicago: University of Chicago Press.

Booth, W. C. (1988). *The company we keep: An ethics of fiction.* Berkeley: University of California Press.

Brennan, T. (1995). Rap redoubt: The beauty of the mix. *Critical Inquiry, 22*, 159–161.

Brody, J. D. (1992). Clare Kendry's "true" colors: Race and class conflict in Nella Larsen's *Passing. Callaloo, 15*, 1053–1065.

Brooks, C. (1947). *The well wrought urn: Studies in the structure of poetry.* New York: Harcourt, Brace & World.

Brooks. G. (1987a). Life for my child is simple, and is good. In *Blacks* (p. 120). Chicago: Third World Press.

Brooks, G. (1987b). Music for martyrs. In *Blacks* (pp. 494–495). Chicago: Third World Press.

Brooks, G. (1987c). Young Afrikans. In *Blacks* (p. 500). Chicago: Third World Press.

Brooks, P. (1984). *Reading for the plot: Design and intention in narrative.* New York: Knopf.

Burgess, A. (1988). *A clockwork orange.* New York: Ballantine.

Burke, K. (1968). Psychology and form. In *Counter-statement* (2nd ed; 29–44). Berkeley and Los Angeles: University of California Press. (Original work published 1924)

Butler, J. (1993). *Bodies that matter: On the discursive limits of "sex".* New York: Routledge.

Callaghan, M. (1971). All the years of her life. In H. Granite, M. Black, & J. Stanchfields (Eds.), *Vibrations* (pp. 84–89). New York: Houghton Mifflin.

Cather, W. (1936). *Not under forty.* New York: Knopf.

Caughie, P. L. (1992). "Not entirely strange, . . . not entirely friendly": *Passing* and pedagogy. *College English, 54,* 775–793.

Cazden, C. (1992). *Whole language plus: Essays on literacy in the United States and New Zealand.* New York: Teachers College Press.

Christian, B. (1985). *Black feminist criticism: Perspectives on black women writers.* New York: Pergamon/Athene.

Coles, R. (1989). *The call of stories: Teaching and the moral imagination.* Boston: Houghton Mifflin.

Conrad, J. (1986). *The collected letters of Joseph Conrad, volume 2: 1898–1902* (F. R. Karl & L. Davies, Eds.). Cambridge, UK: Cambridge University Press.

Conrad, J. (1996). *Heart of darkness.* In R. C. Murfin (Ed.), *Heart of Darkness: Complete, authoritatve text with biographical and historical contexts, critical history, and essays from five contemporary critical perspectives* (2nd ed.; pp. 17–95). Boston: Bedford Books of St. Martin's Press. (Original work published 1899)

Cooke, M. G. (1984). *Afro-American literature in the twentieth century: The achievement of intimacy.* New Haven: Yale University Press.

Cox, J. M. (1986). Humor as vision in Faulkner. In D. Fowler & A. J. Abadie (Eds.), *Faulkner and humor: Faulkner and Yoknapatawpha, 1984* (pp. 1–20). Jackson: University Press of Mississippi.

Dasenbrock, R. W. (1987). Intelligibility and meaningfulness in multicultural literature in English. *PMLA, 102,* 10–19.

Delpit, L. (1988). The silenced dialogue: Power and pedagogy in educating other people's children. *Harvard Educational Review, 58,* 280–298.

Denby, D. (1990, March 26). Dirty Harriet. *New York, 23,* 76–77.

Dewey, J. (1944). *Democracy and education.* New York: Free Press. (Original work published 1916)

Dewey, J. (1964). My pedagogic creed. In R. Archambault (Ed.), *John Dewey on education* (pp. 427–439). Chicago: University of Chicago Press. (Original work published 1897)

Dickens, C. (1907). *Dombey and son.* New York: Dutton/Everyman's Library. (Original work published 1846–48)

Dilg, M. (1995). The opening of the American mind: Challenges in the cross-cultural teaching of literature. *English Journal, 84*(3), 18–25.

Dock, J. B., with Allen, D. R., Palais, J., & Tracy, K. (1996). "But one expects that": Charlotte Perkins Gilman's "The Yellow Wallpaper" and the shifting light of scholarship. *PMLA, 111,* 52–65.

Downing, D. B., Harkin, P. & Sosnoski, J. J. (1994). Configurations of lore: The changing relations of theory, research, and pedagogy. In D. B. Downing (Ed.), *Changing classroom practices: Resources for literary and cultural studies* (pp. 3–34). Urbana, IL: National Council of Teachers of English.

DuCille, A. (1993). Blue notes on black sexuality: Sex and the texts of Jessie Fauset and Nella Larsen. *Journal of the History of Sexuality, 3,* 418–444.

Duffey, Mrs. E. B. (1911). *The ladies' and gentlemen's etiquette: A complete manual of the manners and dress of American society. Containing forms of letters, invitations, acceptances and regrets. With a copious index* (new rev. ed.). Philadelphia: McKay.

Eco, U. (1979). *The role of the reader: Explorations in the semiotics of texts.* Blooming-ton: Indiana Unviersity Press.

Enciso, P. (1992). Creating the story world. In J. Many & C. Cox (Eds.) *Reader stance and literary understanding: Exploring the theories, research and practice* (pp. 75–102). Norwood, NJ: Ablex.

Esslin, M. (1987). *The field of drama: How the signs of drama create meaning on stage and screen.* London: Methuen.

Euclid English Demonstration Center. (1964). Project English materials. ERIC Document Reproduction Service Nos. ED 017 490-ED 017 496.

Faulkner, W. (1938). *The unvanquished.* New York: Random House.

Faulkner, W. (1990). *The sound and the fury.* New York: Vintage. (Original work published 1929)

Ferber, E. (1958). Show boat. In *Three living novels of American Life: Show Boat, So Big, Cimarron.* Garden City, NY: Doubleday. (Original work published 1926)

Fetterley, J. (1978). *The resisting reader: A feminist approach to American fiction.* Bloomington: Indiana University Press.

Fish, S. (1980). *Is there a text in this class?: The authority of interpretive communities.* Cambridge, MA: Harvard University Press.

Fish, S. (1983). Short people got no reason to live: Reading irony. *Daedalus, 112,* 175–192.

Fish, S. (1996, May 21). Professor Sokal's bad joke. *New York Times,* p. A23.

Fishman, S. M. (1993). Explicating our tacit tradition: John Dewey and composi-tion studies. *College Composition and Communication, 44,* 315–330.

Fitzgerald, F. S. (1925). *The great Gatsby.* New York: Scribner's.

Flower, L. (1987). *Interpretive acts: Cognition and the construction of discourse* (Occa-sional Paper No. 1). Berkeley, CA: Center for the Study of Writing.

Foote, D., Forst, M., Hynes-Berry, M., Johnson, J., Miller, B., & Perkins, B. (Eds.) (1992). *Responding to Literature: Multicultural Perspectives.* Evanston, IL: McDougal, Littell.

Frye, N. (1963). Literary criticism. In J. Thorpe (Ed.), *The aims and methods of scholar-ship in modern languages and literatures* (pp. 57–69). New York: Modern Lan-guage Association.

Fuss, D. (1994). Accounting for theory in the undergraduate classroom. In D. F. Sadoff & W. E. Cain (Eds.), *Teaching contemporary theory to undergraduates* (pp. 103–113). New York: Modern Language Association.

Gallop, J. (1993). The institutionalization of feminist criticism. In S. Gubar & J. Kamholtz (Eds.), *English inside and out: The places of literary criticism. Essays from the 50th anniversary of the English Institute* (pp. 61–67). New York: Routledge, 1993.

Garcia, M. (1990). Blue Steel. *Films in Review, 41,* 365–66.

Garner, R. (1990). When children and adults do not use learning strategies: To-ward a theory of settings. *Review of Educational Research, 60,* 517–529.

Gates, H. L., Jr. (1988). *The signifying monkey: A theory of Afro-American literary criti-cism.* New York: Oxford University Press.

Gates, H. L., Jr. (1993). The welcome table. In S. Gubar & J. Kamholtz (Eds.), *English inside and out: The places of literary criticism. Essays from the 50th anniver-sary of the English Institute* (pp. 47–60). New York: Routledge, 1993.

Gilbert, S., & Gubar, S. (1979). *The madwoman in the attic: The woman writer and the nineteenth century literary imagination.* New Haven, CT: Yale University Press.

Giroux, H. A. (1992). Educational leadership and the crisis of democratic government. *Educational Researcher, 21*(4), 4–11.

Giroux, H. A. (1994). Living dangerously: Identity politics and the new cultural racism. In H. A. Giroux & P. McLaren (Eds.), *Between borders: Pedagogy and the politics of cultural studies* (pp. 29–55). New York: Routledge.

Goldberg, J. (1992). *Sodometries: Renaissance texts, modern sexualities.* Stanford, CA: Stanford University Press.

Goldblatt, E. (1995). *'Round my way: Authority and double-consciousness in three urban high school writers.* Pittsburgh: University of Pittsburgh Press.

Graff, G. (1992). *Beyond the culture wars: How teaching the conflicts can revitalize American education.* New York: Norton.

Graff, G. (1994). A pedagogy of counterauthority, or the bully/wimp syndrome. In D. B. Downing (Ed.), *Changing classroom practices: Resources for literary and cultural studies* (pp. 179–193). Urbana, IL: National Council of Teachers of English.

Grossberg, L. (1994). Introduction: Bringin' it all back home—pedagogy and cultural studies. In H. A. Giroux & P. McLaren (Eds.), *Between borders: Pedagogy and the politics of cultural studies* (pp. 1–25). New York: Routledge.

Hamel, F., & Smith, M. W. (1997). *You can't play the game if you don't know the rules: Interpretive conventions and the teaching of literature to lower-track students.* Manuscript submitted for publication.

Hamessley, L. (1994). Henry Lawes's setting of Katherine Philips's friendship poetry in his *Second book of ayres and dialogues,* 1655: A musical misreading? In P. Brett, E. Wood, & G. C. Thomas (Eds.), *Queering the pitch: The new gay and lesbian musicology* (pp. 115–138). New York: Routledge.

Hammett, D. (1989). *The Maltese falcon.* New York: Vintage. (Original work published 1930)

Hanley, J. (1961). The butterfly. In R. Goodman (Ed.), *75 short masterpieces* (pp. 116–120). New York: Bantam.

Harris, J. (1989). The idea of community in the study of writing. *College Composition and Communication, 40,* 11–22.

Hartman, G. (1993). English as something else. In S. Gubar & J. Kamholtz (eds.), *English inside and out: The places of literary criticism. Essays from the 50th anniversary of the English Institute* (pp. 37–46). New York: Routledge.

Hemingway, E. & Perkins, M. (1996, June 24 and July 1). Three words. *New Yorker, 72,* 73–77.

Hillocks, G., Jr. (1989). Literary texts in classrooms. In P. W. Jackson & S. Haroutunian-Gordon (Eds.), *From Socrates to software: The teacher as text and the text as teacher* (88th yearbook of the National Society for the Study of Education) (pp. 135–158). Chicago: University of Chicago Press.

Hirsch, E. D., Jr. (1967). *Validity in interpretation.* New Haven, CT: Yale University Press.

Hirsch, E. D., Jr. (1976). *The aims of interpretation.* Chicago: University of Chicago Press.

Hirsch, E. D., Jr. (1987). *Cultural literacy: What every American needs to know.* Boston: Houghton Mifflin.

Holland, N. (1975). *5 readers reading.* New Haven, CT: Yale University Press.

Iser, W. (1978). *The act of reading: A history of aesthetic response.* Baltimore: John Hopkins University Press.

Johnson, J. (Ed.). (1992). *Responding to literature: American literature.* Evanston, IL: McDougal, Littell.

Kartiganer, D. M. (1988). The divided protagonist: Reading as repetition and discovery. *Texas Studies in Literature and Language, 30,* 151–178.

Kauffmann, S. (1990, April 9). New wave, old tricks. *The New Republic, 202,* 26–27.

Kernan, A. (1993). Plausible and helpful things to say about literature in a time when all print institutions are breaking down. In S. Gubar & J. Kamholtz (Eds.), *English inside and out: The places of literary criticism. Essays from the 50th anniversary of the English Institute* (pp. 8–28). New York: Routledge.

Kolodny, A. (1980). Dancing through the minefield: Some observations on the theory, practice, and politics of a feminist literary criticism. *Feminist Studies, 6,* 1–25.

Langer, J. A. (1989). *The process of understanding literature* (Report Series 2.1). Albany, NY: Center for Learning and Teaching of Literature.

Lanser, S. S. (1994). The T word: Theory as trial and transformation of the undergraduate classroom. In D. F. Sadoff & W. E. Cain, *Teaching contemporary theory to undergraduates* (pp. 57–68). New York: Modern Language Association.

Larsen, N. (1986). *Passing.* In D. McDowell (Ed.), *Quicksand and Passing.* New Brunswick: Rutgers University Press. (Original work published 1929)

Lee, D. (1973). Gwendolyn Brooks. In R. Ellmann & R. O'Clair (Eds.), *Norton anthology of modern poetry* (pp. 1377–1378). New York: W. W. Norton & Company.

Lee, H. (1962). *To kill a mockingbird.* New York: Popular Library. (Original work published 1960)

Lehman, D. (1998). *Matters of fact: Reading nonfiction over the edge.* Columbus, OH: Ohio State University Press.

Littlejohn, D. (1966). *Black on white: A critical survey of writing by American Negroes.* New York: Grossman.

Long, E. (1987). Reading groups and the postmodern crisis of cultural authority. *Cultural Studies, 1*(3), 29–50.

Mailloux, S. (1985). Rhetorical hermeneutics. *Critical Inquiry, 11,* 620–41.

Marshall, J. D., Smagorinsky, P., & Smith, M. W. (1995). *The language of interpretation: Patterns of discourse in discussions of literature.* Urbana, IL: National Council of Teachers of English.

McClary, S. (1991). *Feminine endings: Music, gender, and sexuality.* Minneapolis: University of Minnesota Press.

McDowell, D. E. (1986). Introduction. In D. E. McDowell (Ed.), *Quicksand and Passing* (pp. ix–xxviii). New Brunswick: Rutgers University Press.

McLendon, J. Y. (1991). Self-representation as art in the novels of Nella Larsen. In J. Morgan & C. T. Hall (Eds.), *Redefining autobiography in twentieth-century women's fiction: An essay collection* (pp. 149–168). New York: Garland.

Meek, M. (1983). *Achieving literacy: Longitudinal studies of adolescents learning to read.* London: Kegan Paul.

Miller, J. H. (1979, September/November). The function of rhetorical study at the present time. *ADE Bulletin, 62,* 10–18.

Miller, J. H. (1989). Is there an ethics of reading? In J. Phelan (Ed.), *Reading narrative: Form, ethics, ideology* (pp. 79–101). Columbus: Ohio State University Press.

Moore, S. (1990). Happiness is a warm gun. *New Statesman and Society, 3,* 30.

Morrison, T. (1987). *Beloved.* New York: New American Library.

Morton, D. (1990). Texts of limits, the limits of texts, and the containment of politics in contemporary literature. *Diacritics, 20,* 57–75.

Nabokov, V. (1960). *Bend sinister.* London: Weidenfeld & Nicolson. (Original work published 1947)

Nelson, T. A. (1982). *Kubrick: Inside a film artist's maze.* Bloomington: Indiana University Press.

Newkirk, T. (1984). Looking for trouble: A way to unmask our readings. *College English, 46,* 756–766.

Oxenhandler, N. (1984). Reflections on literature and value. In J. D. Lyons & N. J. Vickers (Eds.), *The dialectic of discovery: Essays on the teaching and interpetation of literature presented to Lawrence E. Harvey* (pp. 32–46). Lexington, KY: French Forum.

Phelan, J. (1989). *Reading people, reading plots: Character, progression, and the interpretation of narrative.* Chicago: University of Chicago Press.

Phelan, J. (1996). *Narrative as rhetoric: Technique, audience, ethics, ideology.* Columbus: Ohio State University Press.

Probst, R. E. (1988). Readers and literary texts. In B. Nelms (Ed.), *Literature in the classroom* (pp. 19–30). Urbana, IL: National Council of Teachers of English.

Probst, R. E. (1992a). Five kinds of literary knowing. In J. Langer (Ed.), *Literature instruction: A focus on student response* (pp. 54–77). Urbana, IL: National Council of Teachers of English.

Probst, R. E. (1992b). Reader response theory and the problem of meaning. *Publishing Research Quarterly, 8,* 64–73.

Propp, V. (1970). *Morphology of the folktale* (2nd ed.; L. Scott, Trans.). Austin: University of Texas Press. (Original work published 1928)

Rabinowitz, P. J. (1980). Rats behind the wainscoting: Politics, convention, and Chandler's *The Big Sleep. Texas Studies in Literature and Language, 22,* 224–254.

Rabinowitz, P. J. (1989). End sinister: Neat closure as disruptive force. In J. Phelan (Ed.), *Reading narrative: Form, ethics, ideology* (pp. 120–131). Columbus: Ohio State University Press.

Rabinowitz, P. J. (1992). Against close reading. In M.-R. Kecht (Ed.), *Pedagogy is politics: Literary theory and critical teaching* (pp. 230–43). Urbana: University of Illinois Press.

Rabinowitz, P. J. (1994a). "A symbol of something": Interpretive vertigo in "The Dead." In D. R. Schwarz (Ed.), *The dead: Case studies in contemporary criticism* (pp. 137–149). Boston: Bedford Books of St. Martin's Press.

Rabinowitz, P. J. (1994b). "How did you know he licked his lips?": Second person knowledge and first person power in *The Maltese Falcon*. In J. Phelan & P. J. Rabinowitz (Eds.), *Understanding narrative* (pp. 157–177). Columbus: Ohio State University Press.

Rabinowitz, P. J. (1996). Reader response, reader responsibility: *Heart of Darkness* and the politics of displacement. In R. C. Murfin (Ed.), *Heart of Darkness: Complete, authoritatve text with biographical and historical contexts, critical history, and essays from five contemporary critical perspectives* (2nd ed.; pp. 131–147). Boston: Bedford Books of St. Martin's Press.

Rabinowitz, P. J. (1997). *Before reading: Narrative conventions and the politics of interpretation*. Columbus: Ohio State University Press. (Original work published 1987)

Radway, J. A. (1984). *Reading the romance: Women, patriarchy, and popular literature*. Chapel Hill: University of North Carolina Press.

Reeves, C. E. (1985). A voice of unrest: Conrad's rhetoric of the unspeakable. *Texas Studies in Literature and Language, 27*, 284–310.

Rich, A. (1972). When we dead awaken: Writing as re-vision. *College English, 34*, 18–30.

Richards, I. A. (1929). *Practical criticism: A study of literary judgment*. New York: Harcourt, Brace, & World.

Ridley, F. H. (1963). The ultimate meaning of "Heart of Darkness." *Nineteenth-Century Fiction, 18*, 43–53.

Robbins, B., & A. Ross. (1996). Untitled reponse to Alan Sokal. *Lingua Franca, 6*, 54–57.

Rodriguez, R. (1982). *Hunger of memory: The education of Richard Rodriguez*. Boston: Godine.

Rogers, T., & O'Neill, C. (1993). Creating multiple worlds: Drama, language, and literary response. In G. Newell & R. Durst (Eds.), *Exploring texts: The role of discussion and writing in the teaching and learning of literature* (pp. 69–89). Norwood, MA: Christopher—Gordon.

Rosenblatt, L. (1978). *The reader, the text, the poem: The transactional theory of the literary work*. Carbondale: Southern Illinois University Press.

Rosenblatt, L. (1985). The transactional theory of the literary work: Implications for research. In C. Cooper (Ed.), *Researching response to literature and the teaching of literature: Points of departure* (pp. 33–53). Norwood, NJ: Ablex.

Rosenblatt, L. (1993). The transactional theory: Against dualisms. *College English, 55*, 377–386.

Rosenblatt, L. (1994). The transactional theory of reading and writing. In R. Ruddell, M. Ruddell, & H. Singer (Eds.), *Theoretical models and processes of reading* (pp. 1057–1092). Newark, DE: International Reading Association.

Rosenblatt, L. (1995). Continuing the conversation: A clarification. *Research in the Teaching of English, 29*, 349–354.

Russo, V. (1987). *The celluloid closet: Homosexuality in the movies* (rev. ed). New York: Harper & Row.

Sadoff, D. F. (1994). Frameworks, materials, and the teaching of theory. In D. Sadoff & W. E. Cain, *Teaching contemporary theory to undergraduates* (pp. 15–27). New York: Modern Language Association.

Savage, W. J. (1992). *Starting points: Canons, genre, the preinterpretive field, and the literary reputation of Nelson Algren.* Unpublished doctoral dissertation, Northwestern University, Evanston, IL.

Schickel, R. (1991, October 14). Hollywood's new directions. *Time,* pp. 75–78.

Scholes, R. (1985a). *Textual power.* New Haven: Yale University Press.

Scholes, R. (1985b). Critical theory and the teaching of literature. *Proceedings of the Northeastern University Center for Literary Studies, 3,* 35–50.

Schroeder, W. R. (1986). A teachable theory of interpretation. In C. Nelson (Ed.), *Theory in the classroom* (pp. 9–44). Urbana: University of Illinois Press.

Sedgwick, E. K. (1990). *Epistemology of the closet.* Berkeley: University of California Press.

Shusterman, R. (1995). Rap remix: Pragmatism, postmodernism, and other issues in the house. *Critical Inquiry, 22,* 150–158.

Singh, A. (1975). *The novels of the Harlem Renaissance: Twelve black writers, 1923–1933.* University Park: Pennsylvania State University Press.

Smagorinsky, P. , McCann, T., & Kern, S. (1987). *Explorations: Introductory activities for literature and composition, 7–12.* Urbana, IL: ERIC Clearinghouse on Reading and Communication Skills and National Council of Teachers of English.

Smagorinsky, P., & Smith, M. W. (1992). The nature of knowledge in composition and literary understanding: The question of specificity. *Review of Educational Research, 62,* 279–306.

Smith, M. W. (1991a). Constructing meaning from text: An analysis of ninth grade reader response. *Journal of Educational Research, 84,* 263–272.

Smith, M. W. (1991b). *Understanding unreliable narrators: Reading between the lines in the literature classroom.* Urbana, IL: National Council of Teachers of English.

Smith, M. W. (1992a). Autobiographical writing in the study of literature. In G. Newell & R. Durst (Eds.), *Exploring texts: The role of discussion and writing in the teaching and learning of literature* (pp. 211–230). Norwood, MA: Christopher-Gordon.

Smith, M. W. (1992b). The effects of direct instruction in understanding unrelieable narrators: An analysis of think-aloud protocols from ten ninth-grade readers. *Journal of Education Research, 85,* 339–347.

Smith, M. W. (1992c). Submission versus control in literary transactions. In J. E. Many & C. Cox (Eds.), *Reader stance and literary understanding: Exploring the theories, research and practice* (pp. 143–161). Norwood, NJ: Ablex.

Smith, M. W. (1993). Interpretive strategies in literature study. In A. Biddle & J. Clarke (Eds.), *Teaching critical thinking: Reports from across the curriculum* (pp. 24–30). Englewood Cliffs, NJ: Prentice-Hall.

Smithson, I. (1994). Introduction: Institutionalizing culture studies. In I. Smithson & N. Ruff (Eds.), *English studies/culture studies: Institutionalizing dissent* (pp. 1–22). Urbana: University of Illinois Press.

Sokal, A. D. (1996a). Transgressing the boundaries: Towards a transformative hermeneutics of quantum gravity. *Social Text, 46/47,* 217–252.

Sokal, A. D. (1996b). A physicist experiments with cultural studies. *Lingua Franca, 6,* 62–64.

Spillane, M. (1947). *I, the jury.* New York: New American Library.

Steinbeck, J. (1992). *East of Eden*. New York: Penguin. (Original work published 1952)

Thomson, J. (1987). *Understanding teenagers' reading: Reading processes and the teaching of literature*. Melbourne: Methuen.

Tolstoy, L. (1960). *The Kreutzer Sonata*. In *The Death of Ivan Ilych and other stories* (pp. 157–240; A. Maude, Trans.). New York: New American Library/Signet. (Original work published 1889).

Treichler, P. (1994). A room of whose own?: Lessons from feminist classroom narratives. In D. B. Downing (Ed.), *Changing classroom practices: Resources for literary and cultural studies* (pp. 75–103). Urbana Illinois: National Council of Teachers of English.

Turgenev, I. (1968). *First Love*. In *First Love and other tales* (D. Magarshack, Trans.). New York: Norton. (Original work published 1860)

Valenti, J. (1996). The voluntary movie rating system. [Web page]

Vidal, G. (1995). *Palimpsest: A memoir*. New York: Random House.

Villanueva, V. (1996, November). *This friend of mine is me: Race, class, and the representation of self*. Paper presented at the meeting of the National Council of Teachers of English, Chicago.

Vipond, D., & Hunt, R. (1984). Point-driven understanding: Pragmatic and cognitive dimensions of literary reading. *Poetics, 13*, 261–277.

Vygotsky, L. S. (1978). *Mind in society* (M. Cole, V. John-Steiner, S. Scribner, & E. Souberman, Eds.). Cambridge, MA: Harvard University Press.

Wadlington, W. (1987). *Reading Faulknerian tragedy*. Ithaca, NY: Cornell University Press.

Walker, A. (1973). Everyday use. In *Love and trouble: Stories of black women* (pp. 47–59). New York: Harcourt Brace Jovanovich.

Wall, C. A. (1986). Passing for what? Aspects of identity in Nella Larsen's novels. *Black American Literature Forum, 20*, 97–111.

Wilhelm, J. (1997). *"You gotta BE the book": Teaching engaged and reflective reading with adolescents*. New York: Teachers College Press.

Wilhelm, J., & Edmiston, B. (in press). *Imagining to learn: Inquiry, reading, ethics, and integration through drama*. Portsmouth, NH: Heinemann.

Wilkinson, J. (1996). A choice of fictions: Historians, memory, and evidence. *PMLA, 111*, 80–92.

Will, G. (1994). Literary politics. In D. S. Richter (Ed.), *Falling into theory: Conflicting views of reading literature* (pp. 286–288). Boston: Bedford Books of St. Martin's Press. (Original work published 1991)

Williams, J. (1982). In defense of Caroline Compson. In A. F. Kinney (Ed.), *Critical essays on William Faulkner: The Compson family* (pp. 402–407). Boston: Hall.

Willinsky, J. (1991). *The triumph of literature/The fate of literacy*. New York: Teachers College Press.

Wright, R. (1966). *Native son*. New York: Harper & Row. (Original work published 1940)

Zavarzadeh, M., & D. Morton. (1991). Theory pedagogy politics: The crisis of "the subject" in the humanities. In D. Morton & M. Zavarzadeh (Eds.), *Theory/pedagogy/politics: Texts for change* (pp. 1–32). Urbana: University of Illinois Press.

INDEX

ABOUT THE AUTHORS

Peter J. Rabinowitz divides his time between music and narrative theory. He has written on a wide range of subjects, from Dostoyevsky to Mrs. E. D. E. N. Southworth, from detective fiction to the ideology of operatic structure, from Joseph Conrad to Scott Joplin. A professor of comparative literature at Hamilton College, he is also an active music critic and a contributing editor of *Fanfare*. He is the author of *Before Reading: Narrative Conventions and the Politics of Interpretation* and the co-editor, with James Phelan, of *Understanding Narrative*.

Michael W. Smith teaches in the Literacy Cluster of Rutgers University's Graduate School of Education. In his research and teaching he works to understand how experienced readers read and talk about literary texts and how teachers can use that understanding to help prepare students to have more meaningful transactions when they read, interests he developed during his 11 years of teaching high school English in suburban Chicago. His research has appeared in a variety of journals, edited collections, and monographs. He has served as chair of the Literature Special Interest group of AERA and as co-chair of NCTE's Assembly for Research and is currently co-editor of *Research in the Teaching of English*.